| ROB FOSTER |

Designing Digital Twins

A Problem-First Approach to Bridging the Real and Virtual Worlds

Designing Digital Twins

ISBN: 978-0-646-74576-3
First Edition

www.designingdigitaltwins.com

Contents

Introduction

I often speak at conferences and corporate workshops, and when I tell people that I'm going to talk about how we work backwards from the real world to design digital twins as applied AI enablers, I am inevitably told:

> *"Oh yeah, we know how to design solutions for [insert their domain]. What we don't know is what a digital twin is or how we can make AI actually work for us."*

This is the world of digital twins and applied AI in the mid-2020s. The concepts are broad and ill-defined and the people building them are domain experts who have been solving their particular brand of problems for their entire careers.

They believe that if they just knew what a digital twin was, or which transformer "worked the best," they'd be able to leap to how to use it to solve their problems and enable effective and repeatable AI-driven solutions.

The last 10 years of my professional career have shown me this view is incorrect.

The problem is not being unable to define a solution. The problem is being unable to design interconnected physical and virtual world systems using domain-specific data models and AI to repeatably achieve real-world outcomes.

The challenges of interconnection

We have not yet thought enough about the challenges and opportunities for deeply interconnecting data models and the real world, and we don't have a playbook for how to approach these kinds of problems to solve them in a repeatable way.

As domain experts, we solve within our domain and stay in our lane. Maintenance is solved by maintenance experts, operations by operations, electrical by electrical, technology by technology, data science by data science and so on.

This has worked for generations because we had no other choice but to make it work – organizations grew massively on the back of economic, education and population growth, and machine and process complexity grew 1000x versus the industrial revolution, where our founding ideas of how to manage enterprises (and people and work) come from.

It was simply not possible for humans to ingest or analyze the ever-growing amounts and complexity of data, and the gathering of siloed data made it very difficult to repeatably solve problems that emerge from systems of systems.

The complexity of siloed systems

Organizations had to reduce complexity by creating siloed boxes for humans to manage and be responsible for, and general management had to find ways to make the boxes work together.

We then abstract the whole and humans fill in the gaps through individual efforts. It works. We have built the modern world on it, and we can then measure success by financial outputs and blame lack of success on strategy or execution or culture.

Management paradigms come and go for how best to manage the boxes, while the impact of market growth and systems complexity are largely ignored, with success and failure attributed mainly to specific leaders (i.e., 0.1% of the people).

It works (on a macro level) – but it's not repeatable. And it's not going to be repeatable in the present state because complexity and the velocity of change is constantly increasing. This results in many more boxes being created, which multiplies the number of relationships between boxes exponentially.

This lack of repeatability, coupled with difficulties measuring what really worked and what didn't, reinforces the Taylorian view that we should stick to our silos, measure our silos, and set targets for silos.

Siloed management dominates all industrial organizations, until you arrive at the GM level and get your first taste of managing and trading off silos you're not an expert in. Silos enable scale, but create cross-silo problems.

The rise of AI as a new and ultra-fast-growing silo is the latest challenge. AI as part of the technology silo has gone from an enabling function, like finance or human resources, to a silo that does work, provides value, links other silos, and in many industries is a fundamental competitive advantage in core products or services.

In industrial organizations, with real-world work and labor, AI is rapidly becoming the most pervasive and cross-silo silo of them all. As the newest silo, it also has the least management depth and experience. Non-technology managers and executives have very little expertise or experience in managing this silo. AI is also bringing forth many probabilistic outputs, which no management paradigm has ever contended with. Perhaps worst of all – the expertise of long experience in "technology" or data science is very often associated with little or no real-world experience in the domain that the technology function now supports.

We seldom promote maintenance supervisors into technology leads, and we seldom promote technology leads into maintenance managers. Their domains are parallel but separate, despite all industrial functions (maintenance being just one example) now being dominated by technology, and much technology now being domain specific.

The fact that the domain, or silo, uses technology from domain specific vendors, does not in any way imply that the silos themselves collaborate or that the domain and the internal technology teams collaborate. We buy and build siloed technology for silos.

Connection between silos is often sought by the introduction of collaborative technology, but in fact the challenge we need to face is that the real world is not siloed – we have imposed artificial organizational boxes over the complexity of the real world in order to facilitate human-led activity at scale.

Why digital twins AND applied AI?

We go into more detail about what digital twins and applied AI are, and mean, in the main text. For now, suffice to say, that digital twins are virtual worlds that reflect the real world, and where we can deploy capabilities to alter the real world, and measure that change in the virtual world.

They are not just "mirrors" of the real world. Similarly, applied AI refers to AI systems and capabilities that are designed specifically to create change in the real world. Applied AI is a subset of the larger AI paradigm and overlaps with Vertical AI (AI designed and trained and tuned for specific use cases, e.g., a HVAC control system) and includes Physical AI (the combination of AI capabilities with physical systems, such as robotics, that enables the AI to directly interact with and manipulate the real world).

Digital twins often incorporate AI models, and applied AI applications are, almost by definition, connected to and from the real world. In both cases, we are talking about **software AND data AND change in the real world**.

In both cases we are judging success on the basis of real-world impact, not just software or data capability and benchmarks. In both cases, we are choosing to go beyond software, and beyond data, and beyond data models, and even beyond users (where users don't directly create the real-world change)... we are choosing to interconnect *real-world problems* and *technology capabilities* together, and *both must be successful.*

We are choosing in other words to make our own lives very difficult in order to maximize the impact we have on the real world.

In this book

In this book I will mostly refer to twins – meaning digital twins that utilize AI and other data and data models to create, measure and improve change in the real world.

I say "other data and data models" because AI itself is already fragmenting, and because a great many applied / industry / use-case solutions incorporate non-AI data models and capabilities. AI is not the panacea. It is not the be all and end all. It is not the only game in town, and in creating change in existing organizations, you will use a lot more than the latest AI model to create, measure and improve change.

This book is the answer to the question:

> *"How do we design interconnected solutions to solve real-world problems using AI and data models?"*

The problem with siloed systems

The advent of scalable data acquisition and cloud analytics has changed the cost and complexity dimension of the root cause (scale / many boxes), but we have been unable to translate this into repeatable cross-silo solutions. Our organizations are still siloed in structure and incentives with abstracted measures of success.

Digital transformation (D(x)) arose to answer this challenge, and we have been D(x)'ing for long enough to understand the main challenges are not digital at all, but rather people and process.

However, D(x) as a process still seeks to insert technology capabilities (AI or otherwise) into the real world, in the hopes that change management and other processes can change the way people think and behave. And of course, it can – to a certain extent, at a certain rate of change, and for certain easy problems (like digitizing manual data collection or natural language search of structured data).

Why digital twins are the answer

We have seen that a great many digital transformation programs fail, and we are approaching that failure from our usual view of management failure - strategy, execution, culture, leaders.

I posit that digital twins are a tool of digital transformation and the best enabler for applied AI.

Digital twins do not replace transformation - they enable it - specifically and repeatably. Digital twins solve specific problems within the context of larger transformations by providing a framework for implementing domain-specific AI solutions.

Critically, they are highly optimized to solve cross-silo challenges. Challenges where the real-world problem crosses multiple organizational silos.

These are the most intractable, hardest to solve problems, as all "organizational" transformations seek to move boxes around or insert new people and processes into boxes. The boxes will never go away and will likely continue to become more specialized, and therefore, we will always have many problems that cross boxes. We need to evolve methods to solve cross-box / cross-silo problems.

This is the level of problem solving and success measurement that provides us with true insight into "what's working and what's not working," below the abstracted level of financial, and organizational metrics, and above the level of user metrics.

This is the level where we can directly measure change in the real world, and make improvements, and measure the impact of those improvements.

By leveraging digital twins as applied AI enablers, we can create more targeted, repeatable, and effective solutions to industry-specific challenges.

Who did I write this book for?

- **You're an AI domain or technology expert** who wants to better interconnect your ever-growing digital capabilities to real-world assets, people, and processes, to create greater value.

- **You're a real-world domain expert** who wants to change how we manage the real world by changing how we design real / virtual world solutions, to better achieve objectives.
- **You're the executive of a real-world business** that owns and operates assets and has people doing work, and you want to understand how we can solve complex and cross-domain problems better, to create better outcomes.
- **You're cynical about "more tech" and "AI everything"** but you believe technology in general and AI in particular have a fundamental place in improving how we work, and want an alternative way to think about applying these technologies to solve real-world problems.

The common thread is:

you want to create change in the real world through the use of data models and AI in concert with existing technologies and data.

This book wasn't written specifically for software developers or enterprise architects or IT administrators – though if that's your job title, don't let it stop you from being that person who wants to create change in the real world.

You won't find landing pads, MQTT pros and cons, or Llama versus OpenAI models. These are all important, and there's an ever-growing body of knowledge around all digital twin and AI solutions, but those are covered in many other works and are evolving very quickly.

Challenges practitioners face

For current digital twin and applied AI practitioners and users, poorly designed digital twins leave a very clear trail – many of which you will be familiar with:

- **As a service provider** (e.g., engineering consultancy), your customers come to you with digital twin and AI ideas or requests for proposals, but they can't articulate the outcome or the method. This translates into delayed decisions, no-decision decisions, and cost pressure to cut scope without regard to impact on outcome (because no one could explicitly link scope to outcome to begin with).
- **As a domain owner or operator** (e.g., maintenance manager), your internal technology teams are pushing AI at you with examples of other successful or well marketed tools, but neither they nor you can answer the question of what and how it will deliver value for you, and no one can answer the "how?" of the "cut 30% of our maintenance costs" promise.

- **As a product manager**, you have features to build, and schedules to meet, but very loose correlation between problems and features, and features and benefits, and you are confused as to why the maintenance teams aren't using any of the things you built last year.
- **As a project manager**, you have a scope of work and an engaged team but every time a "why?" question appears, no one can seem to answer it. And the more you dig and learn, the more questions you have, and the less budget and schedule you have to answer them.

In all cases, it is very common to see data "everything" being pushed and "beyond the scope of work" problems being avoided. We focus on what we can scope and control well, and avoid what we understand least.

The role of connection in digital twins

While technology and fixed scope led building works for many software products (although it is a serious root cause issue for the many features that are never used), for connected solutions like digital twins and applied AI, the problem is magnified.

A twin only exists to connect problem and solution, real to virtual, user to change. Connection is the defining characteristic of twins, and connection implies causality. *We must be connecting them for a reason.*

When the design and build of the twin is decoupled from the connected problem space, we are setting ourselves up for measurable failure.

Similarly for applied AI, and most domain-specific data models, we must be using this particular set of data to train or develop a model that gives outputs that are to be used... for something, by someone, at some point in time. These last three often get very vague, very quickly.

The need for clarity

It's easy to write the scope of work and procure, but we inevitably must answer the why / what questions at some point, and unfortunately, waiting until half-way through the budget or after the thing is built is much too late.

I have been involved in a number – an ever-growing number – of "revitalizations," where I am brought in to diagnose a failed twin project. I no longer begin with investigating data quality, uptime, model test results, or scope compliance. I just start by asking everyone involved:

> *"Why did you build this? What change in the real world were you hoping to create?"*

After the first 10 unique and vague responses, I play this back to the sponsor and say: *"Let's start with this."*

High quality data and test-driven deployments do not necessarily create desirable outcomes. Yes, they are necessary, but they are most certainly not sufficient. Without a coherent view of how the ecosystem should change to create the desired outcomes, and without ways of measuring if it is indeed changing in that way, we create the very high probability that what is built will not deliver the outcome.

Designing for systemic change

Designing solutions to create systemic change isn't impossible. It just seems that way when you don't have a process, methodology or playbook or experience to guide you, and when you've seen so many successes and failures in your professional life.

There *are* trails through the forest, it's just very dark at the moment, and some of the trails don't go where you need to be.

I hope this book can act as a guide to help you find the right trails and to forge new trails that benefit your organization.

Why would you listen to me about digital twins and applied AI?

My hope, of course, is that after reading the above you will be happy to read on as you think there may be something in here to learn.

My background is predominantly in the "real" world. I'm a mechanical engineer (mechanical and space to be exact) with 20 years in heavy asset (mining, power, and oil & gas) and capital project delivery.

About 10 years ago I discovered digital transformation and moved heavily into helping transform enterprises, including my own, and six years ago I stumbled across digital twins and AI, as part of my journey down the rabbit hole of software and SaaS. Since then, I've completed a master's degree in system engineering, have been an executive and GM of SaaS businesses that deliver digital twins, and now am the co-founder and CEO of a digital twin and AI business.

I'm all in on digital twins and AI for industrial organizations, because I love the problems, and I love the people whose job it is to solve these problems. I truly believe that bringing AI and advanced data models into the real world and connecting these new capabilities to ourselves and our world will result in meaningful change to how we create and manage the world.

I am not, however, a digital twin or AI "fan boy." I personally think at least 90% of "digital twins" are not digital twins, because they're not strongly connected to the real world, and they're not designed to create change in the real world. I think a great many AI tools are capabilities, not products, and I know that they are not being used and not being used well, because I make money from organizations that need help with understanding how and why they're even deploying them.

The future of digital twins and applied AI

I also think that in 10 years' time, the digital twin and applied AI paradigm will have evolved greatly, and many more software applications will be designed to create and measure change in the real world... but we won't call them digital twins or applied AI, because they'll just be "real-world solutions." The impact of technology on the real world is only just starting, and the digital twin and AI paradigms of explicitly changing the real world through software and data are in their infancy.

For the tech industry:

- I believe digital twins are a pattern that leads to improved outcomes in the real world.
- I believe applied AI is the AI and AI-enabling pattern that delivers improved outcomes in the real world.

For "real-world" industries:

- I believe digital twins are a pattern that leads to improved value from technology.
- I believe applied AI is the AI and AI-enabling pattern that leads to improved value from technology.

Improved outcomes and improved value. Yes, both. It's possible. I've seen it done many times, and I believe we're at a point where we can do it repeatably.

For me, I think I'm just attracted to my roots of solving problems by creating and measuring change in the real world. That's why I became an engineer, and it's what I love doing, and digital twins and applied AI are very strong levers to pull on. We all seek our "happy place" when faced with stress, and my happy place is solving problems in ways that improve outcomes and value.

In this book we will cover

This book offers a comprehensive exploration of how to design and implement digital twins and applied AI systems that effectively solve real-world problems.

Through a structured and practical approach, the content spans the foundational concepts, design processes, and challenges of integrating advanced technologies into complex industrial ecosystems. Here's an outline of what you can expect:

1. Foundational Concepts
    - Definitions and expanded understandings of digital twins and applied AI, exploring their interconnection and potential to create measurable changes in the real world.
    - The differences between narrow and wide twins, weak and strong couplings, and how these align with specific objectives.
2. The Ecosystem Perspective
    - Insight into domains, ecosystems, and their implications for change.
    - Understanding the interplay of data, processes, and systems within interconnected industrial settings.
3. Value Creation
    - How to design digital twins for usability, viability, and measurable benefits.
    - Key considerations for aligning features, data, and usability to achieve targeted outcomes.
4. Digital Twin Design Process (DTDP)
    - A step-by-step guide on how to work backwards from identifying valuable problems to implementing feasible, usable, and viable solutions.
    - Detailed examples of each stage, including problem definition, ecosystem change, solution delivery, and benefit realization.
5. Practical Applications
    - Real-world use cases and worked examples to illustrate how digital twins and applied AI can be applied to industrial and organizational challenges.

- Case studies of failed implementations, analyzing what went wrong and lessons learned.

6. Advice for Practitioners
   - Guidance on prioritizing problems, managing project roadmaps, and aligning objectives with organizational goals.
   - Recommendations for navigating failure modes, balancing ROI, and developing sustainable solutions.
7. Delivery and Future Insights
   - Strategies for delivering successful digital twin solutions, from project conception to iterative improvements.
   - Exploration of future trends, including the evolution of industrial metaverse applications, ecosystem-wide digital transformation, and the advancing interplay of AI and data.
8. Resources and Tools
   - Checklists, worksheets, and prompts to support practitioners in applying the concepts discussed in the book.

A practitioner-focused style

This book is written in an informal, practitioner-focused style, blending theory with actionable insights. It is designed for those looking to bridge the gap between advanced digital capabilities and real-world implementation, whether you're a domain expert, technology practitioner, or industry executive.

By the end, you will be equipped with the tools and methodologies to drive meaningful change using digital twins and applied AI.

Let's dive in!

Part 1 - What is it?

Definitions, the limitations of definitions, and thinking about how to think about twins and applied AI

Definitions

Digital twin

Let's start with the easiest one: *What is a digital twin?*

That's a lie. It's the hardest one. Not because we don't have definitions, but because we have so many, and so many software solutions are now called digital twins, and new definitions are created to describe what was built.

A digital twin comprises a virtual representation of a selected portion of the real world, with two-way interconnections, synchronized at specified frequencies and fidelities, and designed to create change in the real that can be measured and improved in the virtual.

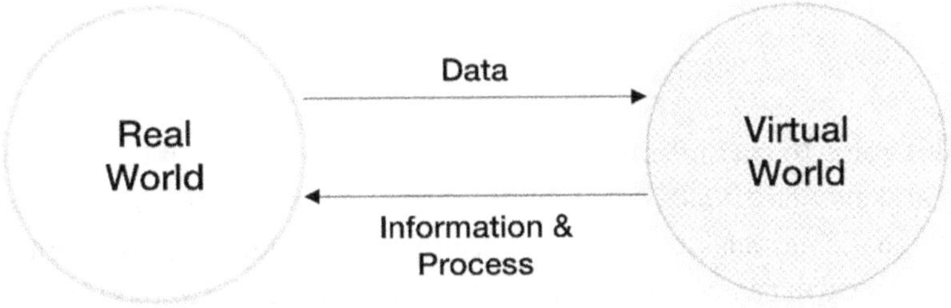

The definition of a digital twin is fraught with controversy and confusion. There are now so many definitions that any attempt to create the single, universally accepted definition is doomed to fail. Similarly, the two component words, "digital" and "twin," have been analyzed and misused through literal interpretations to support or negate other definitions. One of the clearest signs that a category or market is immature is the need for every published paper to define the authors "own" definition of said category. I did, when I penned my master's thesis. I felt like I had to. I did it again when I co-founded Geminum. I think we've updated it twice since.

Applied AI

Vertical AI refers to artificial intelligence (AI) solutions using machine learning and generative AI technologies to solve real-world problems by enhancing software applications and automating real-world tasks. It focuses on practical applications that improve efficiency and decision-making in various industries. Instead of being general-purpose, applied AI is often specialized for one area, such as maintenance, healthcare, finance, manufacturing, or supply chains. The underlying algorithms and models are designed to address unique challenges within that domain, supported by highly specific data sets and industry expertise. The hallmark of applied AI is the combination of domain expertise with problem specific data.

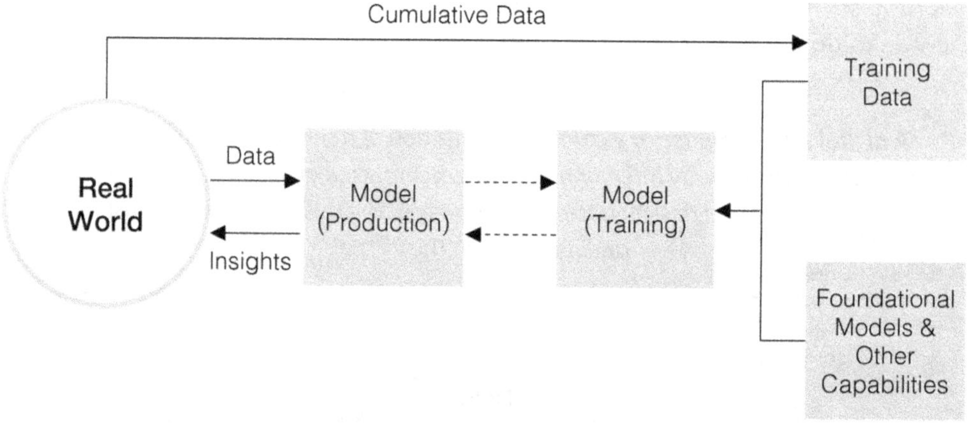

Applied AI is going to revolutionize industrial organizations, as it focuses the rapidly escalating and evolving horizontal (generalizable) AI capabilities such as generative AI (large language models / transformers), and machine learning (ML) onto industry / domain specific use cases, and incorporates domain specific and often confidential / non-open-source data to train and evolve these capabilities.

By 2030, industrial organizations will end up with dozens of unique / proprietary applied AI solutions, hundreds of applied AI solutions (some inhouse, some vendor), and thousands of applications and models built on a small set of very large horizontal models. By this time, the line between trained and unique and applied and horizontal will blur considerably. The rise of agents working across data sets, the burn down and transformation of legacy non-AI (SaaS) systems, and the millions of bespoke inhouse models and agents built that no one uses or even remembers will create a very confusing time for all.

Applied AI as a specific type of digital twin

Looking at the two diagrams of digital twins and applied AI, the resemblance is obvious. Digital twins connect the real world to virtual capabilities, and outputs from those capabilities feed back into the real world.

Applied AI connects AI capabilities to the real world, is used in workflows where real-world information is fed into them, and are trained on data from real and virtual worlds.

Digital twins often incorporate AI capabilities into their specific use case.

Digital twins bring humans and AI together into the same decision space.

Digital twins enhance the trustworthiness of AI.

AI enables twins to do things that neither can do alone.

Applied AI in production needs access to real-world data and is usually used alongside other legacy systems and as part of operational workflows.

The digital twin pattern is the perfect template for applied AI solutions.

The Digital Twin Design Process (DTDP) outlined in this book is explicitly designed to interconnect real-world change, including the decisions and actions of humans and systems to do and manage real work, with virtual capabilities, such as AI, ML, visualization, and legacy IT systems.

Why digital twins at all?

Why not just “applied AI”? The answer is simple. The people who design and build AI systems are about as far from the people who do work in the real world as it is possible to get. They’re not “ignoring” each other, they’re just busy and have very little overlap and each has a whole world of their own problems to solve.

In 10-years’ time, this won’t be true. But today, the gulf between logical systems and human-based governance, and the probabilistic and semi-hallucinatory nature of AI, couldn't be wider. In the real world, people are maimed and die through accidents and misfortune. Industrial organizations have developed 100s of years of domain expertise in getting work done at sufficiently low risk, and 99% of the learnings are captured in the experience and rules and lessons learned, not in structured or mineable data. 99% of AI talent is focused on highly esoteric data models, transformations and compute. It has 10s of years of experience.

Both groups are domain experts. Both groups will evolve and need to evolve in order to maximize positive outcomes and manage risk and cost. The domains are only just starting to overlap, and new domains of cyber-physical knowledge and expertise will grow out of this overlap / collision / transformation.

In 10 years, we will have millions of use cases and data points to guide us.

Today, we have hope and hype.

Digital twins are a bridge between disparate world views, and the DTDP is a process with the goal of bringing them together into common cause and with enough common language and process that every group can contribute to creating value at acceptable risk and cost.

In this book, a twin is a digital twin that may or may not incorporate AI, or an applied AI system that is interconnected with the real world.

Why the clarifier?

Many twins require non-AI data sets, and / or do not need AI at all to deliver value. The overarching purpose of the DTDP is to help you get to value, quickly and repeatably. If you are using or need applied AI to solve your use case, or you are using the DTDP to create repeatable value from your model, great. If you are using the DTDP to design a digital twin of existing data sets in order to solve an existing real-world problem, great. If new AI capabilities arise that can enhance use cases, then incorporating them into the existing digital twins will be a much faster and cheaper route to value, resulting in high-ROI applied AI.

In this book, a twin is a digital twin or applied AI that is interconnected with the real world.

We will cover many AI use cases and some special "hmm" areas where probabilistic, generative, non-explainable, or insufficiently accurate models create particular problems. I think these types of problems will become the norm rather than the exception, and that solving these problems systemically and at the ecosystem level (i.e., not just in the model) will create many paths to competitive advantage.

Digital twins

Conceptual model

No work on digital twins should overlook the contributions made by the fathers of digital twins, John Vickers and Michael Grieves. There are many articles and works detailing the history of digital twins if you are so inclined, and using their names to search / prompt will provide a rich body of work.

The key artifact they gave to the world is the now classic visual depiction of a digital twin, as shown below, reproduced from a University of Michigan presentation in 2002.

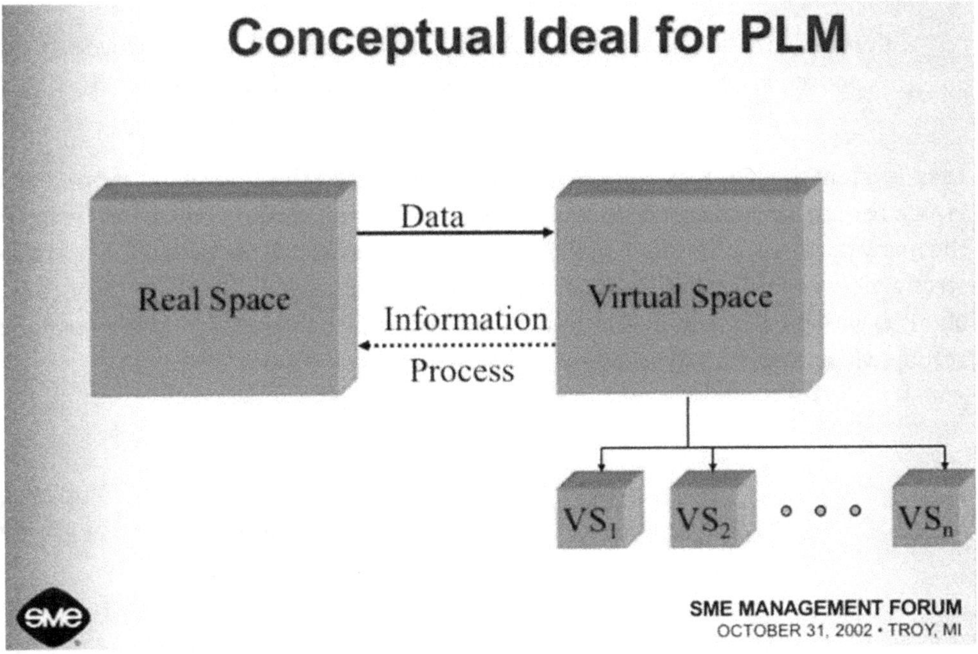

Source: Grieves M. Intelligent digital twins and the development and management of complex systems [version 1]. Digital Twin 2022, 2:8 (doi: 10.12688/digitaltwin.17574.1)

The four elements of the digital twin shown are now widely accepted as canon:

- Real space
- Virtual space
- Data
- Information and Process

Variations on this theme abound, with many different descriptions for the four elements, but the core concept has remained intact for more than 20 years now and continues to drive discussion and, increasingly, literal-but-unhelpful interpretation.

In this book, when we refer to the digital twin ecosystem, and any applied AI system contained within, we are referring to this four-element visual. All four elements of it. The digital twin ecosystem is the system in which the digital twin and all virtual capabilities (including AI models) operate.

If the digital twin requires extensive real-world and virtual-world elements to interact in specific ways, then yes, the ecosystem is big and messy and complex. It's the ecosystem we operate in, obviously, but I would caution you about "bolting it all together."

Connection of all your software systems and data, especially many one-way connections, does not make a digital twin. That's just a highly connected "system."

I say "system" because, as anyone who has experienced this knows, it's more like a Frankenstein, assembled piecemeal and steadily added to and subtracted from by the many parties and vendors who own or control pieces of it. As you will see, I have strong views on why "bolting it all together" isn't necessarily the right way to go about creating value. Equally, if you're well into your bolt-on stage, you're making actual twin and applied AI creation lower cost, so thank you.

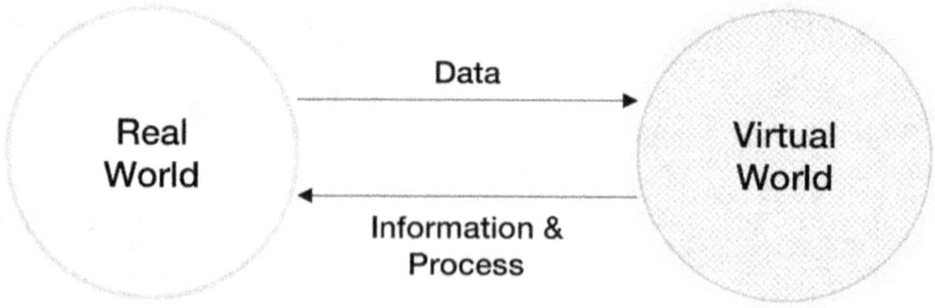

Digital twin consortium

Perhaps the best-known digital twin industry body, the Digital Twin Consortium provides a four-part definition. As an example of how definitions continue to change, below you can see the most recent and the prior definitions by the consortium.

Current definition

"A digital twin is an integrated data-driven virtual representation of real-world entities and processes, with synchronized interaction at a specified frequency and fidelity.

- Digital Twins are motivated by outcomes, driven by use cases, powered by integration, built on data, enhanced by physics, guided by domain knowledge, and implemented in dependable and trustworthy IT / OT / ET systems.
- Digital Twin Systems transform business by accelerating and automating holistic understanding, continuous improvement, decision-making, and interventions through effective action.
- Digital Twin Systems are built on integrated and synchronized IT / OT / ET systems, use real-time and historical data to represent the past and present, and simulate predicted futures.
- Digital Twin Prototypes use data to model and simulate predicted futures before being integrated into IT / OT / ET Systems and before synchronization with the real-world entity or process."

Prior definition

"A digital twin is a virtual representation of real-world entities and processes, synchronized at a specified frequency and fidelity.

- Digital twin systems transform business by accelerating holistic understanding, optimal decision-making, and effective action.
- Digital twins use real-time and historical data to represent the past and present and simulate predicted futures.
- Digital twins are motivated by outcomes, tailored to use cases, powered by integration, built on data, guided by domain knowledge, and implemented in IT / OT systems."

The Digital Twin Consortium's definitions have been a significant contribution to the field, capturing many of the aspects of digital twins. These definitions capture the essence of a digital twin as:

a virtual representation of real-world entities and processes, with synchronized interaction at a specified frequency and fidelity.

Central to this definition, and included or implied in many others, are three descriptors that correspond to the four elements of the digital twin:

- virtual representation (virtual space)
- real-world entities and processes (real space)
- synchronization mechanisms between these two domains (data and information, and process)

The *virtual representation* consists of correlated digital models and supporting data, providing cohesive information about the real-world subjects. The nature of the virtual model is often the first defining point of any twin – most twins today are built on 3D models (e.g., CAD models) or geospatial data, but the use of the word "model" should not be taken to mean a 3D CAD or other geometrical model. A model is a framework of data and relationships. Many twins have no 3D CAD models or have them only to provide context to other data and data models, such as statistical or AI models.

The term "entity" was chosen over "assets" or "equipment" to allow for any type of defined "point" in space, while the inclusion of "process" in the definition emphasizes the dynamic nature of interactions and systems in the real world. These processes can encompass business processes, supply chains, algorithms, chemical processes etc. The key here is that these are parts of the real world that we are interested in.

Synchronization is a critical aspect of this definition. It involves matching the virtual representation with the real-world and vice versa, through various mechanisms like sensors, laser scans, actuators and work. The frequency of synchronization and the fidelity of the representation are / should be tailored to suit specific use cases.

Expanding on the definition

At the time of writing, I am the co-founder of a digital twin business, Geminum (*www.geminum.co*). We design and build digital twins that enable industrial organizations to connect AI to real-world change. Our definition of a digital twin is as follows:

A digital twin comprises a virtual representation of a selected portion of the real world, with two-way interconnections, synchronized at specified frequencies and fidelities, and designed to create change in the real that can be measured and improved in the virtual.

There's a lot of crossover with the Digital Twin Consortium definitions, and many others, which is a measure of growing maturity (where convergence = maturity, but does not necessarily mean value).

Breaking it down again, the key components are:

- virtual representation
- selected portion of the real world
- two-way interconnections
- synchronized at specified frequencies and fidelities
- designed to create change in the real that can be measured and improved in the virtual

Virtual representation

The "virtual representation" is the most obvious aspect of the digital twin, and unfortunately, 90% of the focus and marketing efforts are applied today to the literal meaning of this phrase. The virtual representation is created by software and viewed by the user. It is the "world" in the digital twin conceptual model. The scope and nature of the virtual representation are determined by what portion of the world is being twinned. I will state categorically here that I do not believe that a 3D model alone is a digital twin, nor do I believe a point cloud is a digital twin, and I do not think the method of capturing the visual representation has anything to do with defining the digital twin. Similarly, I do not believe that a digital twin must have a "3D visualization of the real world" in order to be a digital twin.

A twin of a supply chain that seeks to optimize the flow of goods through the system does *not* require a real-time 3D model of the trucks, goods, or warehouses. If the use case revolved around packing and picking, then a machine vision enabled real-time inventory and geospatial model, utilizing an applied AI model optimizer, may be very valuable, as it could help to determine where goods of specific size could be located to maximize packing and picking efficiency. Even in this case, however, the algorithms for determining size, and the algorithms for determining available spaces, would not be amenable to human eyeball tracing and intervention – the idea of moving to an advanced system like this only for a human to say "put that box there" is nonsensical, yet for many other use cases we adopt a similar approach. In an automated warehouse with minimal human workers, it is even clearer that the visual representation is unnecessary, and yet many twin designers spend large amounts of time and money on this aspect of the twin as a high priority.

The rise of digital twins through project and construction phases has been heavily influenced by Building Information Modelling (BIM) and 3D modeling, and similarly, the rise of drones and reality capture has also added to this noise. Even the phrase "capturing reality" is nonsensical, as the LiDAR or photogrammetry captures a tiny sliver of reality, the reflected energy from a surface in a narrow part of the electromagnetic spectrum at a specific point in time. An up-to-date high-fidelity model of the dimension and layout of the real world is valuable in many use cases – but a digital twin it does not make.

Examples of virtual representations:

- 3D models
- Point clouds
- GIS / map-based views
- Dashboards containing graphical interfaces

I prefer to use the phrase "virtual world," as the deliberate juxtaposition of the "real world" (or real life (RL)). Within our virtual world, we will have representations of the portion of the real world we need in order to achieve the desired use case.

Selected portion of the real world

The "selected portion of the real world" may be a building, the building and surroundings, the value chain, a portion of the supply chain, a series of chemical reactions, a plane, a group of people, the weather, etc. etc.

Nearly any aspect of the real world can be virtually represented, however as we shall soon see, a strongly connected twin requires the ability to measure and improve changes in the real world. It is also for this reason that many highly useful digital twins are completely "3D-less" – chemical reactions do not need 3D models, nor Light Detection & Ranging (LiDAR), nor a metaverse. Data visualizations may be the virtual representation of the portion of the real world we are interested in changing.

When speaking of virtual representations, we should always qualify the portion of the real world we are visualizing, the portion of the real world we are seeking to measure and change, and the portion of the real world we have used to train models.

For example, for a building energy efficiency twin, we can visualize the building without needing to visualize the sun and the entire atmosphere, but we will need to collect data on temperature and humidity from outside the building, and we may well need to use real or synthetic values from the changes in the angle of the sun over the seasons. The visual representation is often a subset of the portion of the real world we are twinning, which in itself is a portion of the real-world data we need to build and use specific capabilities within the twin.

Two-way interconnections

The beating heart of digital twins and applied AI is the flow of data, information and processes from the digital twin conceptual model. The selection (number and nature) of these flows is perhaps the most undervalued aspect of digital twins and the biggest component I see missing / under-invested into in applied AI design.

There are two directions to these data flows:

- Real to virtual (R-V)
- Virtual to real (V-R)

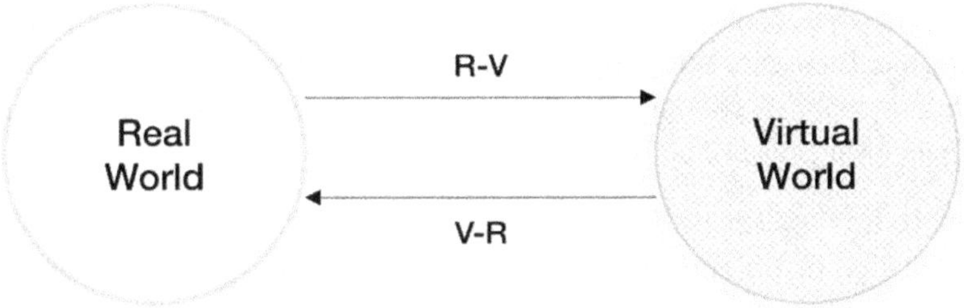

When speaking of digital twins as a concept, I like to refer to interconnections (plural), rather than connection(s), because interconnection explicitly states the two-way nature as fundamental. The R-V must exist, or the virtual capabilities cannot see changes and use that changed data from the real world. In most cases, applied AI requires specific domain data from the portion of the real world being modelled. I say most, because some AI models use wholly generative (horizontal)

data that may not be from the "actual" real world, or which could be from "previous" real worlds where the use case is the design of a new "real world" (e.g., a product lifecycle use case, where previous models of vehicles informed the design of a new vehicle).

All twins have at least one R-V connection, and some have millions of one-shots (think of a complex building 3D model, with millions of static model elements) while others have hundreds or thousands but each has millions of data points over a period of time (e.g., operational data from operating equipment in a factory). The number of R-V connections does not define the quality of a twin, but a twin with multiple connections is likely to be a more robust and connected twin. A virtual representation of a selected portion of the real world that has no connection to the real world is not a digital twin.

An example of this is simulations based on animations alone. Simulation tools abound where the underlying data model has been created to represent a similar environment to the one a human would work in – the conceptual factory, construction site or traffic flow. These simulations provide animated movement of the virtual representation in order to provide context to the user. The user may learn how to disassemble a component, or watch an animation of a potential construction sequence, or interact with a specific scenario. All of these use cases are valuable, but they are not digital twin use cases. They are simulation use cases. A digital twin that is anchored in the real world, and simulates change to that real world, is a digital twin with simulation capabilities. Simulation capabilities are powerful and are increasingly providing significant value to decision makers – but a logical animation of a set of 3D polygons is not connected to the real world and is not a digital twin. One is an apple, the other an orange, both are small round fruit you can hold in your hand, both are good for you, one might be poisonous etc. Labels matter, and change depending on your point of view.

The Virtual to Real (V-R) connection is where many twins come up short, either by concept or design or (in)action. Without a defined connection between the virtual and real, the twin is just a virtual representation of a portion of the real world. A 3D model or Gaussian splat is a virtual representation of a current or ideated portion of the real world. *If that 3D model is not causally connected back to the real world, then it is not a digital twin.*

The most common example of this fallacy may be the naming of a 3D design model as a "digital twin" of a building. The R-V connections may be weaker or stronger, depending on how data of the real world is captured. A feasibility study, or conceptual product design, has almost no R-V – it's just a set of 3D polygons shaped by the experience of the user. The fact that the user knows what to do is not in question (nor does it diminish the value of the 3D model!) – but the 3D model is not *interconnected* to the real world.

When we get to detailed design, or better yet construction, the R-V can be very strong. The underlying structure and dimension of each element comes from the real world. On the return journey, however, the 3D model goes through many phases before it gets back to the Real. The 3D model is detailed. The detailed model is detailed further into fabrication models or drawings. Components are fabricated and may or may not conform to the fabrication models, and by extension the 3D design model. The fabricated components are then assembled, and changes are often made in assembly, especially in construction but less so in manufacturing. The final "as-built" real-world structure bears a strong resemblance to the 3D design model, but the data often does not flow back from R-V to modify the 3D design. Even the process of "as-builting" in construction is a punctuated approximation – a single snap shot in time to update the 3D model (if it's done at all).

The ongoing changes and modification to the building are not updated in the virtual. Changes may be made, manually, to 3D models of buildings over time, but usually only in response to upcoming upgrades or changes, and then the updates are limited to that portion of the building which will be impacted by the change, and changes are rarely (almost never?) made on the basis of an old / unchecked 3D model. The contractor measures the real world, and does their own design, because they are often held accountable contractually to incorrect dimensions.

A digital twin of a building must have a well-designed flow of data from real to virtual, and virtual to real, and that is simply not possible with a 3D model alone, nor is it possible in a siloed design consultancy. BIM was a major step forward in improving the processes of interconnection, between all parties, and its success has arisen directly as a result of creating stronger interconnection. BIM is an interconnection process, 3D models are a virtual representation, and a digital twin requires interconnection and virtual representation – and more – to be a digital twin. They're not the same, and we're back to eating a balanced fruitarian diet.

In manufacturing, the R-V is often strong, and based on known components, and the V-R is strong, and compliance with the V is enforced. Then the V-R repeats, for each specific instance of the product created. Then, each instance of the R (each product) will have a digital twin that reflects the physical state of that specific R (the product being the portion of the real world). In other words, each product will have a digital twin, and often the factory itself has a twin.

It is no wonder that digital twins were born from the manufacturing industry, and in fact were referred to originally as a conceptually "ideal" state for Product Lifecycle Management (PLM). Manufacturing is usually highly repeatable, and small systemic improvements can compound over time, benefiting the improver. Construction projects are often highly unique, and small improvements to the real world are often unique and isolated successes, many times benefiting others.

It should be no surprise that domains with repeatable and connected problems have benefited more from repeatable and connected solutions. Nor should it surprise anyone that the rapid lowering of cost and time to interconnect portions of the real world and create stunning virtual representations is driving an increase in desire for repeatable and connected solutions.

Synchronized at specified frequencies and fidelities

The fourth part to our twin definition is synchronization. In a similar manner to the number and types of connections, how often information flows (in both directions, R-V and V-R) and at what level of detail, are important. Also, in the same way that the number of connections does not determine the quality of a twin, neither does the frequency or fidelity.

To return to our building example – a LiDAR scan from a drone may be at 5 cm resolution and conducted once a year. Is this high fidelity and low frequency? 5 cm may be high when considering building envelope, low when considering crack detection, and null when considering temperature. Once a year may be high when considering subsidence, but very low when considering car park occupancy.

What about the V-R? Collecting mobile telemetry from a motor at 30-second intervals, to an accuracy of five degrees, may be required for a predictive fault model (predicting if a motor might fail). However, if the prediction horizon of the data model is measured in hours (i.e., you only get hours of warning, not days or weeks) and the maintenance team only receives an automated bulletin of predictions at the end of every day, or worse still, a maintenance planner only considers predictions once a week when planning the next 14-day rolling plan, then the V-R frequency is high. Maybe too high, if no one uses it? Unless you're using it to train an applied AI model. Then it might be too low...

Higher frequency and fidelity may seem like the logical path, and in many cases is risk reducing, but two challenges to the "more is better" paradigm arise: overfitting and cost.

Overfitting is a phenomenon in statistics and machine learning where a model is trained too well on the training data, to the point where it starts to capture noise and random fluctuations in the training data as if they were important features. This results in the model performing very well on the training data but poorly on new, unseen data, because the patterns it has learned are not generalizable. Overfitting is essentially a model learning the training data too well, including its anomalies, which detracts from its ability to generalize to other data sets.

Cost is an obvious but very commonly overlooked one, and it's not overlooked because we forget about cost. It's overlooked because determining how much data is too much is impossible without being able to measure what "too much" is, which implies you know what "the right amount" is. In other words, when the data specification is not related, explicitly, to the use case, and hence the problem to be solved, then it is impossible to know what "good" frequency and fidelity look like, and we tend to err on the side of caution – more please, sir.

This tendency is magnified by the data centric mantras of consultants and people who don't need to pay for said data (no skin in the game of outcomes...) and exacerbated by the lack of focus on V-R connections. In other words, many digital twins today are far too heavy on the R-V, and far too light on the V-R, and neither are driven by the actual problem to be solved.

Designed to create change in the real that is measured and improved in the virtual

The fifth element of our definition is the most important of them all, and the least discussed in any forum. Why did we / are we creating this connected thing in the first place? Everyone talks about "solving problems" with technology, but digital twins and applied AI are explicitly interconnected to the real world. The only purpose of these interconnections can be to create change in said world – otherwise, why did we do this? I think this one seemingly simple, but in fact quite fundamental contention has been lost in the marketing and noise of digital twins.

To be explicit:

- If we only want to measure the real world, we have existing paradigms for that – buy a drone or hire a surveyor or install a sensor
- If we only want to design a new world, we have existing paradigms for that – buy a CAD license or generate terrains and go for it
- If we only want to analyze data from the real world, we have existing paradigms for that – statistics and ML for the applied win, generative models for the horizontal
- If we only want to control the real world, we have existing paradigms for that – SCADA / DCS / open / closed etc.
- If we only want to augment our view of the real world
- If we only want to simulate

You get what I'm saying.

The challenge that has arisen for digital twins (and increasingly for applied AI) is in this basic lack of consideration for what makes a twin "different," which is another way of saying "why do we even need it?"

I shall be the heretic in the room and say it out aloud:

- for a great many specific problems, we do not need digital twins or applied AI, and
- for a great many classes of problem, digital twins and applied AI are overly complex ways of solving half the problem, and usually the easier half.

The natural and perhaps final extension of this difficulty in "categorizing" digital twins is the metaverse. The metaverse has been seized on by many as the way to make digital twins more applicable to "everything," because digital twins connect everything, and therefore when you have a metaverse you can do anything. It is an even more generic and fuzzy abstraction of abstractions.

The reason you build a digital twin is that you need to create repeatable and connected outcomes in the real world, and you believe those outcomes can be improved through the use of technology, and *existing specific categories of solutions don't solve those problems well.*

In other words, building a twin to replace an existing maintenance solution should only be done if the twin is fundamentally better than existing maintenance solutions. If that means the twin needs to have all the functionality of the existing solutions, and then you start adding 3D visualizations "because that's what a twin has," then you will quickly find yourself building a maintenance solution with 3D visualizations. Hopefully, your twin will solve the problem better than the dedicated maintenance solution did. Hopefully, there was some problem in the real world that the maintenance solution couldn't solve well, and the unique attributes of representation, interconnectedness and synchronization enabled the twin to do better.

If not, then you have probably built a poor and unique maintenance solution. And worse still, if you're a software vendor, you're playing the wrong field entirely, and don't know who you're competing with, and your "twinny" maintenance solution is twice as costly to support and improve than your competitors' domain-specific solution.

Our goal is not to solve every problem with a twin – it's to solve problems in the real world in a better way than they are currently being solved. Knowing which problems don't require or are not amenable to twin solutions is as important as designing great digital twins and great models. The definition as it stands is:

"A digital twin comprises a virtual representation of a selected portion of the real world, with two-way interconnections, synchronized at specified frequencies and fidelities, and designed to create change in the real that can be measured and improved in the virtual."

A digital twin that meets this definition would, I hope, be widely considered a "digital twin" by most. More importantly than pleasing people – and let's not forget that many of the strong opinions in any arena are driven by commercial incentives of one form or another – the above definition is meant as a guide to understanding what a "good" digital twin should be designed to do. In practice, vendors and creators can brand and market anything as anything, and the market decides what becomes commonly referred to as a digital twin. For practitioners, (i.e., those who build), I hope that this definition helps you when you are faced with the many competing or contradictory statements you will continue to face.

Mental models

With this in mind, let's tackle some of the implications of such a definition, to deepen our understanding of the why and the what of digital twin types.

Software versus framework

One of the most divisive debates in digital twin land is software versus framework. The debate can be boiled down to this: is the digital twin a piece of software, or is it a framework for building software? A framework is generally considered a structure or system that provides support or guidance for building something. Software is... software.

I have vacillated on this issue many times over the years. The Digital Twin Design Process we discuss in this book is evidence of my views. But let's examine the alternatives.

First and foremost, the original digital twin ecosystem model is composed of the real world, the virtual world and the interconnections. If we take the software view, we are effectively discarding the real world, and often the real-to-virtual connection. The virtual-to-real is usually limited to data acquisition and ignores synchronization, as that is not required when we have discarded the real world. In this view, the digital twin is reduced to "just" software and the data required to enable the internal features and capabilities of the software. I think this covers 90% of digital twins ever built. It's also becoming the dominant paradigm for applied AI. I think it's simple but I don't think it's very helpful to builders.

In the framework view, the fundamental model provides a baseline but provides almost no guidance on what to build and what needs to happen in the real world. Various frameworks have been developed, and for professional twin developers (e.g., service providers) they are almost a necessity to enable repeatable delivery processes. The challenge with frameworks is that they are all unique, and are proliferating faster than definitions. When large customers, say asset owners, define their own frameworks for twins, they frequently reference engineering and software standards. This makes complete sense for a guide on how to build a digital twin. What makes less sense is that most frameworks are designed to provide consistency in *how* to build, but no guidance on *what* to build. This also makes sense, as the people who develop frameworks are not the people responsible for defining problems in the real world or accountable for outcomes or lack thereof – they are software architects and developers.

Thus, the software and framework views cover the same portion of the ecosystem: the data acquisition and software parts.

So, software or framework?

I think, sadly, it's both. And both are useful, but neither is enough on its own if misapplied to only one part of the ecosystem.

Service providers build software. They don't use digital twin frameworks to build software products – they use software products and engineering management.

Problem owners benefit from frameworks if they are going to repeatably buy or build digital twins. Internal technology teams sometimes use software product management, though more frequently they use project management methods.

> *My hypothesis is that the digital twin is the connected elements of the ecosystem that create, measure and improve the specific changes we desire. The digital twin design process is the design of the changes to the ecosystem, via those connected elements, both real and virtual.*

I'll repeat it: My hypothesis is that twins are the connected elements of the ecosystem that create, measure and improve the specific changes we desire. i.e., it is more than the "digital twin" you bought from a SaaS vendor or built with your dev team. It is very important to note, however, that this definition differs from many others. There are many people who are selling "digital twins" that are just 3D models, and "digital twins" that are platforms for connecting data, and "digital twins" that are specific data instances of specific physical objects, and so on. They're all "digital twins" to someone, and some are more twinny than others, but critically, they are all excluding (implicitly or explicitly) the real-world elements of the ecosystem.

How can things be more than one thing at once? The pump that is twinned becomes part of the digital twin. It is still a pump. It is also part of a process plant. It is also a class of equipment. It is also part of a balance sheet. It is still a part of the digital twin. If there are multiple digital twins in operation, say one for predictive maintenance, and one for production optimization, then the pump is part of 2 digital twins. It is still a pump.

How do I handle this multiplicity?

For starters, I hardly ever say "digital twin". I don't argue with people about their digital twins. I don't produce maturity matrices that rank features of the software components of a digital twin and exclude the real-world components. And I for sure don't get hung up on someone who says "that's not a digital twin, it doesn't have [insert favorite capability here]". Everyone is entitled to their opinion, and the generalized labelling of specifics is a game as old as religion (or politics). We all play it, whether we like it or not, and it most certainly changes what we do and where we spend our time and money, but it most definitely doesn't alter the laws of thermodynamics, or the interconnectedness of a process, or the accuracy of a data model. That's my world, and the level of abstraction above that I call "marketing" – and I do enjoy marketing as a game to be played – well. But I never confuse marketing with entropy.

Throughout this book, you will likely notice that at times I refer to digital twins as software, and I use the product software paradigm (discover & iterate) to describe the ways of delivering and improving change in the virtual and real worlds. Roll with it, and you'll see that the very multiplicity which creates anxiety for academics creates flexibility for thinking about how to solve problems.

Twin types

When conducting my Masters of Engineering research in 2020-21, I reviewed over 200 academic and open-sourced references on digital twins. From this work, it was clear that digital twins have generally aggregated around the type of physical phenomenon they are twinning, and thus are often represented by the particular lifecycle paradigm that the phenomenon is contained within. Applied AI is 10 years behind and is following the same path.

The main categories of digital twins I discussed are:

- product
- operations
- project
- algorithmic

Note that these categories are not mutually exclusive. A digital twin is an amalgam of capabilities and the specific configuration is, by definition, a mirror of the physical object / process / reality being replicated. Thus, a digital twin may be asset-oriented and contain specific algorithmic capabilities, or be some other combination of the above categories, in order to best achieve the desired outcome. However, it is clear that the diversity and confusion of posited digital twin use cases is leading people to subcategorize in order to reduce uncertainty. In particular, potential customers are confused about what a digital twin is, and technology vendors are narrowing their messaging to attract the right kind of customers. In all cases, the domain expertise / background of the owner has a massive impact on how they frame the concept.

Product digital twins view the conjoined real and virtual ecosystem through the product lifecycle management paradigm and seek to optimize product outcomes. Product twins will often incorporate advanced analytics related to manufacturing and supply chain quality and cost, high-fidelity 3D models (typically of parts / product components), and material / cost simulations (to understand the impact of changes to materials / supply chain / design) as part of their capabilities.

Operations / Facility digital twins view the conjoined real and virtual ecosystem through the Operations and Maintenance (O&M) or Facility Management (FM) portion of the asset lifecycle (depending on the industry), and seek to optimize the operation and management of physical assets such as buildings or power plants. Operations twins typically incorporate advanced analytics related to equipment faults, maintenance works, and operations, and may have several product twin components (e.g., original equipment manufacturer (OEM) supplied digital twins).

Project digital twins view the conjoined real and virtual ecosystem through the design and build (creation) portion of the asset lifecycle and seek to optimize project delivery outcomes related to the creation or modification of physical assets. Project twins are typically built on or are extensions to existing 3D CAD (computer aided design) software, with specific use cases in progress measurement, risk analysis, or construction sequencing. Many project twins have weak or non-existent Virtual-Real connections, due to the unique nature of construction projects.

Algorithmic digital twins view the conjoined real and virtual ecosystem through one of the physical world process-oriented paradigms, such as supply chain management or chemical process design and optimization. Algorithmic twins utilize AI, simulation and analytics to optimize complex problems and / or to simulate / generate / predict future events. Algorithmic twins are usually built to solve specific problems in the real world that are represented by domain-specific data models, and are grouped with a corresponding product, operational or engineering twin capability for visual representation and user context.

Solution focused

While the above groupings simplify the comparison of one digital twin to another (the purpose of categories), in reality digital twins and applied AI (like most technology solutions) are often designed to solve a class of problem and named after the corresponding solution. Examples include predictive maintenance twins, process control twins, carbon twins etc. As with any software-defined solution, the degree to which a digital twin can be compared with a similarly focused solution is largely based on specific features and specific problems that are solved, and how well those problems are solved. In many (most) cases, a [solution] digital twin will be competing with an existing incumbent non-digital twin solution, and this comparison serves to further complicate and perpetuate the "what is a digital twin" question. The often-asked question is "If my non-digital twin solves the same problem as the [solution] digital twin, then is my non-digital twin also a digital twin?" The answer, of course, is maybe – but probably not – because the question is meaningless / academic.

A similar and non-sensical question would be, "If my horse gets me to the shops and your car gets me to the shops, is my horse a car?" Equivalently, "If my animal gets me to the shops and your vehicle gets me to the shops, is my animal a vehicle?" hmmm... no? And if we then take it to the logical extreme, "If my means of non-bipedal conveyance gets me to the shop and your means of non-bipedal conveyance gets me to the shops, are our means of non-bipedal conveyance equivalent?" Well... yes? They are both means of non-bipedal conveyance.

Similarly, you can ask if the digital twin is "better" or "worse" than the non-digital twin... a better means of non-bipedal conveyance? A better vehicle? Lower emissions? Lower cost to build? Better fuel economy? Better companionship?

Comparing solutions only makes sense in the context of what you are comparing against or measuring for. Worse still, comparing features ("connections," "data") may be as silly a comparing the number of wheels to legs between the car and the horse. Equivalency in data and connections in no way implies value for money, and yet these are the typical solution-focused features that are discussed.

Technology led

The other large driver of digital twins is the specific technology that the twin is built around. Digital twin solutions are often driven by the underlying capability, infrastructure or visualization engine.

For example, simulation twins abound. Many of these digital twins are designed to provide high fidelity visual simulations. The virtual representation is typically underpinned by 3D CAD models or 3D animations, and some simulations are algorithmic in nature (e.g., a simulation based on a physics model) while some are animated (pre-programmed to follow a specific sequence). Many algorithmic digital twins are built on simulation capabilities, as that is their primary reason for existing.

Infrastructure providers who power many digital twin applications have been developing digital twin platforms for many years now. The two most notable are Microsoft's Azure Digital Twins (ADT) and Amazon Web Services (AWS) IoT TwinMaker. In both cases the vendor refers to digital twins as the specific instance of each entity that is twinned. Thus, an operational digital twin built on ADT may have thousands of "digital twins" within it, each one corresponding to a piece of equipment or structure that makes up the overall building. The clarifying terminology of digital twin "instances" has now appeared, thankfully, though many end users do not use this yet. A digital twin may be made up of thousands of digital twin instances. The twin is at the "system" level, while the instance is at the "component" level.

The final technology category is the gaming visualization engines, such as Unreal, Unity, and Omniverse, which are claiming some mindshare with the use of "industrial digital twin" and "industrial metaverse" applications. These solutions, which provide extremely high quality and low latency visualizations, and upon whom many digital twin applications are being built, are attempting to capture market share by reinforcing the increasingly common definition of digital twin as "real-time 3D visualization."

Internal feature versus connected capability

If a twin utilizes a capability of a connected system, is the twin doing the work or is the connected system? More importantly to many, is the twin responsible for the value created when that capability is already extant inside the ecosystem? Similarly for applied AI, if the domain specific model serves to filter more than generate, and the underlying vector or graph provides definitive and separate value, and it is connected through a gaming engine for 3D visualization, is it still "applied AI"?

If a twin is defined by the features it contains, rather than the change it creates in the real world, then the features inside the twin will dominate, and the value of the twin will likely be limited to the direct usage and impact of those features, both by the user and the designer of the twin.

If a twin is defined by the change it creates in the real world, then the internal features will provide value if and only if they contribute to creating that desired change – features that are internal but not related to desired outcomes are as "disconnected" as other systems that are not connected to the digital twin and do not contribute to the desired change. Similarly, connected systems that are not directly related to the desired change will also provide no value. *Features and systems that are integrated but are not connected to the desired change are not value-adding features or integrations.* In fact, they could be judged to be wasted effort and cost, and complexity, at least for a specific desired change in the real world, albeit they may be connected to other use cases or be planned to be connected to future use cases. The purpose of the twin determines what features and data are valuable, not the extent / breadth / fidelity / quality of the features and data.

Additional versus replacement

This difference in how a digital twin is framed is related to the classic "additional" versus "replacement" system discussion. If a twin is brought in to replace another system, then feature parity / direct replacement of capability / comparative cost will be the primary decision criteria. If the twin is seen as being additional to existing systems, then additional value / return on investment / additional complexity / change / total cost of ownership will dominate.

Note that these criteria are standard software buy / build criteria. They are also one of the major impediments to envisioning, specifying and creating change across ecosystems of people, assets and work. The standard procurement process defines the battery limits of a new addition to that ecosystem, and this implies the value created by that addition as being limited to the value created by the addition. The problem here is that to create connected change across the ecosystem, one may need to buy digital twin software, add sensors, train models and change business processes.

No value can be created without approval to add or change existing systems, and this approval is contingent on business cases, which are usually siloed to department budgets, which usually only have approval to use or modify or add systems that are already within their control.

The result is that many digital twins bought and built today are single-use-case and narrowly defined precisely to optimize for procurement and internal approval processes. They deliberately limit their interaction with the real world, or limit their need to rely on data or change from non-buying silos, as these introduce buying friction and adoption friction that undermines vendor revenue growth aspirations.

At the other end of the spectrum, the opportunity to create value from existing data and systems, regardless of ownership or legacy, has led to the rise of "platform" twins, where many use cases can be configured through a single system, and many data models can be connected to user actions. These types of platforms are usually bought by the technology silo, and extensive vendor services are required to configure and integrate as the final leg of delivery into hands of users, who again have little or no authority to create up or downstream change to enable their new capabilities.

Vertical organizational silos are far bigger impediments to connected change than most realize. They have shaped our very ideas of what could be done, limiting what is even attempted by the majority of people. We have narrowed down our aspirations to the silos we can directly influence.

Narrow versus wide

The concept of solution versus platform is very common in twins and AI. It's worth us digging down into this to better understand the difference between capabilities and use cases, and transformation versus solution. My mental model for this is "narrow" and "wide" twins.

Narrow twins

Narrow twins are digital twins and applied AI designed to solve specific problems. The choice of problem specificity (and it is a choice) determines if a twin is designed to solve a problem (working backwards from the real world), or if a twin is a coupling of capability and data that may serve a wide variety of purposes (working forwards to the real world).

Narrow twins have strongly coupled problem-change-capability-data loops. The problem determines what change needs to happen, which in turn drives the capability required, which drives the data required. Narrow twins are inherently better able to measure benefits (as the problem and change are clearly defined), but may not be able to solve other problems, even within the same problem class, without modification and additional cost. Narrow twins need "strong and complete" data – data directly enabling the capabilities and change, available at the required frequencies and fidelities. Weak or missing data directly undermines the ability of the narrow twin to solve the selected problem.

A narrow operations twin may be a digital twin of a HVAC system, designed to optimize energy consumption versus occupant comfort.

A narrow-applied AI may be a twin of a specific chemical reaction, designed to optimize reaction rate versus reagent usage.

Narrow does not imply non-reusable, nor does it imply non-extensible. A narrow twin built on an open architecture with multiple modular capabilities may be quickly applied to many adjacent problems. Critically, multiple narrow twins may solve multiple problems in the same class, e.g., maintenance problems. But if each narrow twin was born of a problem, and worked backward, then it is a set of narrow twins.

Wide twins

Wide twins are at the other end of the problem specificity spectrum – non-specific problems. Non-specific problems can include classes of problems, such as "risk," or opportunities, such as "improvements," but unlike narrow twins where problem, change, capability, and data are strongly coupled, in wide twins the problem is diffuse or abstracted and thus the capability and data are weakly coupled to the real-world problem.

Wide twins typically start from data related to a problem type (e.g., equipment faults), or capabilities known to be beneficial to a problem type (e.g., simulation). Wide twins are often technology led solutions. A specific technology has solved similar problems, or proponents believe it can solve similar problems, and the technology leads the design of the solution. This is working forwards to the real world. I have grouped non-specific problems and technology led solutions together as they have the same challenge: defining what changes need to be made in the real world in order to create improved outcomes.

In a similar way to many digitization and digitalization motions, deployment of more advanced capabilities underpins digital transformation. More capabilities are generally seen as increasing maturity. Maturity roadmaps are generally sequential lists of "increasing" capabilities, with the clear implication that greater capability implies greater value.

The benefits of wide twins are that increased capabilities or more highly connected capabilities can be brought to bear in the real world. The challenge is measuring success and ROI. Wide twins also suffer from difficulty in attributing user behavior – some users use it, some don't, and understanding why is very difficult when there is no clear user journey or relationship between features (capabilities) and value.

More advanced twins coming into market now often combine wide capabilities with specific, narrow problem solving, to provide a base problem-solving capability to then extend upon. We'll touch upon this again later.

Weak versus strong

Weakly coupled twins

A twin with only R-V (real to virtual) connections, or a single R-V update at a point in time (think 3D model to create the twin virtualization), are examples of weakly coupled twins. As argued earlier, a twin with no V-R connections is difficult to categorize as a digital twin, but frequently this is because the V-R is ill-defined, not missing altogether.

What makes twins weakly coupled:

- No V-R connection (lack of interconnection)
- V-R connections that are diffuse or multi-step (poor interconnection)
- A single initial R-V "creation" event (lack of synchronization)
- Misaligned V-R and R-V synchronization (poor synchronization)
- Loss of some R-V connections (weakening)
- Loss of all R-V connections (decoupling)

Wide twins often suffer from this weak coupling, as the majority of the data flows are R-V to enable the capabilities, and existing business process is trusted to provide V-R change. There is no doubt that a wide, weakly coupled twin can create benefits. However, defining and measuring those benefits will likely be very difficult, and the product owner will discover that there is little pattern to the requests for additional capabilities. In fact, nearly everyone will want their current tools and processes replicated and bettered.

Wide, weak twins often suffer from feature-itis: the twin is (inadvertently) positioned as the new and improved way of operating, and every user who has to spend time with their existing systems and the twin, in order to accomplish the same thing they used to do in one system they know well, either demands the twin replace the old system (leading to runaway feature requests) or they just don't use the twin at all (leading to runaway roadmapping to try and get them back). In either case there is friction to user adoption.

Strongly coupled twins

At the opposite end of the interconnection spectrum, strongly coupled twins have strong V-R connections and R-V connections driven by measurement of change. Note again that the absolute number of connections is not necessarily an indicator of coupling strength or value. Rather, the relative strength of the V-R and R-V must be assessed against the real-world change desired and cost to achieve.

Strongly coupled twins with multiple R-V at high frequency and fidelity often require higher costs and time to create and higher ongoing costs to maintain (versus weakly coupled). In particular, the cost to change or update the R-V connections when the real world is changing rapidly is often overlooked. The higher the rate of change of the real world, the more important the type of connection to ensure this change is accounted for and / or that the virtual representation and corresponding capabilities remain synchronized. A decoupled twin is the result of losing the R-V connections. A strongly coupled twin with some loss of connection becomes weakly coupled.

Strongly coupled twins with high rates of change in the real world need very robust connections to avoid progressive decoupling or intermittent weak coupling. As with all software, even short periods of decoupling can quickly erode user confidence, with commensurate falls in value creation and rises in change management effort and / or features to recover. Beware creating overly strong couplings if there is no need to.

Fit for purpose

Bringing the concepts of width (narrow versus wide) and coupling (weak versus strong) together, we can begin to see that different combinations suit different situations, and certain combinations may be problematic.

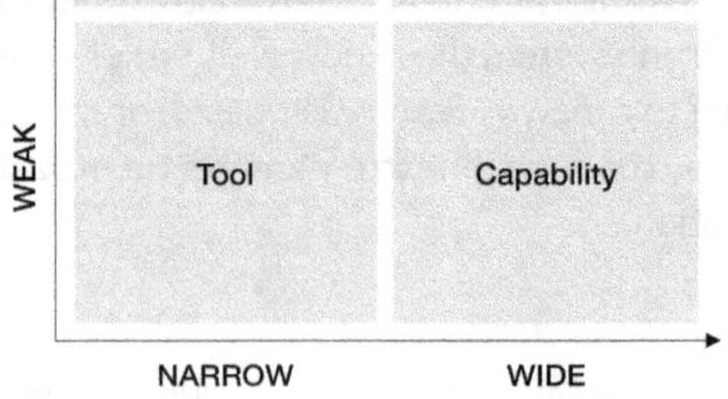

Wide, strongly coupled twin

A wide and strongly coupled twin may look the most robust from a data strategy and extensiveness point of view. The risk here is ROI: the investment is likely to be large and high to maintain, and the return may be difficult to measure. Many digital transformation initiatives driven by large consulting firms fall into this category. "Get all the data and connect it to every kind of capability" and you will be transformed. In 2025, the mantra has become "connect all your data to generative AI" and [insert positive transformational outcome]. The failure modes and statistics for digital transformations are well known and beyond the scope of this book to analyze. I will say, however, that I think the days of extremely large consulting engagements to "digitally" "transform" organizations that are now built around and upon technology are coming to an end. Large orgs will be far more likely to Palantir than McKinsey, in my humble opinion.

Narrow, weakly coupled twin

The narrow and weak twin is likely to be a low-cost, highly specific tool. If the correct data set and connections are chosen, it may be highly valuable. On the other hand, if the V-R is absent, it may be an existing software solution masquerading as a twin.

Wide, weakly coupled twin

The wide and weak twin looks like a set of capabilities. Visualization twins, showing as much high-fidelity visuals as possible, often fall into this category. The usual wide challenge of difficult-to-prove-ROI exists, however when selected properly, wide and weak can be very useful for piloting specific new capabilities that are required to underpin other initiatives or other narrow twins.

Narrow, strongly coupled twins

The narrow and strong twin is a product. It is designed to solve a problem and the interconnections are implemented to solve and measure the solving of that problem. If the problem is rapidly changing in the real world, the connections will need to be robust to avoid weakening / decoupling. If the product does not solve the problem, the twin will prove that the twin is not solving the problem. If the architecture is not sufficiently open, or the capabilities not sufficient modular, then solving adjacent problems may require new products.

What then is "fit-for-purpose" in a digital twin or applied AI? The answer lies in the objectives that led to the creation of the twin in the first place. A digital twin that is strongly coupled is not better than a weakly coupled twin, nor is a wide twin better than a narrow. A well-designed twin is a twin that is optimized to achieve the objectives, both problem-specific and ROI. All twins are solutions and require changes to existing capabilities. All twins reflect their real-world paradigm, with correspondingly fast or slow or unanticipated changes. Similarly, problems in the real world often have a "natural frequency," that drives the need for data acquisition at a certain frequency and fidelity, and drives actions in the real world at a certain frequency and fidelity (often by business processes and decision-making / governance).

A twin that achieves its objectives with a high ROI is a well-designed twin. A great twin is one that continues to achieve objectives, over a long enough period of time, with feasible changes in the real world and improvements in the problem space. A fit-for-purpose twin achieves the objectives with the minimum problem specificity and coupling required to achieve and measure the achievement of the change required. You can tell a fit-for-purpose twin when you see one, because it is obviously a part of the overall ecosystem, and people love using it to solve problems in the real world.

Solution patterns

There are four common solution patterns typically seen in the wild:

- Bridge
- Tool
- Wrapper
- Enhancement

Bridge

The Bridge Pattern (Bridge) occurs when a twin is used to connect multiple existing systems under a single engagement layer.

Existing infrastructure remains unchanged, and various systems and data models can be connected together. The engagement layer will likely encompass front and back-end elements (e.g., UI and APIs).

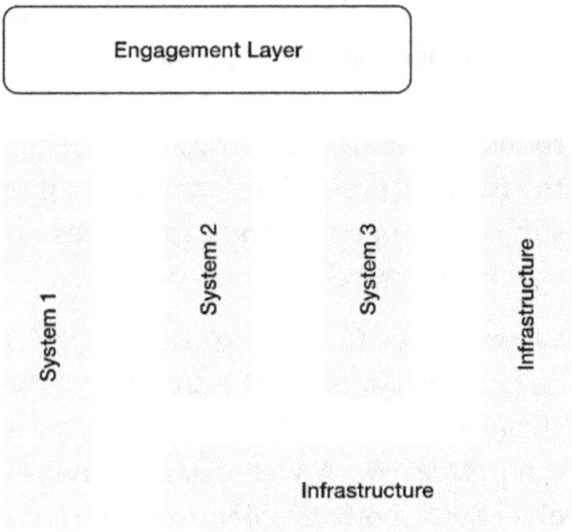

A Bridge is often present when a twin is used to:

- Create cross-functional workflows
- Connect multiple existing applications together
- Create an organization-specific and controllable engagement layer / user interface

Depending on the existing software ecosystem and connected systems, in particular with existing SaaS solutions or older solutions without any API, or coded in older / unsupported languages, the Bridge may be quite difficult to build.

A Bridge may be wide or narrow. Wide Bridges are usually an attempt to standardize or control what a user in the field sees. Narrow Bridges are now commonly being used to bring together multiple related systems (e.g., all work management systems), or existing systems with new data models (e.g., the enterprise work management system with inhouse AI predictive maintenance models).

Tool

The Tool Pattern (Tool) is the classic software product – a Tool to replace an existing system or solve a specific problem or support business process change. Most applied AI solutions are Tools.

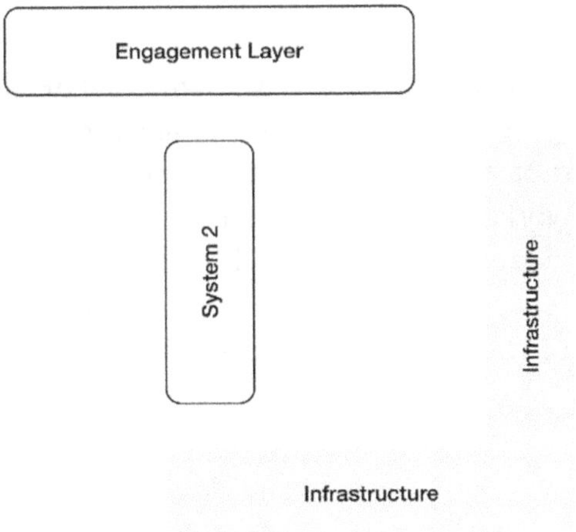

A Tool is most often used when:

- Bringing new capability (application) into an organization
- Converting manual processes into system / product workflows
- Replacing legacy systems

A Tool is typically narrow and often contains a bespoke data model – in some cases developed independently of the twin.

Wrapper

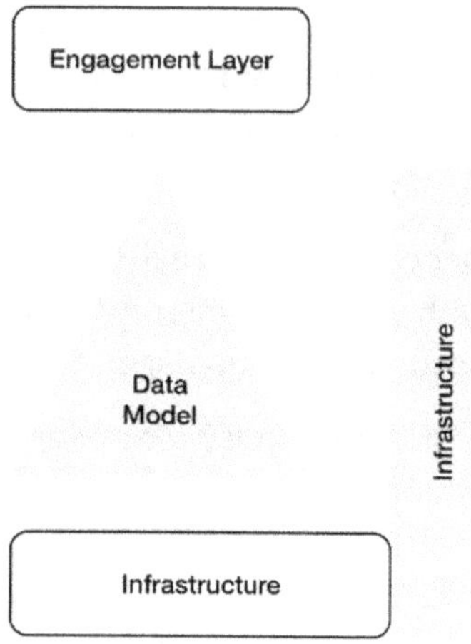

The Wrapper Pattern (Wrapper) is an emerging pattern that enables data models (e.g., ML models or AI products) to be used for field testing or in production (user-deployed, not data engineering / software dev production).

Wrappers are used when:

- Bringing new data products and data model capabilities into existing workflows
- Testing new and multiple data models (or rapid iterations) in field production environments
- Productionizing data models, especially to incorporate user feedback, or reinforcement learning from human feedback

Wrappers are a rapidly growing segment of twins, driven by the rise of AI and genAI growth. In-house AI models and products in particular, often the province of internal data science teams, are experiencing low success rates. Of the companies I have worked with in Wrapper-type situations, the lack of success has not been due to model inaccuracy (which is usually well quantified), but rather lack of connection to real problems, or lack of usability, or lack of explicit connection to how the problem can be solved in the real world.

Enhancement

Twins that enhance existing systems are also a growing segment.

Enhancement twins solve problems with combinations of existing systems and new capabilities.

Enhancement twins often include aspects of Bridges and Wrappers, combining existing systems and new capabilities within a single engagement layer.

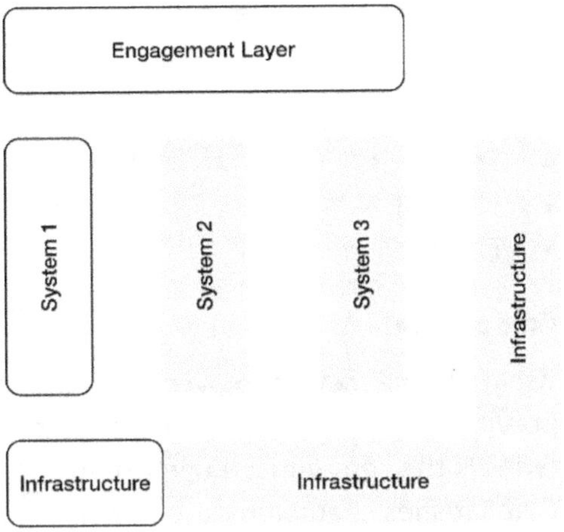

Visualization twin

Visualization of the real-world domain is a very frequent first step into "twinning," especially in asset intensive industries such as manufacturing, airports, mining, power and construction. I would say that visualization twins are the most common "first" twin for many organizations, and seem at first to be the easiest to do, but in fact have one of the longest "tails" of confusion, "incomplete" features and low adoption.

Visualization twins usually include the following Capabilities and Data:

- 3D visual representation (3D CAD models or LiDAR / point cloud / photogrammetry models) of fixed assets and / or terrain
- Spatial location and navigation (moving your point of view to various places to observe the 3D visual representation)
- Static "equipment data" related to equipment or assets (e.g., pump tag name and number)
- Real-time operational data of fixed assets (e.g., the pump operating curve, head pressure, current / voltage etc.)
- Real-time location of mobile plant / vehicles (e.g., forklifts or truck with real-time location sensors (RTLS))
- Ability to interrogate objects "embedded" in the visual representation (e.g., clicking on a pump brings up its static and real-time operational data)
- Ability to make and place notes "spatially" so that other users can see / interrogate later (e.g., make a note when pump real-time data looks "wrong")

What challenges do visualization twins often have?

Visualization twins offer suffer from five typical wide twin issues:

- Gold plating
- Low adoption
- Featuritis
- No-ROI
- Decoupling

Gold plating

"Gold plating" refers to over investing into things that don't drive returns or don't provide benefits to users or consumers. The most common issue with Visualization twins is the sometimes-huge expense and effort to acquire "excellent" spatial data that satisfies champion requirements. What do I mean by this? Champions – those who passionately believe in an innovative change, are often over-zealous in their beliefs about detail and perfection. They have a vision of what something could be. Vision driven visualization twins typically try to perfectly mirror reality. This can be unintentional and usually comes from a well-meaning place. But the downstream effects often result in spending millions of dollars on data acquisition projects.

Worse still, accuracy and fidelity become absolutes, with people sometimes insisting that every bolt and nut needs to be "visible", while entire areas that are not of interest to the champion / buyer are left "empty," resulting in very mismatched and patchy mirroring of the real world. This is very typical when BIM type processes are considered "necessary" to create a digital twin, and exacerbated if project / design people are the project sponsors. Very often the discussion becomes what Level of Detail (LOD) is required, and project execution people will often stipulate LOD400 as a minimum requirement.

Extremely heavy / large visual data models lead to all sorts of technical issues with browser-based systems (though this is getting easier with game engines, tiling and clever memory management), but they also create an enormous future synchronization cost. The greater the detail in the creation of the twin, the greater the detail required to synchronize the twin. This detail is often overlooked in project delivery motions, where a fixed budget and scope need to be delivered, and downstream costs are "someone else's problem."

The upshot of gold plating fidelity is that the very detail that is unutilized is often shown off to highlight how detailed the twin is... and if the purpose of the twin is to highlight how detailed 3D models are, then this is no longer gold plating, but rather making 3D models accessible.

Low adoption

Visualization twins are typically built for "anyone" to use and pitched that "senior managers" will love to log in and check on things in real time from anywhere. They do love this, and they do check in, about twice. Then they go back to their meetings, their PDF and PowerBI reports, their subordinates who need to report on progress, and their financial metrics.

For technical workers who work at the site in question, or who support it from afar (e.g., engineers), there is low adoption because they know the site, and they know the parts of the site they care about very well, and they still must use their designated systems of record to conduct their work.

If there is a narrow use case built in, then this cohort may use it more frequently, but I have found many visualization twins have not explicitly built themselves into workflows, even for the narrow use case, because the team in question still needs to use all their existing systems and processes. The visualization twin is not displacing anything or altering business processes.

Featuritis

The main consequence of the wideness of visualization twins is potential champions requesting more features. I say "potential" champions, because these well-intentioned individuals usually have a love of technology, and can envision how a near real-time or very high-fidelity visualization could benefit part of the organization, "if only it had two more things." This is not to say they are incorrect. Rather, that they are not typical [insert job title here] and their peers and co-workers may very well not share their fascination of technology and desire to "change how things are done around here." Building features from fascinated parties is rarely high-ROI work. The features look good, the champion uses them, but others rarely do, and the champion has not thought through the little details of process changes and data availability and impact on other areas. This isn't their job, of course – it's yours. The lure of "one more feature" is very hard to resist, when 99% of your intended audience doesn't use your product, and the two who do are happy and very engaged and give you lots of time and attention.

No ROI

Low adoption + featuritis = low or No ROI. The visualization twin may be a showcase of capabilities, and this is a benefit in many organizations who are struggling to show outputs from investments into innovation. But without strongly defined use cases, and without buy-in from people who are responsible for real change in the real world, it's very unusual for Visualization twins to have any measurable ROI. They can provide some organizational benefits, as we'll see next, but without measurable returns and with a very small number of users, ROI is likely to be nil or made up.

Decoupling

The final nail for many Visualization twins is the progressive decoupling from the real world as changes are made to assets / areas / equipment / processes, that are not reflected in the visual representation. Many Visualization twins need data updated every hour, or day, or week, and the cost to do this and manually integrate data and push revised static models out to users is prohibitive. Additionally, when specific items in the real-world change, static and operational data feeds must be recoupled with the new visualization elements. Decoupling is usually progressive, i.e., 1%, 2%, 4% of the relevant portion of the real world is no longer synchronized. The real challenge is not keeping the virtual 100% coupled and accurate at all times. The real issue is determining what parts of the real world need to be tightly coupled, and what parts only need to be synchronized every X time periods, and what parts are context and only to create awareness of the users' point of view or navigation.

When Visualization twins are pitched to be "the virtual representation of the real world," there is a strong and persistent tendency to try and make all parts of the representation of equal fidelity and synchronization. I hope you will agree by the end of this book that this is not the ideal way to approach a wide twin. Some data is >>> more important than other data.

What benefits do Visualization twins offer?

Visualization twins are a common stepping stone on the journey from siloed, abstracted in-arrears metric management to holistic, situation-aware management. They are also ideal "bridges" between siloed systems and departments, bringing together people who work together every day anyway, and enabling people who are often struggling to "see" what is happening "across" an organization, to do just that. Remote worker collaboration is a particularly valuable benefit.

Visualization twins with narrow use cases embedded in them are often valuable and provide ROI. They do sometimes have challenges with "gold plating" visual data, but when visual data provides context to multiple narrow use cases then the investment may provide genuine value. Visualization twins can also be valuable for genuinely challenging non-line of sight problems. Use cases involving subsurface work, e.g., drilling or utilities, or work across large linear distances, or work inside sealed pressure vessels, are all good examples of situations that humans were never well suited to, and removing humans and providing increased "visibility" (even where light rays literally cannot penetrate) can provide immense benefit.

We'll return to Visualization twins later in the book, after we explore some concepts for how to design valuable twins.

Part 2 – Ecosystem

Explores the interplay between real, existing virtual, and new virtual worlds, highlighting the challenges and opportunities in designing interconnected systems for impactful change.

Ecosystem

- Real
- Virtual (existing)
- Virtual (new)
- Ecosystem
- Methods of change
- Implications

Returning to the existential question: *Is a digital twin a technology solution or a pattern?*

Yes.

😊

Ok so we've established that the nature of the portion of the real world should drive much of the design of a digital twin, but how do we reconcile this real versus virtual problem?

If a digital twin is a software solution, or a framework for how to build a software solution, we know how to design those, let's just do it. If applied AI is an AI that we think will be better than other people's AI, let's just build it and try it.

That's exactly what many vendors and internal technology teams have done. They have created standalone solutions, based on classic software principles, and used APIs and integrations to connect data between systems. The challenge inherent in creating highly interconnected solutions is that we should optimize for change in the real world, not to connect data for the sake of more data. When we design software, the furthest we normally go is the user. What actions did the user take *in our software*? North star metrics optimize for user behavior, as that is the furthest we can feasibly control into the real world as *software* builders.

The reality though is that there are a great many use cases where the V-R connection is multi-step beyond the user and includes business processes and manual work. Literal, walking somewhere to look at something and use your hands work.

Is this the purview of the software designer? No – or perhaps not, or perhaps maybe if you're not in a SaaS business. If you own the outcome, however, then you and your team need to have sufficient expertise across the real world and the virtual world. For a twin where you are seeking to maximize the actions of a user in a reasonably simple ecosystem, then the classic software research, discovery and design methodologies are ideal.

For those who operate in complex industrial environments, where the laws of physics are the ultimate arbiter, the user may be but one of many interfaces with the real world, and acquiring sufficient domain expertise to enable product discovery will take infeasibly long. For many experts in their domain, it has taken decades of work to achieve sufficient knowledge to be considered expert.

It is, therefore, not feasible to assume that software teams alone can consistently create highly interconnected technology solutions whose purpose is to create change in the real world, if that change requires more than use of the software. It is possible, and exceptions and world changing software abounds, but for the types of problems that digital twins and applied AI are optimized for, it is unlikely that a software team alone will strike gold repeatably.

Domains

The real world

In the real world, domain expertise is commonplace. We have experts in every field of human endeavor, and every organization aggregates domain expertise to solve their domain-specific problems. The challenge in the modern organization is that all of this expertise resides in silos. In most organizations, the first level of cross-functional management is the General Manager, and all of them grew up in silos. In projects, the project manager is cross-functional, but they live in the silo of delivery, usually not being judged if the thing they build works as designed. Silos within the organization and silos that sometimes cut across other silos.

The siloed nature of the organization does not mean that the problems faced are siloed. Mother nature and the laws of thermodynamics care little for the last corporate restructure. The real world contains the problems we are seeking to solve.

Actions are taken in the real world, whether by actuators or hands, and decisions are made in the real world by humans and in the virtual world by machines and models. These actions and decisions are governed by business processes.

The real world contains the problems we face, the actions we take, the decisions we make and the business processes that bind them all together. The growth of AI demands that we now also encompass decisions in the virtual world, non-human decisions, adding yet more complexity to the real-world problems.

Virtual (existing) world

Every organization has an existing virtual world. We all use computers, and store data, and communicate via email and IM, and use domain-specific software to do and manage work. Every organization of any scale has authentication tools, permission rules, security standards, and a plethora of other process and tooling requirements.

Every twin, therefore, is created inside or adjacent to an existing virtual system. There are no "standalone" solutions in an existing organization, though there are many de-coupled and sitting-on-shelf solutions.

As connection machines, twins are very often (almost always?) connected to existing organizational systems. The twin uses data from the existing virtual world, whether it be just cloud storage, or the ERP, or EAM, or CMMS, or CRM, or bespoke data models, or any other TLA. Very often, one or more of the real to virtual (R-V) connections are already in existence and are then plumbed into the twin.

The virtual world also contains decisions, in the form of rule-based logic or numerical computation or AI. The rapid rise of AI is leading to rapid rises in predictions, which are, in turn influencing decisions and actions in the real world.

The virtual world is full of capabilities and these capabilities are fed by and produce data.

Every twin must, therefore, be able to work with the existing virtual world. And every virtual world is unique to every organization. Common capabilities and common data types are determined by the industry and problem space, but unique software and data types are very common across different organizations.

Virtual (new) world

The virtual part of the twin is new software. It contains all the parts that all industrial software requires, and all the parts that the twin design requires that are not already in the existing virtual world. The new capabilities are built to deliver change into the real world, and data to feed these capabilities comes from either the existing virtual world or the real world.

Putting these together, we have a revised ecosystem model that more accurately reflects the relationships between existing and new.

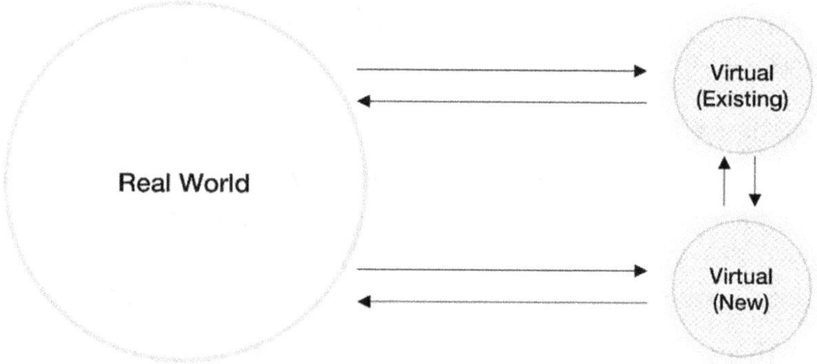

I have also taken the liberty of making the real world much larger than the virtuals. The twin, in particular, represents a portion of the real world, while existing virtual worlds are not really comparable to the real in any meaningful way.

The building of the twin, the Virtual (new), is thus an exercise in placing the correct additional capabilities and interconnections into the existing real and virtual worlds.

Ecosystems

The concept that links everything we have discussed so far is the ecosystem.

An ecosystem is a complex network that consists of all the organisms / elements, the relationships between those elements, and the physical environment with which they interact. A biological ecosystem is a structural and functional unit of ecology where the living organisms interact with each other and the surrounding environment. These interactions create a web of relationships that sustains life and maintains the balance of the ecosystem.

Examples of natural ecosystems include:

- Forests
- Grasslands
- Oceans

Examples of combined natural and artificial (human) ecosystems, where the artificial is seeking to enhance the natural, include:

- Urban parks
- Green roofs
- Sustainable farms

Examples of combined natural and artificial (human) ecosystems, where the artificial is impacted by, but does not seek to enhance the natural, include:

- Mine sites
- Power networks
- Cities

Examples of artificial ecosystems where the natural world is largely "outside," but the very nature of the interconnections resembles a natural ecosystem, include:

- The internet
- Data centers
- Management of groups of humans

The common thread that links all of these domains together is interconnection – ecosystems are domains where many individual elements are interconnected with many other elements. Changes in one element, or one relationship between elements, can create changes in and between many elements, including ones that are often not considered "adjacent" or "related" to the original elements that were changed. As such, the relationships between elements have a disproportionately high impact on ecosystems (compared to how we traditionally think about linear processes), especially when we try to manage ecosystems via individual elements only. Similarly, the behavior of any one element in an ecosystem can be very hard to predict, as the forces and relationships can be fluctuating in unexpected ways over time.

Consider a refinery. On paper, the fundamental elements that determine the success of the refinery are the machines that store, transport and process material. This material starts as "raw" material and is transformed (processed) until it becomes the final product, and the remaining materials (waste) are disposed of. The design of such a refinery is an exercise in systems engineering and domain engineering (e.g., chemical, mechanical, electrical etc.). The refinery consists of many systems, from equipment such as a pump (a small interconnected system of components) to a compressor (a larger system of components and equipment such as pumps) and so forth up to the refinery itself. The refinery is a system of systems. Adjacent to the refinery is the administration office, workshop and other infrastructure. These are also systems, of buildings, equipment, HVAC, etc. The infrastructure system is separate but interconnected to the refinery system.

Across all of the fixed systems are the systems of people, vehicles and moving material that operate in and on the fixed systems. People do work and change the elements of a system. Material flows change and impact many nodes in multiple systems, and energy flows among nodes of multiple systems, forming its own system. The refinery system of systems has many interconnections, far too many for a human to hold in their head, and so we simplify the complexity and manage work and decisions at the most discrete level possible, typically "assets" and "work," such as pumps and work orders. A specific person does a specific task on a specific asset at a specific time. In reality, this person is part of a system, and their movement and work impact multiple systems, and very little of this non-work-related impact is planned or monitored or managed. We provide the human with rules to follow and those rules include risk assessments, "being careful" and "using good judgement." We do this because we know that the refinery is an ecosystem. Simple things on paper can have unintended consequences. We hire experienced workers from the domain who have first-hand knowledge of what and how things go wrong, and we pay them to prevent problems and mitigate unexpected changes.

When we come to designing systems, however, we go back to drawing a strong little box around the system we are interested in (or responsible for). The pump designer has a data sheet that specifies maximum and minimum voltage, temperature, humidity etc., and the pump is tested to ensure it continues to operate at these levels. This limits the risk of the pump vendor from warranty claims and gives the user confidence it will work as advertised. At the pump level, this kind of strong interface provides assurance that the system within the box will perform across the envelope defined. Operating envelopes are critical items for the user of any system to understand and stay within. Inside the envelope, low risk. Outside the envelope, all bets are off.

The problem, of course, is that when we apply "in the box" thinking to a system of systems, the place where we draw the lines has a massive impact as it determines the elements we are ignoring in our design. The degree of interconnectedness between elements in a system drives the complexity of the system. To limit this complexity, we draw tight lines, and we make strong specifications, and we say "if you cross outside the line then it's on you, all I can control is what's inside my box." And thus, the ecosystems of large organizations, or refineries, or complex supply chains, are a superposition of all the various things that are changing and their impacts on all the other elements around them. And within them, the artificial boxes of budget, team, schedule and plan try to paper over the complexity of the system of systems, which sometimes reacts in highly unpredictable ways to highly structured in-the-box change.

What has this to do with digital twins? Let's revisit the fundamental diagram.

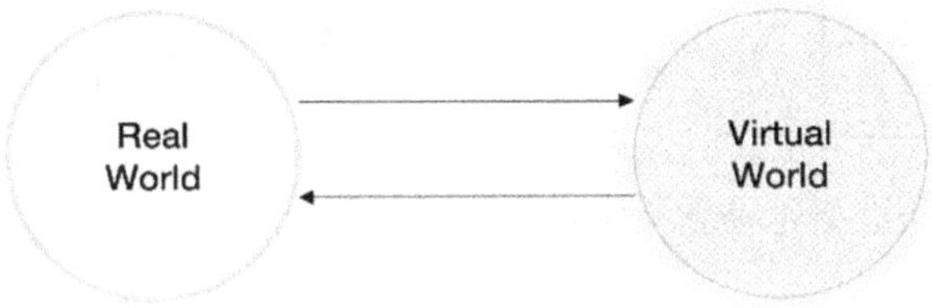

The papering over that is occurring here is the elements within the real and virtual worlds.

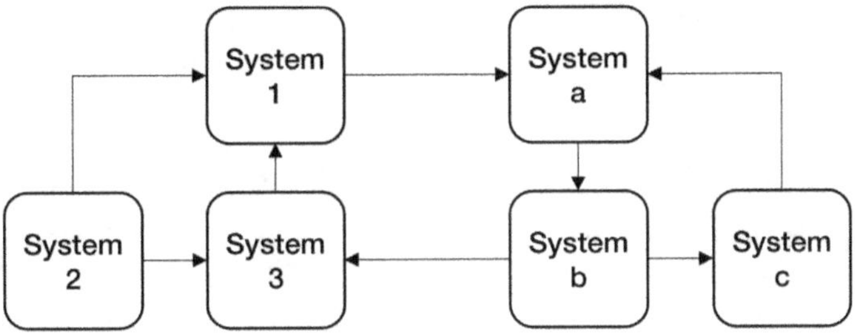

How many systems exist in the real and virtual worlds we are interested in?

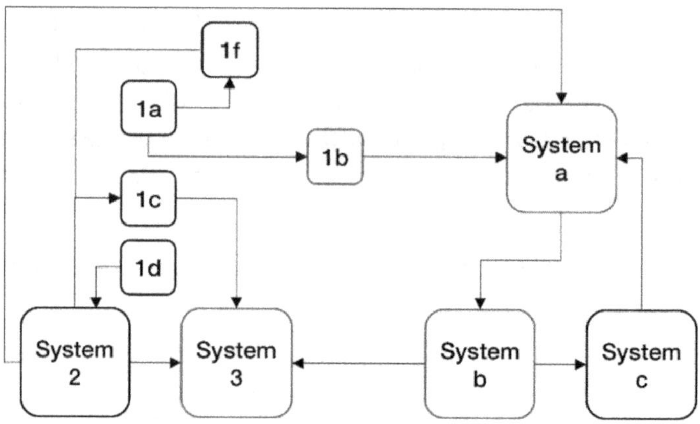

How many elements exist inside those systems?

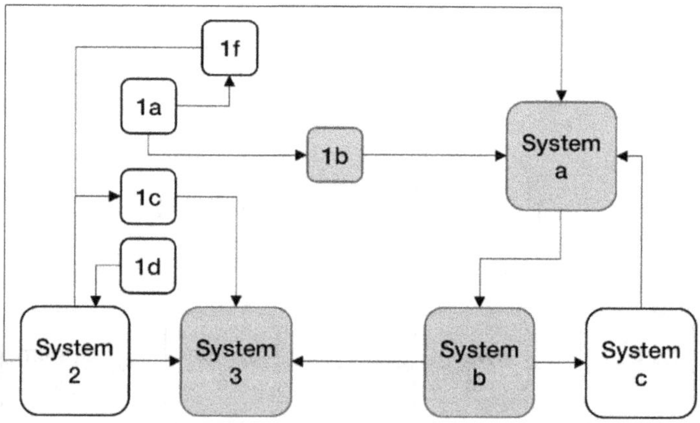

And of those elements and systems, how many are we "interested" in? If we draw our boundary conditions by source of data alone, how many interconnected elements are excluded?

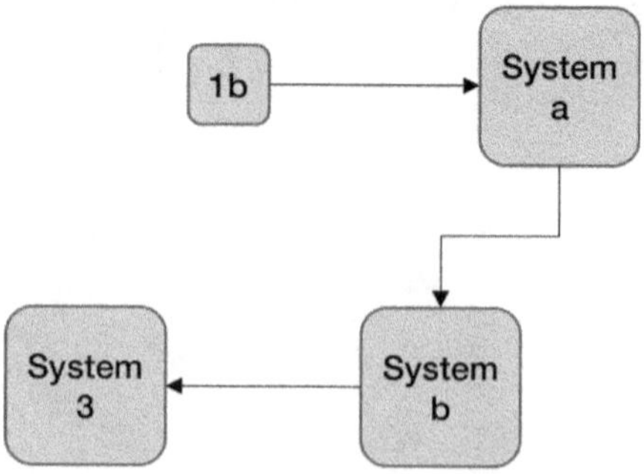

Let's put some real numbers down. 10,000 elements (components) in the real world? That's a small real-world industrial system. 1000 elements in our virtual world? That's a medium sized enterprise stack. 1000 connections from R-V. That's SCADA alone, not even the human feedback loops to the many systems of record, which are low in data but high in information. 100 connections from V-R. That's the many data points that are displayed or pushed to users or control valves to make changes in the real world.

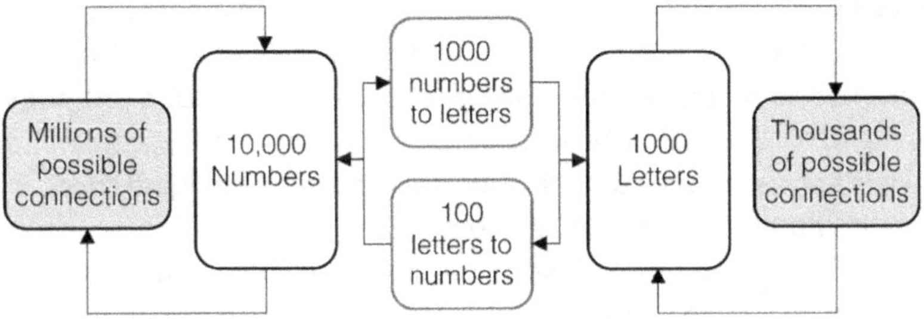

This is not a huge system in the real world (when measuring nodes and relationships). But the number of possible interconnections between elements in each portion of the real world is staggering, and the number of interconnections between real and virtual worlds is actually tiny in comparison.

Software is eating the world, but 99% of the impact on the real world at this time is via changes to human behavior, not connected change to the real world. The real world is still largely isolated from the virtual, precisely because it is too complex to logically analyze and control, and because the vast majority of it is not directly connected to the virtual at all.

The real world is still mostly dumb and dark, and only now are we truly seeking to connect the virtual world to it in order to measurably and repeatably improve how things work. The last 20 years of software building have been mostly aimed at improving the virtual world – building the foundations, creating capabilities and educating ourselves on what can be done inside this new universe. And we know that we've barely gotten started there. In parallel, humans still make 99% of decisions in the real world, and change comes from isolated machines that do our bidding. It works, it totally works, and it's taken us from steam boats to satellites, but the next leap is taking the burgeoning superpowers of the virtual world and bringing them into the light of the sun, not the light of the fiber optic cable. And to do that without creating chaos in our existing ecosystems, natural and artificial, we are going to need to think differently about how we solve problems with highly connected solutions.

Implications of thinking about ecosystem change

Isolated

Truly isolated physical systems do not exist in the real world. Every system is subject to influence by gravity and electromagnetic radiation and most to rain and dust and the oil from human fingers. If it moves, it creates heat from friction (superconducting magnets aside, and remember the trains above them have a lot of other moving and interconnected parts and that pesky air resistance thing is still a problem), and things wear out. If it's an asset of an organization, then people visit it and check it and work on it or use it. If it provides no value and no work is done on it, then we can say it's practically isolated from the real world we seek to change, but it's probably not of much use in any given scenario.

There are also systems that are isolated from virtual worlds. The water pump sitting in the dam for the last 10 years. The shipping container that last saw a ship in 1999 and doesn't even have an RFID tag. The footing of the building you're sitting in or walking past right now. These systems aren't isolated from the real world, but they are isolated from the virtual world. In an industrial setting, there are still a great many large real-world machines that are virtually isolated, with only local measurement and monitoring. The vast majority of static structures (roads, bridges, buildings) are virtually isolated (even "smart buildings" are typically monitoring occupancy, and internal temperature, and which lights are on. They are not monitoring the building structure or foundations or windows or air currents or toilet habits). In the natural world, most animals, trees, icebergs, clouds and dust storms are virtually isolated. Of course, many of these isolated structures are monitored, or some aspect of them is captured remotely by satellite photos, or inspections by humans. What then is the difference between monitoring and connection?

Connected

One-way systems fall into two categories:

- Real systems connected to the virtual world
- Virtual systems connected to the real world

Real systems that are connected to the virtual world are increasing rapidly. The rise of low cost and low power Bluetooth and almost ubiquitous Wi-Fi in urban environments has enabled mass wireless connectivity. Today, most R-V only systems are legacy products (e.g., older style fixed, wired, security cameras, or HVAC systems that send one-way telemetry) that were never designed to be interacted with virtually. Interestingly, with the rise in IoT and machine vision applications that utilize electromagnetic radiation to create the R-V connection, we are connecting and monitoring many previously virtually isolated systems without creating any hardwired connection.

In an industrial setting, the increase in capability and decrease in cost of Internet of Things (IoT) technology and sensors is increasingly connecting real-world assets. Retrofitting of sensors is now a multi-billion-dollar industry, and extends to artificial structures and natural world elements that are of interest or create risk (water bore monitoring, wall / slope geotechnical monitoring, air pollution monitoring etc.).

Virtual-to-real systems that do not include any real-to-virtual connection are rare. There are few valuable use cases for sending one-way messages / data / instructions to a real device / human without any feedback loops. Emergency warning / broadcast systems are one of them (e.g., tsunami alerts), as are long-range submarine communication systems. Real-world systems that use electromagnetic radiation to map / measure the real world are, of course commonplace, in our phones (e.g., cameras and video), within surveying and optical measurement systems (e.g., light detection and ranging (LiDAR)) and in sensors (e.g., ultrasonic sensors in piping and radar sensors on cars and aircraft), and all of these are physical sensors that receive feedback from the real world to generate a virtual representation.

Note that a formal definition of an "open" control system says that there is only a virtual-to-real connection - the control signal. In reality, even "open" control systems have feedback loops, but they are typically human or other system observation and then manual changes are made as the virtual-to-real signal, to correct / improve the control signal.

Interconnected

Virtual systems that are interconnected to the real world (real-to-virtual and virtual-to-real) are becoming the norm for new technology products. A map application that is not connected to the real world for updates is an oddity, but of course, the primary connection back to the real world is the human looking at the map. A toy that isn't controlled by a smartphone is a blessing for many parents. At the application level, many systems connect to other virtual systems that reside in mobile real-world products. Most applications include mobile and web versions, and in the industrial setting, the web is still often the "master" and the mobile app is the subset, while in retail / consumer the reverse is increasingly true.

Control systems, such as HVAC controls that utilize remote temperature and airflow sensors to automatically change compressor and flow rates, are interconnected systems. Data flows from the real to the virtual via sensors, and the control system interprets these inputs to make changes to the real-world hardware, which creates change in the real world being monitored, which passes back into the system via the sensors.

Control systems are typified in two ways: open and closed. Open control systems have no explicit feedback loop - the virtual-to-real connection is the "control" signal, but the control signal is not necessarily coupled back into the control system. Closed control systems have a defined feedback loop, which changes the control signal to achieve a desired state in the real world. Closed loop control systems are perhaps the ultimate version of "strongly coupled" systems. They are not, however, the only form of strongly coupled system, and the first order coupling of direct feedback is not a necessary precondition for a digital twin.

Sidebar: the confusion between control systems and digital twins

Common questions from control systems professionals are:

"Isn't a digital twin just a control system with a pretty picture?"

"We've had closed-loop control systems for decades, why call it a digital twin and confuse things?"

"If all digital twins are control systems, then any digital twin must have a defined control loop, or it's not a digital twin."

Much of the confusion comes from the original picture of the digital twin, with the "closed loop" of information and data flowing around the system.

The resulting literal interpretations of digital twins as closed-loop systems, and then the confusion of digital twins being the software, not the system, has added further confusion.

Many control systems people I speak to are offended in some way that digital twins have come into "their" space and are confusing people and / or competing with their chosen / preferred control system. This is exacerbated by digital twin sales that represent they are, or could be, a control system, and this leads to the obvious software trap of feature parity, which is leading to digital twin vendors building control system features, and control system vendors building pretty UIs, and buyers being confused by what they should buy and users still using what they used 10 years ago. Of course, software being highly malleable, and software categories being dotted line boxes that are drawn by marketing and redrawn by the market, digital twins can incorporate control system features and security, and control systems can incorporate non-control system functionality to better represent and interconnect with the real world.

Thus:

- Digital twins are not control systems
- Digital twins can control the real world directly or indirectly
- Control systems do not twin the real world they control – they take (for example) temperature sensor data and make changes to throttle settings. They control the real world, but they generally do not twin the portion of the real world that they control, because this is not necessary for their purpose
- Control systems can be digital twins
- Digital twins can be control systems

Or in summary: they're different things, but depending on how you build them, they can do some of the same things, and if you wanted to, you could make any digital twin look like almost any other type of software that interacts with the real world, but more than likely you would be confusing buyers and users and misunderstanding who you compete with.

Personal opinion: I think some of the new generation of control-like systems should be digital twins, because the models they incorporate require many different inputs and feedback loops from the real world, in order to both use and train and improve said models. This kind of heavy multi-data type, 2-way interconnection is what twins are great at.

Multi-step interconnections

A source of confusion for digital twins and applied AI is the presence of multistep interconnections. In other words, where there are multiple steps beyond the user to create the change in the real world.

The driving paradigm of data, as the source of truth and objective itself at times, and the ever-increasing paradigms of AI, IoT, integrations and control systems (all data-driven paradigms), has created the implicit idea that unless a digital twin is *directly* connected with the real world, it is not a digital twin. A subset of this view is also used by proponents of control systems: unless a digital twin is directly connected to and controlling the real world, it is not a digital twin, and once it is directly connected to the real world, it is a form of control system. Ergo, control systems are digital twins, and we've been building control systems for 30 years etc. In my experience, both cases are driven by people seeking to reduce the influence of digital twins, either because their company / industry is being impacted by the rise of digital twins, or because they perceive digital twins as a hyped upstart that offends their deep domain expertise in a field impacted by digital twins.

Let's look at multi-step interconnections.

We return to the foundational concept. You will see that we can anchor a great many ideas in this one concept, which is why it has lasted the test of time. Simplicity is a strength. Equally, you are perhaps seeing why it is so often the root of confusion. Oversimplification can leave too much to interpretation.

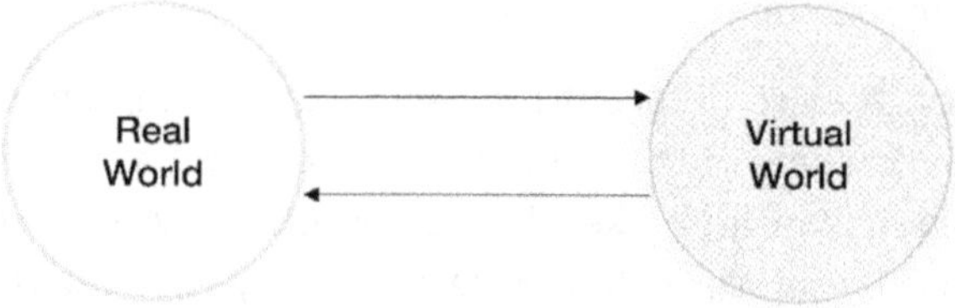

Let's breakdown the concept diagram again into some elements.

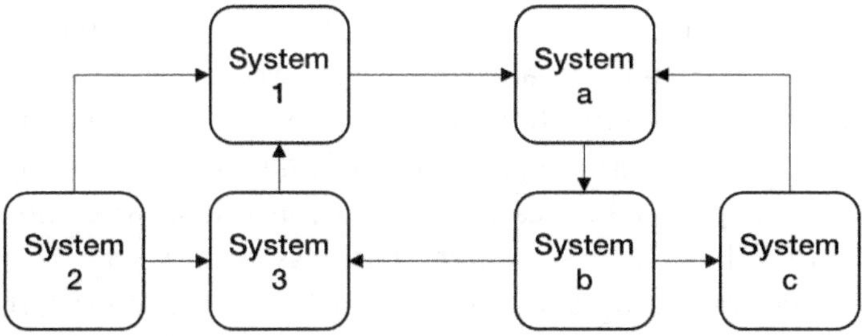

Now let's suspend the use of the term "digital twin" for a moment, and think about a common business process, maintenance, and arrange the key elements of a maintenance system into "real" and "virtual" elements.

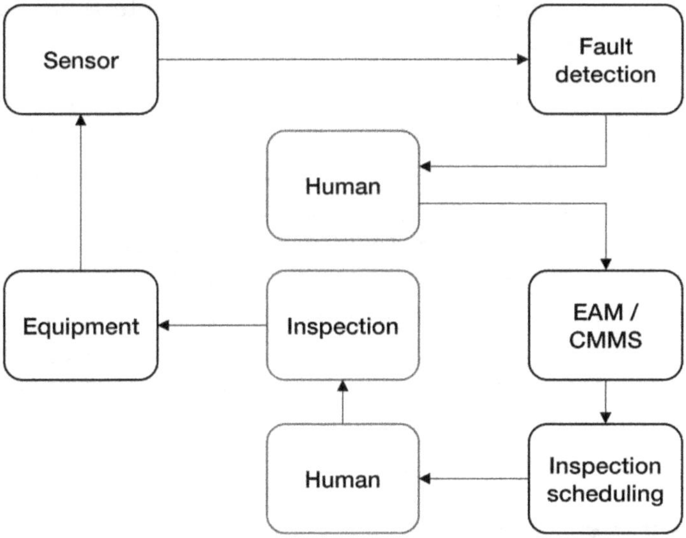

Equipment operates, or is operated (if another human is connected to and controls the equipment), sensors collect data, and fault detection systems alert humans when things are going wrong. Humans interact with the maintenance record system, prompt or create inspections that are scheduled to other humans to do at certain times, and these humans perform inspections, the results of which are put back into the system of record for work activities. Action may or may not be taken to correct faults / inspection results, and the equipment continues to operate and the wheel keeps turning.

The interconnections between real and virtual world elements are undeniable, and no one would say that the machines are not "under control," but we cannot say that the virtual world is acting as a "control system." Thus "control of real-world systems," as a solid and direct line from virtual system to real-world system, and "management of real-world systems" as a function of multi-step processes, seek to achieve the same thing but live in different categories. It is fair to say that most multi-step interconnections are people + process + system connections. A person uses a system or systems in accordance with a specified business process to make a decision or take action. The business process constrains and defines the scope of the action, and which human(s) are involved in the action(s). A modern industrial organization has both control and management mechanisms acting across its assets, people, and places etc.:

- Control system interconnections (systems controlling the real world)
- Multi-step interconnections (people and systems interacting with the real world)

Digital twins do not need to be narrowly framed to one or the other. Whatever the interconnections from virtual to real, the twin design should take them into account in order to achieve the desired outcomes. The types of interconnections required for the specific twin design will then set the capabilities required which in turn will drive the data and business process requirements. Many twin use cases involve control system and multi-step actions in concert. In fact, many twin use cases exist and are valuable *because* these two methodologies are considered in isolation and are designed and implemented in different ways by differing groups of subject matter experts. When a digital twin incorporates existing and new types of control and multi-step interconnection, new ways of working, and in particular coherent cross-functional ways of working, are opened up.

Implications of attempting to create change in an ecosystem

Ultimately, we are seeking to create change in an ecosystem. The ecosystem contains the existing problems, the existing solutions, the existing data and the existing people and processes. The ecosystem is complex. There are many, many relationships between elements, far more than any (human) mind can puzzle out, and many of these relationships are only "active" for brief periods, or when things go wrong, or new ones are created when things change (e.g., a vehicle moves into an area where people are working - a whole new set of relationships appears between vehicle and people).

The primary risk in creating change is unintended consequences. Ecosystems are intricate webs of interconnected elements, and changes to one part can have ripple effects throughout the system that are difficult to predict. Even well-intentioned interventions aimed at solving one problem may inadvertently create new issues or exacerbate existing ones. This fact is exacerbated by the common paradigm of abstracting and oversimplifying complexity by measuring purely financial outcomes. The financial "outcome" may be the result of one intended and five unintended consequences, all occurring in the ecosystem at places that are unmeasured. The resulting "superposition" of results is then interpreted through the lens of only the designed change, not the unintended changes. This becomes even worse when we fail to factor time into our measurements. Problems have a natural frequency. They occur as a result of actions and changes in the real world, whether natural or human or artificial, which are in turn driven by production, or customers, or weather etc. Changes to the ecosystem and hence the elements and relationships are then also connected to these timings and frequencies, as are the unintended consequences. The result is that over time, the outcomes can change multiple times, as the various consequences ripple through the networks or relationships. The problem is not just delay in knowing if a change is "working," but also that the results at any point in time are the result of many small changes, often both positive and negative. Unintended consequences can be positive or negative, and often both, and often delayed.

The other main failure mode for system change is misidentification of the locations and means of leverage. Leverage is a simple concept: where and how do we make changes to get the benefit we want? The subtlety of leverage is that certain places in the ecosystem are highly sensitive to change, and other places are not just insensitive but also actively resist change. Without considering the resistivity of the ecosystem, or the connectiveness of the elements, it is easy to form a view that we should just "save five minutes here" and the result will be a five-minute saving for the entire system. This is what has driven productivity app growth and what drives change management as the primary tool of adoption. We tend to view the ecosystem as "flat" and assume that all elements and relationships are equal, and that they follow or respect the organizational boxes placed over them. In fact, the terrain is highly variable and moving, and starting in some places requires a very steep climb up a big mountain to make any change. Misidentification of leverage points, or selection of the wrong type of change at a leverage point can drastically reduce effectiveness and can feed into unintended consequences.

If you are interested in learning more about systems thinking and design, I highly recommend any of the works by Donella Meadows.

How then do we make changes if anything or nothing could happen?

Change fatigue

We address the above challenges head-on in the Digital Twin Design Process. But first, it's worth noting that the fear of change, and the fear of creating more change, has led a lot of improvement programs and managers into the trap of continuous tiny improvements in areas of little consequence. In other words, the people responsible for creating change are themselves afraid that there is too much change already. Change fatigue is a real thing. I often hear that the cure for change fatigue is to make fewer changes and to make them smaller and to spread them out more. In other words, we seek to minimize the impact of each change, while desiring "real change."

Projects

This is further reinforced by the project view of the world. If every change is a project, and every project is managed individually, then we must manage each project to the scope and budget of the project. A successful project is a project delivered on time and under budget. Our current inability to truly measure success of the change we seek to create leads to "real world" changes being heavily discounted. If a project is on time and under budget but didn't create the change we wanted, well that's the fault of whoever designed the change. If the benefit is not able to be measured until far after completion, well we've moved onto the next project by then. And if the change required is the sum of many projects, well I just need to worry about my piece.

Programs (programmes) of work are just the summing of individual project values. We very rarely "address" a problem with multiple changes. We line up the first project, see how it goes, then the second, then the third. We want to minimize change so we break large changes up into discrete projects, often managed by different people, and approach the same problem through their own personal lens / style / capability etc. Tackling a big problem with tiny individual projects that don't have any measure of success related to the ultimate change desired is not the way.

Perfect information

A complementary challenge today is the ongoing fallacy of perfect information. With the proliferation of IoT and the rise of AI, there is a growing chorus of technical managers who believe that we just need to "analyze everything and then we'll know what to do." For students of history, we have had many iterations of this since the advent of mechanical calculators. We are always on the cusp of "knowing everything" and increasing computer power and analytical techniques are always about to "tell us what we need to know." AI is the latest magic wand to help us, and while it is yet another leap forward, it is also not the tool of measurement or change. It is a decision aid, and a great one, and we are at step 1 of 1000, but AI alone is not the panacea. For real-world problems that have had very little data collected except abstracted outputs, there is not a large enough or accurate enough corpus of information to train and learn from, nor are there many models or applications where hallucination and / or inaccurate outputs have been truly solved. Yet. I say yet, and tomorrow is another day, but creating positive change today is what we're all about, and thus we need to work with what we've got.

Emergence

The unknowableness (this should be a word) of ecosystem change seems the great barrier. How do we breach it? We accept, embrace and iterate. We accept that we do not and cannot know what exactly will happen when we create change, and we embrace that unintended change can be beneficial, and we plan to iterate changes to overcome unintended consequences and inconsequential outcomes and increase beneficial outcomes.

To complicate the complex, probabilistic virtual outputs have entered the fray. Most existing software is deterministic (if this then that) whereas most AI and ML model outputs are probabilistic (if this then maybe that or they or them).

Thus, we are combining probabilistic inputs into complex ecosystems. The likelihood of deterministic outputs is.... low? Yet we write business processes on the basis of logical and deterministic rules. This too will change.

What this all means is: problems will emerge from the ecosystem as we make changes, so we plan to make multiple changes to overcome unforeseen problems and we measure both activity and outcomes in the real and virtual worlds to give us the best chance of identifying emergent behavior early, while still having budget to do something about it.

We treat emergence as both the challenge and the opportunity, and we explicitly seek to take advantage of this fundamental property of complex systems. This, of course, has profound implications for how we think about creating value.

Part 3 - Value creation

How digital twins and applied AI create value by solving validated problems through actionable change in the real world, emphasizing measurable outcomes, decision-making, and designing solutions for high ROI and sustainable benefits.

The purpose of deliberate change is value creation. Value is created by solving problems, if and only if the problem being solved provides benefit to the organization, and that benefit is greater than the cost and risk of creating the change.

Problem solving

The solving of problems is the province of domain expertise. In industrial settings, we hire people with experience in the relevant domain and set them to do work and overcome challenges. Problem solving does not require or belong to digital twins or AI. But digital twins and applied AI should be designed to solve problems. Preferably, they should solve valuable Problems. What is a valuable Problem? It's a problem that the solving of, creates value. This isn't semantics. The value of the problem is determined by the question "What is the value of solving this problem?" All problems have a financial value. Ultimately, they must, even if that calculus is very difficult, because all investments are made on the basis of budgets, and budgets without prospective returns in the same denomination are just expenses, and expenses are subject to cuts and value engineering. If the problem isn't valuable, then it's likely to not be solved. Perhaps worse still though, if the problem isn't valuable, but it is invested in, and there is no return on that investment, then there is less to invest in valuable Problems. The valuable Problems kept causing downside while you spent time and effort solving non-valuable problems.

Problem validation

To judge if a problem is valuable, the problem needs to be validated. We cover validation in the Digital Twin Design Process (DTDP). Suffice to say, I always advise that every problem is a potential problem, until proven to be a valuable Problem.

Every idea, every complaint, every financial metric is a potential problem. Of these, there is a subset of valuable Problems. And of these, there is a subset of valuable Problems that we believe we can feasibly and viably solve.

Validating problems is difficult because there is no universal language for problems, and because most problems are really groupings of many smaller problems and issues, some of which are not valuable Problems at all. One of the key challenges in modern corporate life is the use of highly abstracted financial metrics to determine what problems we have. If we define "high labor costs" as the problem, the solution writes itself. If we define "low labor productivity" as the problem, the solution is more complex. In both cases, the solution will certainly have unintended consequences, the impact of which is abstracted in arrears into revenue and EBITDA impacts. The reason for this is not that we don't "know" we have high labor costs – it's because "high labor costs" is a terrible problem statement. It provides no guidance on how to solve the problem, or what changes we would make in the real world to solve this problem, or whether those changes are feasible (possible) or viable (economically attractive).

For digital twins and applied AI, we are creating solutions connected to our problems. Problem definition and validation is a key skill, because if we cannot define the problem, and we don't know if it's a real problem, then we'll soon be measuring our lack of value creation. Digital twins are somewhat unique in the solution pantheon in that they usually measure their own success or failure. Defining and validating valuable Problems is perhaps the highest leverage step in the process.

Sidebar: Model outcomes versus problem solving

A key facet of applied AI and all data model-based solutions is the difference between model outcomes (e.g., accuracy and precision) and problem solving. Many problems have multiple facets, or are somewhat "grey" in the sense that there are variations to each problem. A "problem" is often a bundle of smaller problems, or a superposition of multiple changes in the real world, none of which present as "problems" alone. Some problems are defined as "things not going according to plan."

On the model side, accuracy is determined by measurement against training and then production data. A "highly accurate" model that doesn't solve the actual problem in the real world, because the problem was slightly different, *this time*, to what was modelled, does not invalidate the accuracy of the model. But it can cause the model to give outputs that do not help the organization solve the problem.

Highly accurate models that aren't used, are blocked by other workflows / lack of approvals, only give the correct output after the time to intervene in the problem has passed, etc., all reduce the effectiveness of the AI solution, because they prevent the model from solving the problem in the real world.

If we define success as the "accuracy" of the model (measured against known data) rather than the solving real-world problems, we are at great risk of over investing into models that don't or can't solve our problems. No ROI models are a bigger issue than model accuracy.

Opportunities

I am often asked something along the lines of, "what about opportunities? Can we use the DTDP for opportunities, instead of problems? We don't like saying problems at our company. It's too negative."

Yes, you can use the DTDP for opportunities.

Problem is a negative word. And in a similar vein to risk and opportunity, the word opportunity has come to represent the benefit of avoiding / mitigating / eliminating downside. In this context, an opportunity is a problem waiting to be solved, and we should seek to take every worthy opportunity we can.

My only concern with opportunity is that it can so easily be turned into Shiny Thing. It can so easily be turned into Pet Project. It can so easily be turned into New Capability. If you are using opportunity instead of problem, I strongly urge you to double down on validation. I have also broken out some different starting point patterns in the DTDP so that you can think about whether your opportunity is really a capability in disguise and still use the DTDP to assure value creation.

For those of you who work in organizations where saying problem is a problem, I would recommend you say opportunity and think problem. Be opportunity focused and you'll have less opportunities... wait. Yeah, changing words is risky. Be problem focused and you'll have less problems (and more opportunities).

Real-world change

We have spoken around this but let's make it crystal clear:

- Digital twins and applied AI create value by creating change in the real world that solves valuable Problems.
- We design the change we want across the ecosystem of real, virtual (existing) and virtual (new).
- Change in the real world is how we solve problems.
- Change in the real world creates other changes, some of which are intended and some of which are unintended.
- We make these changes through decisions and actions in the real world, informed by the capabilities and data in the virtual worlds.
- We measure the changes and actions and decisions to learn what is happening, and we measure the outcomes to determine how much value we are creating.

Actions and decisions

Actions are the actions that humans and machines take in the real world to create change. Decisions are the decisions that humans and machines take in real and virtual worlds to initiate actions. They are part of the V-R interconnection.

Decision-Action chains are often multi-step and can cross into and out of the virtual world. Humans receiving orders, entering data into other systems, for other humans to get instructions, to then walk over to a machine, to check something, to enter data back into another system, which flows back into the twin. The control room operator who sees an alarm, presses a button, and the control system takes action by closing a valve, which changes a sensor reading, which flows back into the virtual, which changes the display on the operator's dashboard. Decisions and actions create change, which creates other changes, some of which create value.

Measurements

Measurements are critical across and adjacent to the value creation activities. We measure not just the output of all these activities, but the decisions and actions themselves (where we can), so that we can learn what we are doing (and not doing), what works and what doesn't, and better correlate what changes cause other changes. Correlation and causation are known challenges and direct measurement does not solve them well. Measurement of change, as well as outputs and inputs, does however provide a much richer data set to analyze and learn from. In particular, measurement of non-domain actions and decisions is often the missing link in domain specific problems. We know unintended consequences will emerge, so we design measurements to learn quickly to enable the next set of feasible changes to be designed.

Measurement enables learning. Learning drives repeatable value creation. Without learning what has happened, and where and when, it is very difficult to determine what to do next.

Product creation

The science and art of repeatable value creation is best encapsulated in product management. Products, tools, projects and transformations are all cousins, but there is nuance in how we apply them and where digital twins and applied AI fit it. There are known strategies for creating good products, and each area is a world of its own. Below is a primer on a few of them, and you can find more resources online at *www.designingdigitaltwins.com.*

Tool versus Product

I have posited that twins should not be projects, as projects are effectively decoupled from real-world change (because they measure project success, not real-world change), and that problems emerge and change beyond the end of the project, and the team and capabilities best suited to handling that change are gone.

What's the alternative then?

In the game of technology, there are many "products" but seemingly few product businesses. A great many software products are project driven, especially inside large non-technology companies that have built their own software teams. In the world of SaaS, product management has been elevated to somewhat of an art form, with the science following on behind.

Digitization and digitalization have been significant drivers of change for more than 20 years now. Within the umbrella of digital transformation, the conversion of manual processes to digital has entailed the building of millions of tools by internal teams and has been a major driver of the explosion of enterprise SaaS products.

What is the difference between a tool and a product, and why does it matter?

In today's corporate world, internal product, data and technology teams are continuously building and deploying tools to improve efficiency, reduce risk, automate processes, analyze their own data etc.

Tool building has become an accepted part of every organization, and low / no code and AI tools are accelerating this beyond Excel lookups and macros. People have long built their own tools (think craftspeople building tools they used to build a house, thousands of years ago), and often tools are built to be used by the builder, and then become used by the builder's associates or team members. These are internal tools. When people see a tool that works well or enables the user to do something faster or better than the current way, they often desire it and adopt it. This demand can create commercial markets, which creates the opportunity to supply tools to external customers. These are external tools.

Modern organizations do not have "tool" teams, they have product teams. These teams are often composed of product, software engineering, domain expertise and data professionals. Many internal product teams are led by domain experts, who combine the problem knowledge with the solution ownership. Product owners seem to be more prevalent than product managers in these organizations, while in tech companies the opposite is true.

Other organizations do not have product teams that build, but they do have technology teams responsible for managing the build of bespoke tools. In these cases, the team may or may not have product in the title, and the key coordinators may be called product owners or project managers.

Finally, procurement and technology teams collaborate to purchase or lease (SaaS) products from vendors.

Organizations are investing heavily to create tools and to buy products, and the two terms are often used interchangeably. What then is the difference between tools and products?

Tools are built by the builder, thinking about how they would use the tool to solve the problem. Domain expertise is a fundamental requirement of this, as is the need. A carpenter is unlikely to build a multimeter, but a carpenter who tinkers in the garage repairing old computers might. The domain expertise and need are based on the jobs that the user does, not necessarily the job title they hold, and doing these jobs is what builds the expertise of both the problem and potential solutions.

Products, on the other hand, are built for others, by thinking about how they would use the product to do the job in a way that solves the problem. Domain understanding is similarly important, in order to understand the job and the constraints and needs of the user. The builder of the product often does not have the specific personal experience of doing the job and they don't have the need to do the job themselves. The product manager building a product for the carpenter might be an avid amateur woodworker, but in all likelihood the product is not targeted at "amateurs" – it's targeted at a large enough group of carpenters who can pay, or in the case of internal products, at people who have a well-defined enough need that they get budget to solve that problem.

In both cases, understanding of the jobs that the user does is paramount. The way that this understanding is acquired, however, can be radically different. Those who have done the jobs, usually rely on their own experience. Those who haven't, need to learn from those who have. In both cases, there are many pros and cons.

The summary looks like this:

- Internal tools – built and used by the builder, or the builder's associates, without any commercial transaction
- External tools – built to be used by the builder, sold to others via commercial transactions
- Internal product – built to be used by others, without any commercial transaction
- External product – built to be used by others, sold to others via commercial transactions

For some tools / products, the distinction is subtle, or even ambiguous. For others, it may start as an internal tool and become an external product when it is sold to others. Many great products we use today started as internal tools built by experts in their trade.

Another way to look at it is in terms of what defines success. This is important to us as digital twin designers as we are often called upon to define, and prove, "success." Failing to define success is a common failure mode of solution providers.

Escalating measures of success, from builder sufficiency to user desire:

- Solves the problem for the builder
- Solves the problem for the user
- Solves the problem for the user sufficiently well to create demand by other potential users
- Solves the problem for the user sufficiently well that prospective users will pay for it (directly or with internal budget / time)

We can immediately see that measures of success will influence (or should influence) the requirements of the solution. The tool that you have built, that works for you, is not necessarily the solution that others would pay money for. Perhaps more importantly, the tool that you can easily use is the tool that you understand intimately, because you built it. For the stranger that picks it up and needs to get value from it quickly, what seems "natural" or "common sense" to you may be alien or confusing to them.

For the product creator, this necessity to build something for someone else is the first and biggest hurdle. The second hurdle is whether it appears attractive enough that the stranger would "buy" it.

Many solution designers forget that their intended users are busy and already have a full plate of tools and products and processes and systems and... the coin of the internal user is time. The coins of the external user are money and time. In both cases, the user needs to believe the solution will solve their problem *and* they need to believe they could solve that problem with this solution. Only then will they try / buy the solution, and only then will they find out if it actually solves their problem.

To summarize:

- A product is a solution that is designed for others to use.
- A product is a solution that is designed to be desirable enough for others to want to try it.

This sets the scene for the intended application of the twin.

If you are an internal product team, building a connected solution for your team, you are building a tool. It needs to be effective enough to create value, but it can be rough and even complex because you know how it works and what you built. Think EFFECTIVE.

If you are an internal product team, building a connected solution for another team, you are building a product. It needs to be effective enough to create value, and it needs to be usable enough that the cost and effort to train / support / incentivize to keep using it is low. Think USABLE.

If you are an external product team, building a connected solution for a customer, you are building a product. It needs to be desirable enough that people will consider changing from how they solve that problem currently, effective enough to create value, and commercially viable enough that the value created is much higher than the cost to procure and change how they work, and usable enough that the cost and effort to train / support / incentivize to keep using is low. Think VALUE FOR TIME and MONEY.

You might ask, what is the most important thing to focus on: usability, desirability, value for money? The answer depends on who your user is. User-centricity provides the answer to most questions about prioritization. When in doubt, ask yourself two questions, in this order:

1. What does the user need?
2. Can I satisfy this in the solution?

If the user needs a business case to justify investing in the twin, then measuring the value created in a way that is easily explainable is the priority. If the user needs consistent help with how to do a certain action, then the solution interface or user flow needs to be looked at. In every case, solving problems in the solution (rather than outside the solution, say with "more training") is the right place to look first. Your users may well need more training but if you can solve the problem they're having – without them having to do anything else – they will be happier, they'll use it more, and it has a chance to create more value.

The full array of skills and things a product team needs to manage is beyond the scope of this book. But it is worth reiterating some of the core and fundamental needs, and highlighting their importance in digital twins.

Design

For many, design is synonymous with aesthetics – the way things look and feel. While aesthetics is certainly part of design, they only represent a small portion of the discipline. At its core, design is about understanding problems, generating potential solutions, and creating meaningful outcomes.

In this context, we're not just talking about designing products or services, but about designing change across ecosystems. Ecosystems can be anything from a natural environment to a complex social network. They are made up of many interconnected elements, each playing a vital role in the overall system.

A great way of thinking about change in an ecosystem is through *design thinking*.

Design thinking is a human-centered approach to problem-solving that can be applied to understand ecosystems in a holistic way. It involves:

Empathizing: Understanding the needs, wants, and challenges of the various stakeholders involved in the ecosystem. This includes not only humans but also other living things and the physical environment.

Defining: Clearly defining the problem or opportunity that needs to be addressed. This involves gathering data, conducting research, and analyzing the information to understand the root causes of the issue.

Ideating: Generating a wide range of possible solutions to the problem. This is where creativity and brainstorming come into play.

Prototyping: Developing low-fidelity models or simulations to test the feasibility and usability of the proposed solutions.

Testing: Evaluating the prototypes with stakeholders to gather feedback and refine the solutions.

Iterating: Repeating the process of prototyping and testing until the optimal solution is achieved.

By applying design thinking and committing to iterations, we can gain a deeper understanding of how the different elements of an ecosystem interact and how changes to one element can impact the entire system.

Designing change: Existing and new elements

Once we have a thorough understanding of the ecosystem, we can begin to design changes that will improve its overall health and sustainability. This may involve:

Redesigning existing elements: Modifying the function or form of existing elements to better serve the needs of the ecosystem.

Adding new elements: Introducing new elements that address gaps or weaknesses in the existing system.

Creating new connections: Facilitating new interactions and relationships between different elements.

Managing the system: Establishing processes and structures for ongoing monitoring, evaluation, and adaptation.

The goal of designing change is not to impose rigid *control* over the ecosystem, but to create the conditions for the desired change to have the desired impact, and the means of measuring what change occurs due to our actions. This requires a deep understanding of the system's natural dynamics and a willingness to experiment and adapt. Rigid design of change in a complex ecosystem is almost certain to fail. That's why so many products and transformations fail. The unexpected happens, and we need to design the solution and the change knowing that unexpected changes will happen, and give ourselves flexibility to make further changes.

Features and capabilities

All digital solutions are composed of features. We think of features as we think of the components of a system. I like to talk about capabilities in twins, not features, because many twin features have multiple aspects of capability and interconnection. But it's important to understand what features are, and what problems can arise from being too feature-focused. The problem that features present in digital twins generally fall into two categories:

1. The solution has poor or missing features that are needed to solve the problem.
2. The solution is full of features that do not solve the problem.

In some cases, a digital twin will suffer from both problems: It is full of "shiny" things and doesn't solve the problem.

Over featured

The presence of multiple unrequired features is sometimes called "featuritis." It is an issue in software development generally, and studies abound on feature utilization showing that the problem still remains – the usual number quoted is 20-30% of features are ever used, and only a percentage of these are used often. With such a high percentage of features in conventional, siloed software remaining unused, what does this say for digital twins and applied AI? The problem, of course, is compounded by the vague nature of twins and the need to utilize an external ecosystem to create the desired change in the real world. The twin by itself can almost never create the change required, and relies on external elements (systems or people) to "do their job" as well. Even a properly closed loop control twin, where virtual changes are directly connected to real-world changes via a control system, may not solve the problem. The valve may open when instructed, but that is not the problem being solved (reducing pressure). If we set the bar at "solving problems for users," then we as solution designers must go beyond "opening the valve." For most twin use cases, the V-R connection is less directly causal, and a number of other things need to go right in order for desirable change to occur (multi-step interconnections).

In the presence of this external uncertainty, it is natural for the solution designer to focus on "the twin" or "the model" (i.e., the software and data parts), and to add features that are known to be "twinlike." 3D visualizations, simulation, OT / operational / real-time data. Many twins thus end up as a laundry list of capabilities, branded as features, and the implementation of the solution is left to others, and the desirable change in the ecosystem is left to the end user to manage. Many product people would recognize this "technology first" pattern – start with the tech you think is needed, and once it's built, start to figure out how someone could use it to solve their problem.

Missing / poor features

The other issue of course is that the solution does not contain the feature required to solve the problem. Note that above I referred to capabilities masquerading as features. This is an important point. Even where a problem requires a specific capability, e.g., analytics, the specific analytics that are implemented, the types of data it can ingest, the transformations that occur, whether the user sees the outputs in time, all have a massive impact on the real-world change. Simulation is a capability. Simulation of physical and chemical reactions in an aluminum potline, designed to provide analytics engines with predictions of potential pot health issues, is a feature. Capabilities are components of a generic system. Features are the specifically designed components of a solution. If the features in the twin don't enable the desirable change in the real world, we have failed as product designers.

The consequences from these are:

- Featuritis makes the product more complex, harder to learn and use, and more costly to support.
- Missing / poor features either eliminate the ability to solve the problem or transfer tremendous burden to other parts of the ecosystem (usually the user).

In the extreme case, the twin solves no problem. I say extreme, but the amount of "3D visualization" systems is proliferating rapidly, and a great many of them are just that: visualizations. The entire V-R loop and any change in the real world is left to user discretion. In some cases, the user did not want any change to their ecosystem, and visualizing a point cloud is exactly what they want. Of course, I think you know that in this case I do not think this is a digital twin. Not designed to create change, or measure it, or improve it – not a twin. Still a solution, might be commercially viable, might solve a problem for a user. Not-a-twin doesn't mean can't-be-a-success, it just means it's not-a-twin.

In most cases, the poor outcomes are a combination of the two problems, with many unused features and some undesigned use of capabilities to half solve a problem. The underlying root cause of this is that the twin designer had no methodology for designing a twin solution. The contributing factor was that the user couldn't describe their need, as per every user, and that in the case of twins, the capability / tech first factor is so dominant because of the lack of a methodology to design... you can see what I'm saying here. When you don't know where you're going, any direction is as a good as another. If you've heard all twins must have 3D visualization, then that's a good place to start. It's not the designer's or the user's fault – it's just where we're at in time and space right now. Conventional, decoupled software solutions have very low feature usage and high failure rates. The virtual side of digital twins are a subset of software solutions, with higher uncertainty and ambiguity, and a distinct lack of playbooks and methodologies for what works and what doesn't.

Usability

We mentioned usability a few times above. I feel it needs further highlighting because usability is the gateway to adoption, and therefore a major blocker to value creation. If we set the bar at "creating desirable change," then a first big milestone is "I logged in" and a second is "I used it today" and the biggest one is "I have been using it every day for the last year and I can't live without it."

Usability is so important that the entire SaaS industry over the past 10 years has steadily narrowed down on user metrics as the primary determinant of success. The Venture Capital (VC) industry has similarly brought user metrics to the forefront of early evaluations and valuations. Products with good user adoption and retention are far more valuable to their owner than products that create great outcomes but hardly anyone uses them. That's a very powerful incentive. The external product owner may live and die (at work) on their user numbers. Interestingly, internal product / tool builders often don't track user metrics at all. I have worked with many internal product teams that have to build the thing they're told to build, and the measure of success is completion of the approved scope on time.

When a solution is a project and the definition of success is completion of the build, rather than creating the desirable change, the natural inclination is to not collect data that confuses the situation. Finish the build, throw it over the fence, and move onto the next one. In many internal product teams, there is 1-2 years of backlog already in place, and there is no time or resources allocated to measuring outcomes and aiding users by improving "old" solutions. The project that is completed represents measurable progress for the builder. Improved outcomes for the user are, of course, to be hoped for, but if the solution is difficult to use, well... that's the users' problem. The internal product team is usually commissioned to create solutions, not to make their users' lives easier.

The benefits of usability are widely documented. Some examples are:

- Improved usage (and usage always precedes value – if they don't use it...)
- Increased efficiency (users can complete tasks faster and with less errors)
- Reduced training costs (users can "pick it up" much faster)
- Reduced change management costs and time (when users are happy using a solution, there is always less resistance to change)
- Reduced support costs (users ask less questions, make fewer mistakes and / or can solve some of their own problems e.g., password resets)
- Enhanced accessibility (color blindness, font size, ability to easily use in very bright and very dark conditions)
- Increased likelihood of user testimonials and product feedback scores (happier users not only give better scores, they are often happy enough to give a score at all)

The upside of all of these is that highly usable solutions cost less to roll out and support, create more value, create value faster, create less administrative problems, and succeed more often.

The downside is that the product team needs to change some ways of working. However, given that we're talking about changing how we design solutions in order to create great twins, change is going to happen anyway. As a twin designer, we are usually called upon to solve cross-functional problems, or problems with mixes of IT / OT / ET systems, or near real-time problems... in other words, non-trivial problems. Trivial problems generally don't need a twin, and we should always strive to simplify rather than complexify.

In the case of usability, the key is the user. User centric design is an entire group of disciplines, but usability is also an ethos. Product teams that strive to create "usable" solutions generally create solutions that are far more usable... sounds silly, doesn't it? But it's true. Intention counts for much. Let's discuss some ways to ensure usability is a part of your ways of working.

Ways to make usability a core part of your ethos:

- Educate yourself, your team and your leaders on usability and its positive impact on adoption and value creation
- Conduct user research to better understand user needs, behaviors and pain points
- Conduct usability testing to test your hypotheses

- Iteratively design the solution, incorporating feedback early and often, and allowing for iterations after delivery
- Create and mandate usability metrics and ensure that these measurements are made regularly after go-live (e.g., 3, 6, 12 months)
- Understand accessibility needs and create a checklist or process that ensures your team meets minimum requirements
- Try to create an intuitive design through the use of familiar design patterns and consistent locations / designs
- Provide clear and comprehensive documentation and make this available and consumable by users (without needing to ask you)

Education

The first step in change is getting buy-in from those who control the solution creation process. For external product teams, usability has a definitive impact on retention in conventional sales led motions and an even more dramatic impact through acquisition, activation and retention in product led motions. In both cases, external teams should strive to bring usability into the center of their delivery process because it makes the product more valuable. Building a business case for internal teams is often made easier by talking to users and their managers. Go talk to the maintenance manager, or the finance manager, or the supply manager and ask them how their team uses the solutions you've built, and what their feedback is. Do the same with the actual users. Nine out of ten times you'll get feedback about usability. You might also find out some solutions have never been used... this is not unusual, unfortunately. You might also find that some of the people ragging on a solution have never opened it up... word of mouth inside an organization is even faster and more powerful than it is for social media. Get buy-in from your customers to support your business case that this change will be good for your teams standing in your organization and provide examples of "successful" projects that have never been used. It's not heresy to speak the truth, and if you are serious about creating better business outcomes, this is a good place to start and one of the highest value changes you'll ever make.

User research

User research is the discipline of investigating the needs of your future and current users, in order to understand their specific user needs. User needs aren't necessarily the same as solution needs. A user who has to wear gloves will have problems using a touchscreen in the field. This isn't the shortcut to features – it's the effort that goes into understanding who your user is, what their jobs are, how they do their jobs, and what constraints and issues they overcome every day in doing their jobs. The key to user research isn't being an experienced researcher – it's empathy. If you care about your user and put their problems at the center of your mind (rather than your solution), then you will come out of research sessions with a real sense of who you're trying to help. Remember we said that teams that want to create usable solutions, do? This is the heart of it. Wanting to create usable and valuable solutions means caring what and how your users do, not just whether the solution solves the business problem. I have encountered many product builders though my career who think this is wishy-washy stuff. I feel bad for them, and I feel bad that I am often unable to state this case strongly enough to convince them. On the other, more mercenary hand, I create better products than them. People like my products because I care about them more than my product. I don't care because I'm a nice guy, I care because I have set a bar much higher than others. I care because I have done this many times, and when I care about users, they can feel that, and they respond in kind – they give and give and give because I have been giving and giving and giving. We become a team, collaborating to solve problems, freely sharing information and advice. We challenge each other, we disagree, we sometimes passionately disagree, and five years later when I see them again, we are both happy to see each other. Everyone remembers being a part of a high performing team, and as a solution creator, you have a unique opportunity to help catalyze many high performing teams in the service of causes greater than yourselves. The key is to care about their problems more than you care about your own ideas.

Iterate

A big process change for some teams is to iteratively test ideas with users, and then to iteratively alter the product once users have been using it for some time. I have grouped the iterations together to cover the whole lifecycle:

- Iterative research and design
- Iterative delivery and testing
- Iterative measurement and upgrades

Research and design

There is a concept in product circles called the double diamond. It is not universally accepted, and many versions or alternates exist, but for the purposes of using a single explanatory concept, I think it's a very useful theme. I highly recommend researching the double diamond to learn from the many excellent texts available.

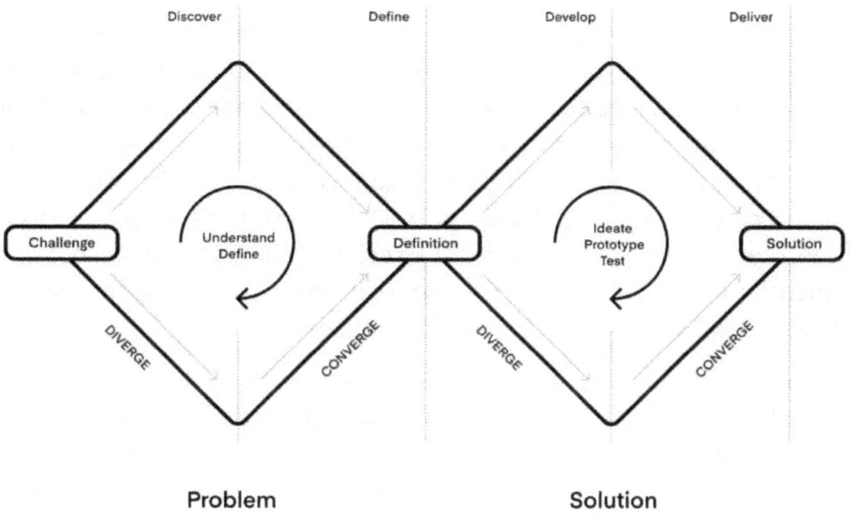

Source: Productboard: The Double Diamond Framework for Product Management. www.productboard.com/blog/double-diamond-framework-product-management

Research: start with a known problem or user, go wide to find out all you can related to the problem, and then narrow down to the specific problem or aspects of the problem you are going to solve.

Design: starting from the problem you have selected, go wide to consider options for how to solve it, then narrow in on a specific solution.

The theory is simple – research the problem by interviewing prospective users and investigating the problem, and playing back findings to them to confirm you understand both their user problems and the business problem. The selection of the problems (user and business) that the solution will address is often defined by the budget holder for an internal team, and is a commercial decision for external teams. External teams have the added challenge of considering competitors, though many product teams ignore competitors and the current user ways of working as they are more focused on their features. It's a very hard mindset to shake. Remember also that we want to validate the problem (more on this soon). Research is an excellent form of validation.

Prioritization

The other challenge is prioritization. When solutions do not use business outcomes as their measure of value, the task of prioritization is usually political or budget driven. Buyers with budget can "buy" the services of product teams, and senior managers have more influence than junior. The upshot of budget-driven priorities is that solutions are usually only commissioned to solve siloed problems. Budgets live in silos, and decision makers live in silos, and therefore solutions are created to solve siloed problems. No budget, no solution. The result is that potential revenue or cost improvements can languish for years without sufficient political sponsorship, and cross-functional solutions often never see the light of day.

A recent conversation with a customer went like this "We really need to fix this problem, it's been ongoing for longer than I've worked here, but we've been told it's on Tech's roadmap for delivery in the next two years, so we can't engage anyone to solve it." Seems reasonable, and every fixed resource team has to put something earlier than later. When I enquired if the two-year estimate was recent, he paused for a moment and said "well, actually, that was the update they gave me about two years ago, and then again two months ago, so I guess it's still two years away?" I didn't respond, because what can you say? The problem his team has is very real, with very significant implications, and their current method of solving it is Excel and a graduate engineer. But he's far from the decision-making center and he's trying to solve a cross-functional problem. That's a terrible combo in many bureaucracies.

We will return to measurable change in the next chapter, but for now the important lesson is that very often the end user does not know or cannot clearly articulate the exact problems they have when trying to solve their problem. This is very common. In fact, it's so common that a common maxim in product circles is "never ask the user what they want." That might sound crazy to you, but it does not refer to a fear of being lied to or that users will ask for outrageous things (though occasionally they do), but rather that people are just not skilled at describing the *real problems* they have in sufficient detail. The panacea to this is to focus on the problem, and what job the user has to do. If you focus on the problem, you'll have a much better chance of not building the shiny thing that no one will use. That won't stop people asking you for more shiny things – oh, no – in fact, the more empathy you show, the more they're likely to ask – I didn't say this was the easy path – I said this was the path to solving real problems, repeatably.

Data

Where would we be without data? As twin and AI designers, we'd be nowhere. Data is very often the answer. Interestingly though, the question often had nothing to do with data. Very often the question is about how to solve a problem. When "better data" or "more data" is the answer, I tend to squint a little bit. I try hard not to, but it's a reflex. My theories on wide and narrow twins were actually borne of data conversations, not twin conversations. So many times I have seen teams failing to start work, or failing to complete work, or failing to deliver value, and data is blamed. Data has become the panacea to all problems, it seems. However, being the slightly contrary person that I am, I can't help but ask "What data do you need to solve the problem?" I would have to say, that in all the years I've been doing this, I have perhaps received three specific answers to this question. It's worth noting that all three also stated that before they started working on the problem, they didn't know what data they needed. For all the others, however, I generally get a version of:

- We need better data
- We don't have enough data
- The data we have is terrible
- We can't get data from team (x)
- We can't get budget to improve the data
- We'll never be able to fix that data

Often these are true statements (and I'm an outsider, so I always err on the side of believing them), but rarely are they the whole truth.

I like to ask, again: "What data do you need to solve the problem?"

It's a hard question. It's not hard because they're not smart people, they are. It's hard because they haven't done the hard work of actually mapping data to change in the real world. Even when people show me data maps and data-value maps and solution designs and model outputs, I am always asking "ok, but what action or decision or capability is that data, right there, used for? When is it used? Who needs it? How often do they need it? How long before or after the problem arises, do they need it to be of any value?"

I would say, in 90% of cases, when I ask this of technology people, they cannot answer it. They cannot answer it because they don't have a plan to create change in the real world. They have a plan to build capabilities in the virtual world.

When I ask data engineers, they can tell me all the issues with collecting the data, and validating the data, and connecting and transforming data.

When I ask the data scientists, they can tell me what the accuracy of their models are and the weights and the tests they are doing. They can tell me what other or better data they need, or think they need, to improve the accuracy of predictions. They can tell me about their hypotheses for how their data products could change real-world outcomes.

When I ask the domain experts, they can tell me what capability and when they need it to make changes in the real world. Often, they can articulate the outputs from the capability. They always tell me what they won't use, and why, and why they're frustrated that none of the above people understand the conditions they work in, and the business processes and governance they have to comply with.

Data, and the information produced by utilizing capabilities to transform data, seems to be... everyone's and no one's job. And because it's no ones, the answer is always: more and better data.

It was the repetition of these events that led me to the theories of "wide twins" and "weakly coupled twins," and their opposites the narrow and strong twins.

Without being able to link real-world change, to actions, to decisions, to capabilities, we can very rarely align data quality, data types, and data frequency to our design to create that change.

Why is more and better data a problem?

It's not! Not for the data team. It is for finance though. It is for the end user. After a few years it is for the CFO, and then sometimes the CEO. More and better data means more cost and longer times before change can be made. More data projects without corresponding ROI creates the feeling of spending more on data just because we keep saying we need more data, which leads to cuts in data budgets, which increases the time before changes can be made. For 99% of organizations, data is not the new oil. We don't sell data. It doesn't sit there waiting for someone to extract it. We create the data. We manufacture it or buy it. We then use it to create value. Data is an output of our investment that is an input into other parts of the value chain. No one buys more oil than they need, at least not very often. No one stockpiles oil out the back and brags that they have "more oil than they know what to do with" (no, they don't. Sometimes they over supply and have large holding costs and then dump oil and create problems for others, but outside of very rare geopolitical / state-controlled shocks, rational actors do not stockpile oil for no reason other than "more is good"). No one quietly admits under their breath that they use 1% of all the oil they have bought... I've had that conversation about data more than a few times. In any real-world business, anyone who does that in public gets fired. Data maximalists exist because we're in a data bubble - we're so excited going from 1 to 10, and the cloud computing explosion reduced some costs so dramatically, that many organizations have overinvested in one part of their supply chain and underinvested in the other parts needed to create value. It's a bubble. They happen. Organizations correct. It's happening now, though genAI has again brought data back to the fore. But most of you reading this aren't training LLMs - or are you? I mean, you want the right data, for your domain problems - don't you? What data do you think you need? How will your data product be used? Who will use it?

In summary

To sum up, product creation is as much art as it is science. I know that's not a great statement, but it is a truthful one. And, I think, it's a hopeful one, because you don't need to be called a "product manager" to make great products. You don't need to be ex-google or be a guru in Figma or have worked in a "growth team."

To have the best possible chance of making a great product, twin or AI or otherwise, you need to:

- Want to solve real problems, not create shiny things, AND
- Want to create great outcomes for your actual user, including making their life better, not just solving the business problem they're responsible for.

That's it. If you can hold these two things up in front of you every day, the problem and the user, and accept that they are your reasons for doing this work, you will be a long way ahead of most of your peers. I say if, because there's a heap of organizational and other pressures that make these two things hard. It's simple, but not easy. There will be plenty of days where your boss doesn't understand why you care about this stuff, and your user will cancel your meeting for the fifth time because there's a problem elsewhere, and your project deadline is looming.

Take a breath, keep believing that solving real problems for real people is a worthy problem to spend your life on, and you'll be a better person for it. You will for sure build better digital twins and applied AI.

Part 4 - Digital Twin Design Process

The reason for this book.

A structured, iterative approach to designing digital twins and applied AI, focusing on solving real-world problems, enabling change, and ensuring measurable value through validated solutions and user-centric design.

Why do we even need a process?

A major current challenge with digital twins and applied AI is that everyone does them differently, and everyone starts a new process or way of thinking each time, and those processes are discarded almost before they're used in anger. Most of these new starts are done under extreme time pressure (after the contract / project / runway time has started ticking), and no small amount of new twins are reverse engineerings of ideas that a budget holder had. This is very normal in the early years of a new paradigm, and older readers will be able to name any number of "paradigms" that swept through our professional lives and were marked by extreme uncertainty in ideation and haphazard execution. Eventually, as we learn the hard lessons, ways of working emerge that deliver benefits more often than not, and the long climb of professionalization and deeper learnings begins.

Digital twins and applied AI are no different. A key difference, however, is that these connected solutions are explicitly designed to create change in the real world. The real world, therefore, has an integral place in digital twin and applied AI design. We address this by explicitly considering the ecosystem around the twin, as well as the actual software.

In the land of software, I will focus on products as they are a higher bar than tools, and by definition any product can be used as a tool, while the reverse is not necessarily true.

The ecosystem encompasses the real-world elements that must be understood and / or changed to enable the product to create value (i.e., it is the portions of the real and virtual worlds that we are interested in). Note I do not mean designing and building the real world – there is no need to know how to build a jet engine in order to create a digital twin of one, but if you don't understand the problem the jet engine has that you're trying to solve, and how whatever portion of the surrounding ecosystem of fuel, air, structure, controls etc. impacts that problem and solution – then the probability that your twin or AI model solves the real-world problem is low.

Digital Twin Design Process – Summary

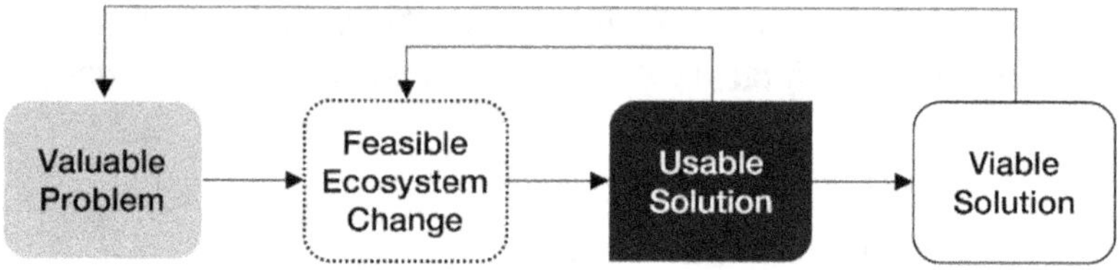

The Digital Twin Design Process (DTDP) has four stages that drive the iterative process of designing a valuable, feasible, usable and viable industrial digital twin and / or applied AI solution. Following this process drives the right behaviors and vastly increases the probability of positive change in the real world and subsequent ROI.

We call this highest level the Level 1 DTDP. It explains the why of the process stages and the intended outcomes. It also shows the deliberately iterative nature of the DTDP.

Valuable Problem

Twins as products or tools must solve real problems in order to create sufficient value to justify the investment and cost. Unlike many software products, digital twins and applied AI are highly connected to the real world. This strong connection is what drives much of the change in the real world and it is also what enables twins to measure the change created. The flipside of this is that twins measure their own success or failure. All software products are meant to "solve a problem," but twins are in the unique position of measuring the effectiveness of themselves.

The outcome of this stage is a well-defined problem that is at least partially validated in terms of cost and complexity. Executing this stage well results in the selection of a problem whose solution will create real and measurable value for the organization.

Feasible Ecosystem Change

The heart of the DTDP is analyzing and defining the change required in the real world to solve the selected problem, and the linking of capabilities and data to create and measure change. The process in this stage works backwards from the desired change in the real world, to determine what actions and decisions will need to occur to create these changes, and what capabilities enable the decisions and actions. Desired Changes, Decisions, Actions and Capabilities all create and / or require Data, and the final step of data requirements brings together the complete data acquisition and measurements of the virtual and real worlds.

The outcome of this stage is a solution specification for the software and hardware components of the twin, a data strategy, and a change strategy for business processes and user activities that enable the solution to work in the real world. Executing this stage well results in a feasible twin design, which is technically capable of creating the required changes to solve the problem in both the real and virtual worlds.

Usable Solution

Many industrial products suffer from very low adoption rates and products that have many interfaces with existing products and processes suffer the most. When users encounter complexity, and when users in one department need to work with users in another department to execute new or changed business processes, the inevitable result is confusion, friction, frustration, Excel and WhatsApp. To combat this, solutions and changes must be designed with the users in mind – both users of the solution and users of changed business processes. Change, in all its forms, must be designed for the humans who make the decisions and take the actions. Measurement of adoption enables the digital twin product team to target features and actions that do not work for the users, and to continuously improve these to increase ROI.

The outcome of this stage is the solution design, the change related products for users (business process redesign, training programs, change management etc.) and delivery of the final solution. A critical outcome of these steps is the instrumentation requirements to measure adoption and use of capabilities. Executing this stage well results in a digital twin that is used in its intended manner, and that provides the right feedback to designers to improve the product further, increasing value and ROI.

Viable Solution

With a validated problem that defines the change required and potential value created, and a technically feasible solution that measures the change created – we are now setup to determine viability. The success of a product is often measured by its adherence to cost and budget. In a digital twin, we have defined success by the change in real world, and thus we measure success by the benefits created in the real world versus the increased cost of virtual world capabilities and real-world changes. Pre-deployment, this is a calculation, that must be weighted by the risk of failure and the risk of unintended consequences as a result of change. Post-deployment, this is a measurement that is highly impacted by adoption of users and successful change of business processes and actions. We measure the benefits and cost across the real and virtual world, to obtain the true "round trip" cost and value, and hence determine the viability of the product.

The outcome of this stage is a business case before we build the product, and cost / benefits analysis three, six and twelve-months post-deployment. Executing this stage well results in approvals for digital twins that are highly likely to create value and positive ROI, ongoing measurement and improvements of success, and reinvestment to iterate more and increase value creation.

> Sidebar: How to Read this Part
>
> The remainder of Part 4 is heavy going, as it is designed for the practitioner to learn from and use as a reference. If you are not designing or not about to build a twin yourself right now, you can skip straight to the summary at Part 5 and continue on, and return to Part 4 as a reference when needed.

Digital Twin Design Process – Detailed

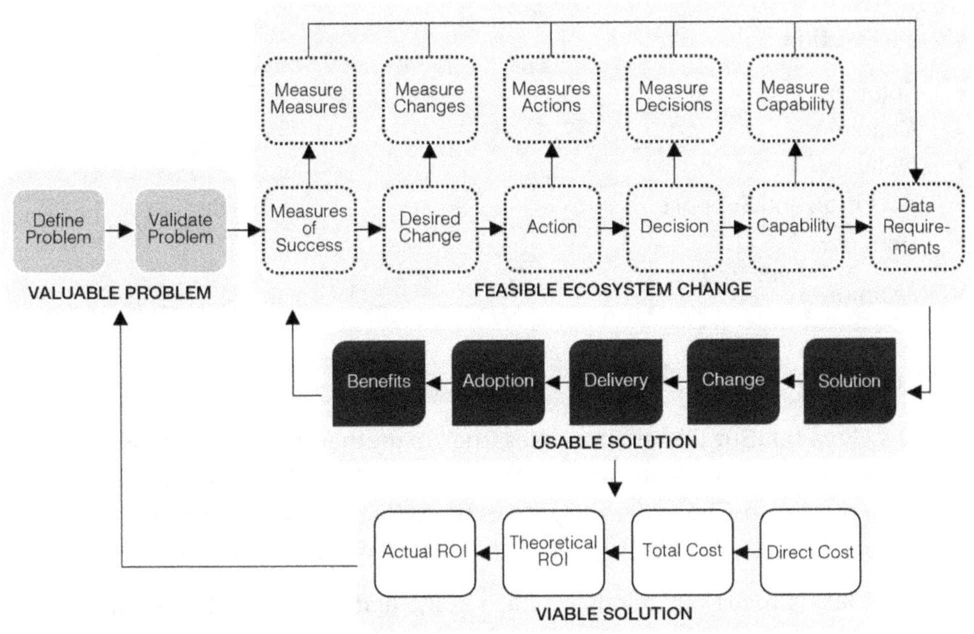

In detail, we see the major steps in each stage, and the feedback nature of the process becomes clearer.

Stages

- Valuable Problem
- Feasible Ecosystem Change
- Usable Solution
- Viable Solution

Within each stage, there are a number of recommended steps.

Valuable Problem

- Define Problem
- Validate Problem

Feasible Ecosystem Change

- Measures of Success
- Desired Change

- Actions and Decisions
- Capabilities and Data

Usable Solution

- Solution
- Change
- Delivery
- Adoption and Support
- Benefits

Viable Solution

- Total Cost
- ROI

It looks like a lot. But like all processes, there's method to the madness, and I will show you how we work iteratively to make quick decisions on what is worth investing more into. The entire purpose of the DTDP is to **maximize the probability of high-ROI change.** The cost and time of the DTDP itself is part of our investment.

For now, let us focus our minds on each stage and each step. In this section we provide a summary starting with what and why and then driving down into the how. I have structured this in what I hope is an easy to digest fashion: each step has a summary, and then detail. The detail is meant as an aid that you can refer back to. I have also included recommendations based on the work I have done myself and with help from reviewers of this book.

In the following chapter, we then look at how we apply the DTDP iteratively, starting with fast checks on feasibility and working up to sustainment of deployed twins.

For checklists on each step, you can refer to Appendix 1, and you can go to *www.designingdigitaltwins.com* to find downloadable templates, tips and tricks, and articles. I'll be updating these regularly until such time as I find a better way to design digital twins, and very likely many of these individual steps will stay with me forever. Use them in good health!

Stage 1: Valuable Problem

Ensuring only problems worth solving are assessed, this stage focuses on defining and validating problems to prioritize impactful solutions, enabling measurable ROI and reducing wasted effort.

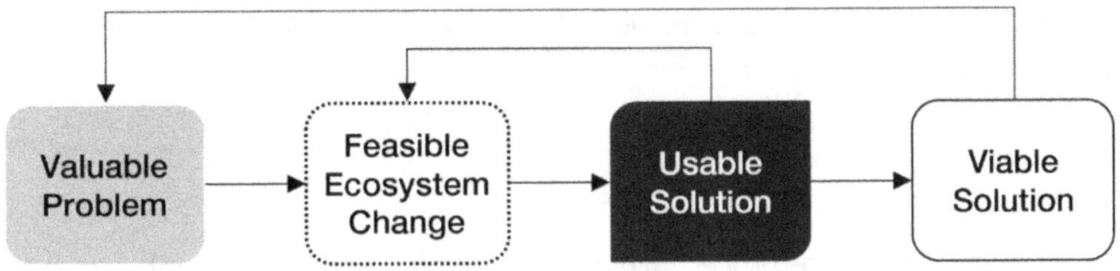

Purpose: Ensure that only problems worth solving are assessed for feasibility.

In the Valuable Problem stage, we have two steps:

- Defining the Problem
- Validating the Problem

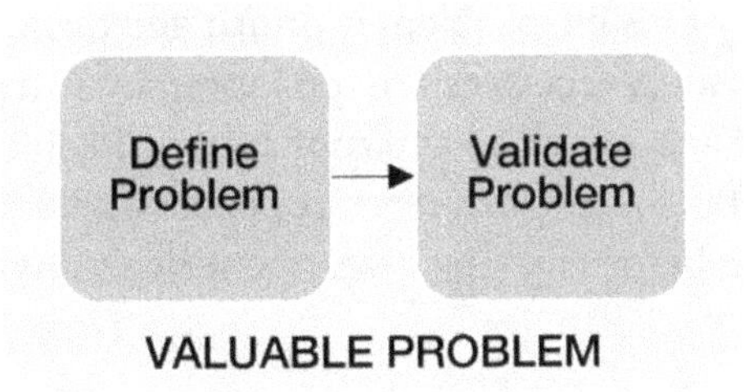

Stage 1, Step 1: Defining the problem

Summary

What: Problem definition is the process of defining problems with sufficient detail, context and impact for an organization to be able to decide if they should invest to solve the problem.

Why: Digital twins and Applied AI are immature and frequently technology led. Far too many twins reach 6-12 months after deployment, and cannot show ROI or justify why they were built in the first place.

How: Use well known frameworks such as Double Diamond, Design Thinking, Root Cause Analysis and Re-framing to examine possible problems, and determine if they are real and measurable.

Use a repeatable template for your problem statements to force you to be specific. An example is:

The Problem is [What], it affects [Who, Where and When]. We need to [Change], because [Why].

Detail

What is it?

Problem definition is the process of defining problems with sufficient detail, context and impact for an organization to be able to decide if they should invest to solve the problem.

Why do we do it?

Prioritization of investment is problematic at the best of times. Many ideas, problems and corporate themes compete for attention in any given budget cycle. Often, the latest or most visible problem is prioritized over systemic and recurring problems. Equally as often, executives are too far removed from the ground truth to be able to understand and prioritize the root causes. Problem definition mitigates this risk by forcing the business to examine proposed problems and understand their impact and root causes before making investment decisions or proposing potential solutions.

Additionally, proper problem definition provides the solution design team with sufficient information that they can validate proposed solutions before and after building and implementing them. This is the beginning of the powerful closed loop that provides ongoing ROI measurement and targeted improvements. When we can measure the problem, we can better measure the solution effectiveness, and that means we can decide to invest more to solve "more" of the problem.

A final benefit is that problems that don't need digital-twin-like solutions are not pushed down a digital twin path. Twins and AI aren't silver bullets. Worse still, digital twin and applied AI expertise is still very thin in most teams. Spending 6–12 months getting approvals and building a solution that isn't solving a real problem is a very large opportunity cost, and if it's the first, could be the last.

What problems does this solve?

Problem definition helps to solve the twin problems of:

- investing to solve problems that are not worth solving
- attempting to solve problems that aren't real problems

Many solutions are ideas in search of problems, and many problems are defined in such a way that the solution does not solve the actual root cause of the problem, but rather another problem altogether (or just an idea). In these cases, the root cause is usually masked, or is an inter-related series of problems, and very often a solution will be designed to solve the problem that is under the control of the team who allocates the budget. In other words, functions engage solution providers to try and solve cross-functional problems through changes to only one part of the problem.

The solution to this problem is to define the problem sufficiently to enable decision makers to invest based on expected changes (increase or decrease) in fundamental business metrics, and to link expected changes (increase or decrease) in user metrics to these business metric changes.

How do we do it?

Problem definition is not unique to digital twins or applied AI. There are many processes and frameworks in use across product and service industries to define problems, such as:

- Double Diamond
- Design thinking
- Root cause analysis

Any of these frameworks, if used well, could provide decision makers with sufficient context and expected value to make a Go / No-Go decision.

For organizations that wish to further de-risk this process, and increase the probability of positive ROI solutions, the follow-on step "Validate Problem" exists.

The key to making the Problem Definition step work well for highly connected solutions is to ensure that the problem is expressed in terms of business metrics *and* user metrics. This is the most vital requirement, and it is a high bar. Many business problems are expressed in one or the other – either business (e.g., financial / safety) or user (e.g., time taken to complete a process), but not both.

Most of the time we *emotionally* connect one to the other. We tend to create causal connections between what we experience and what happens to the business, and the first explanation is often the one we emotionally choose as the "root cause."

This returns us to the statement – "if done well." The key here is, that "well" = business and user metrics. That's the gold star. That's the intent. That's the outcome we strive for.

Use a standard template for your problem statements. When you are defining multiple problems – it is much easier to assess problems relative to each other, and for your solution teams to understand the problem – if you use a standard template.

An example problem definition template is:

The Problem is **[What]**, it affects **[Who, Where and When]**. We need to **[Change]**, because **[Why]**.

Appendix 2 has more details on Problem Definition, and you can find links to additional resources such as a Miro board template at:

www.designingdigitaltwins.com.

Here's two examples of defined Problems, from real digital twins, showing varying levels of details:

Problem definition 1: The Problem is [Increased downtime of HVAC systems when predictive maintenance tools reduce planned maintenance], it affects [Building tenants, in Buildings where we have introduced predictive maintenance, 3-6 months after introduction of predictive maintenance].

We need to [find a balance between planned and predictive maintenance and unplanned downtime], because [our reduced costs of planned maintenance, as a result of introducing predictive maintenance, are being offset by increased costs and complaints from tenants from excessive unplanned downtime].

Problem definition 2: The Problem is [Excessive recharge stops and depot returns when performing maintenance callouts], it affects [Drivers of Battery Electric Vehicles (BEVs), Maintenance planners and Customers, in Callouts from depots who have introduced BEVs, at unknown times, though anecdotally it is increasing].

We need to [understand what needs to change in order to make BEV operations profitable], because [we have committed to converting 50% of our fleet to BEV by 2027].

The exact wording of the template is much less important than the forcing function of specificity. Be more specific, and call out specific uncertainties. Create clarity on what is known and what is uncertain.

Recommendations

Your first twin

I recommend that businesses embarking on their first twin, front end load problem definition. "Over" invest on definition and the following step, validation, to maximize the probability of solving a problem that is worth solving. Over invest (perhaps 5x what you would "normally" do) on defining the user problems. If you have not executed a software discovery type process before, consider bringing in someone who has, and template the discovery / interview / data exploration processes. For those who live and breathe discovery, note that I have broken the normal process into a few parts, in order to better align to traditional transformation / technology / program processes. As stated previously, I am unapologetic about this.

If you are the team leader, push back on building solutions to ill-defined problems. Push to prioritize real problems, regardless of size, and take a careful look at problems where you know significant cross-functional business process change is required. The ratio of cultural change versus technology change is a good barometer of the kinds of problems you'll have, and you will know if you have the relationships to effect or influence this change with those teams.

Software + real world

If you are in an industrial organization, then processes like root cause analysis (RCA) will be familiar and well bedded in with real-world business leaders. I recommend combining a design thinking type process like Double Diamond with a physical world process like RCA. Run RCA to drill to the business and process problems and run the first half of Double Diamond to drill to the user problems. There will be overlap, and there will also be things that appear in one that are not caused by the other… this is the point of maximum danger, because the tendency will be to create a relationship in order to test potential solutions in your head. This will also be exactly what your team naturally does and what the users do.

Talk to users

There is no substitute for being close to the people with problems. Empathy is your key to opening this door. Being willing to travel to and align with the users' work is a huge step forward. If you can – go to them. Work alongside them and walk as many miles in their shoes as you can. The things you learn outside of structure interviews are almost always the things that make you go hmmm the most. Remember as well that users do not know how to describe their problems. They are not trained to dissect their own actions and decisions. People are paid to get outcomes. Sometimes that means moving a ball along a prescribed path, and sometimes it means making tough shots in the dark. There is a wealth of information available on user interviewing, user research, and discovery. Spend an hour reading and / or prompting.

Premature solutionizing

Premature solutionizing is a common and treatable problem. You engage with experts on the problems they have. You are paid to create solutions, and you care enough to want to help them. Both of you want to jump to the solution, and both of you are proud of your capabilities and intelligence.

Protect your emotional state by documenting user and design team feedback and ideas. Write them all down beside your boss's and the executive ideas, in a file called "Ideas." Remember that ideas are like... problems. Everyone has them. Don't create a solution yet. Find a good problem to solve. When empathy turns to sympathy, you have found another rabbit hole called "building what the user told me." It is no different from "building what the executive told me." In both cases, people used abstractions driven by emotion to try and explain complex issues. Listen. Learn. Do not leap to the solution.

Wide twins

If you have a mission that requires a certain capability that must be deployed (probably an Idea in the Idea file), you're really working forwards from new / desired capabilities to a class of problem, and then backwards to design a solution. In this case, the problem definition process needs an additional step in Validation – preliminary capability validation. See the next step, and the discussion later on starting point patterns. At this step, you still need real problems. Resist the urge to screen too many problems because you think your selected capability won't solve them. Creating a body of real problems is high future ROI work. They'll very likely be there for another mission, or another year, because they don't usually solve themselves. If anything, they grow and morph and people rarely create budget to define them properly. See the Problem Bank described later on.

Proceeding with multiple problems

Sometimes a selected Problem is a grouping of related problems, and Problem Definition pulls this out into the open. This is great. A twin often needs to solve multiple problems, especially if they are adjacent and you have enough budget and capabilities. Business problems often have multiple user problems and multiple data problems. This is different to multiple business problems. In this case, selecting the business problems that the team will move forward with is critical. Triaging which problems can be missed / ignored / de-prioritized is equally critical. Having a primary business problem, and multiple secondary problems, should be viewed as an opportunity for the team to crack the nut properly and deliver higher ROI and happier users. Having 10 primary problems and 20 secondary problems means you're trying to digitally transform a team or function... beware this scenario. Where you go next depends on your situation, budget, team size, problem value, internal capability etc.

When in doubt, force the question: are you building multiple narrow twins with shared capabilities where you will measure effectiveness by problem, or are you building a wide twin with shared capabilities that you hope will be able to solve these adjacent problems? Both can work, but consider the odds of hitting many targets with one arrow, and then think about how you stack the deck in your favor. Less problems, closer problems, more arrows... the analogy breaks down. The point is, that Problems are often messy, and you will nearly always move forward with business and user and process problems, but you should think hard about moving forward with multiple business problems under the same heading. It's doable, but far more complex, and usually results in a wide twin and crossed fingers. I'll show you a way in connect multiple narrow twins together to solve related problems.

Proceeding with ambiguous and uncertain Problems

Some Problems resist being defined. This is normally because there are multiple business problems, either within the target Problem (i.e., you're working at too high a level) or inter-related with the Problem (i.e., you're looking at only part of the Problem). Then there's the Problems that are just really hard. For whatever reason, it happens that you set out to define the Problem and you end with... a bunch of interesting information and opinions. Time and budgets are finite, and you need to close off the definition and make a decision.

Whatever the situation, remember that you need to provide an outcome to enable downstream or you need to pull up and reassess. Ambiguity does not imply failure. It merely means that your target is less certain than you'd like it to be. See below for ideas of what great outcomes look like, and use what you have to make an informed decision. Sometimes... you need to make a decision.

Proceeding with ill-defined Problems

We all take orders from someone – for whatever reason. When you have an ill-defined problem, you have four realistic choices.

You can:

1. Salute and hope for the best, remembering that if it doesn't provide value, they'll look at you first.
2. Ask for more time / budget, to try and define the real problem now.
3. Ask to validate the problem, before moving into solution mode.
4. Shift / continue problem validation further downstream, and focus it on the selected problem to try and maximize the chances of identifying at least a valuable sub-problem.

I personally try 2, then 3, then do 4. I am not a fan of 1 at all.

Whatever you choose – or have thrust upon you – remember that you need to provide an outcome to enable downstream steps. So do this. See below for ideas of what great outcomes look like and use what you have. Don't let ambiguity and uncertainty prevent clarity for your team. Be a leader and make a decision.

What if we can't say problem?

In a business where problems are not to be discussed openly (I have worked at one, and seen many now), the reframing can be easily accomplished to Opportunity or Risk. My word of caution is to never let semantics interfere with reality. An opportunity to reduce waste is a waste problem. Validate the problem, "waste," not the upside opportunity of "no waste." If you only validate upside, you will only prioritize increasing upside, not decreasing downside. Real problems are real because they are problems right now – not because they are missed opportunities in the future. Similarly, but less so for risks. Real risks are potential future problems. Reducing risk is a very viable and potentially valuable exercise, but it may not solve real problems today, and measuring future risk reduction can be a difficult exercise. Where risks have been realized historically, then reduction in risk can be measured directly and statistically. But for many long-tail risks, the expected frequency may be many years, and the absence of risk realization in the short term does not tell us much about the effectiveness of the change we have created. A good bank of problems will undoubtedly include risks and opportunities, but it should be anchored in real and present problems. See more later on the Problem Bank and Problem Roadmaps for more discussion on this point.

What does great look like?

A great problem definition is a series of artefacts that are tailored to the creators of the products, and clearly link user problems to business problems.

The business problem is defined in terms of impact to the business and is supported by evidence of impact that is translated into financial and / or operational terms. Strong problem statements include direct and indirect financial calculations or estimates, but more importantly, include the assumptions and calculations themselves. A strong business problem definition provides the foundation for measuring the positive or negative impact of changes, which anchors value, ROI, risk etc., through the rest of the process.

The real-world problem is defined in terms of physical processes and includes probable causality where possible. Friction, fatigue, unintended impacts, people / vehicle interactions etc. Investigations are appended where possible, and specific instances of failure or failing to meet planned targets are documented, preferably with eye witness / user interviews and statements.

The business process problem is defined in terms of failures of or conflicts between existing business processes, or instances where business problems fail to work due to specific circumstances (e.g., edge cases), or where business processes have been interpreted differently to intended.

The user problem is documented and includes discussion of where / when / how the problems occur, with lower emphasis on why. The point is, not to discount the users' view. Rather, to try and separate the natural inclination of people to judge, defend and solutionize, as part of any discussion of their problems. The user will hopefully be included in the solution stage, but at the problem definition stage, the vital aspect is gathering data, and, this includes points of view of people who do the job. That may not be the people who "have the problem", or who are responsible for fixing the problem.

The virtual world problem includes hardware outputs that are missing or invalid or incorrect, as well as missing or unsatisfactory capabilities and known missing data.

Do not overly stress on this last one. The DTDP helps to define the data that is required, and it's meant to be more comprehensive than any cursory examination.

What are the minimum outcomes required to enable downstream success?

At a minimum, the problem definition should describe the prioritized business problem, the users involved and their problems, and the business processes that are associated with the business and user problems.

When do we stop at this step?

Problems that cannot be defined in terms of business metric changes and user metric changes should be closely examined as to whether they are candidates for digital twin solutions. The lack of either creates a fundamental downstream gap for solution creators.

For all proposed problems, this should trigger a Go / No Go decision. A problem that cannot be defined is a problem that is unlikely to be measured. Therefore, it is very difficult to provide an ROI or to measure whether the problem has been reduced / solved.

In an ideal world, for problems that are clearly a business issue, this lack is the subject of further investment to investigate the problem further in order to define and measure the problem. For many problems, we "know" there is a problem, but we can't point to what is causing the problem.

Problems that are well defined, and where the problem does not require any technology-based solution, should similarly be No Go-ed for digital twin solutions. A digital twin is not a panacea. Many problems are political, or cultural, or relate to lack of resources. No Go-ing a proposed solution should not No Go solving the problem. Digital twins and AI are merely tools in our arsenal.

How does this step fail?

The primary failure mode is skipping the step altogether. In many cases, perhaps most cases in some organizations, the leadership feels that it understands problems in enough detail to make investment decisions, without properly defining the problem. Frequently, this is a cultural norm. Where leaders and experts must have the answers to problems, or else they should not be leaders.

The lesser failure mode is ignoring the users' problems and needs and only treating the problem as a "business" problem. This is recoverable further downstream, but is usually a symptom of lack of experience in the solution team regarding user needs, and the impact of not designing solutions to help users. This symptom can result in solutions that could solve the problem, but no one uses it, and hence the gap between theoretical and actual ROI is often high.

Who should be involved?

The Problem Definition step is rarely a "Standalone" step. Businesses generally don't stop to consider and rank problems. The first step officially starts when the digital twin design team gets involved. The problem itself may have been extent for many years, and examined multiple times. Solutions may even have been attempted a few times. A "good" problem is rarely "new." It's usually old and gnarly, and others, more learned than you, have tried to solve it.

The solution team should therefore seek to involve:

- the probable problem owner (or the budget holder as an abstraction)
- people who live with the problem
- people who are impacted by the problem
- people who have tried to solve the problem

Expected effort / duration

With access to the right people, and a problem that has been previously examined, a strong problem definition can take as little as two weeks – with another two weeks to write up and playback to participants.

At the other end, if a problem is complex, and the relevant parties cannot agree on what the problem is, or it turns out that the problem is really 5 or 6 inter-related problems, or if key stakeholders are unavailable or unwilling, then Problem Definition can be 2-3 months of hard work. This doesn't mean 2-3 months of continuous work. Problem definition is a process. It involves finding time with others, and considering what has been learned. 10 hours of work a week is what I budget for.

An additional benefit is that problem definition provides the solution design team with sufficient information that they can validate proposed solutions before and after building and implementing them. Pre-deployment validation is rarely invested into sufficiently, with technology teams preferring to jump straight to building, and business problem owners not understanding how low the likelihood of successful solutions are.

Stage 1, Step 2: Validating the Problem

Summary

What: Problem Validation is the process of measuring the scale of and relationships between the defined business, user and process problems.

Why: Many "problems" are really ideas. They may be good ideas, but problem thinking is difficult for solution-oriented people to do. Validating that a problem is real, is the key step to ensuring there is real Return for any proposed Investment.

How: Describe, specifically, who the problem impacts. For how long, and how often. Use this as the basis for calculating a cost to the business, and hence a potential benefit if the problem was partially or wholly solved.

Detail

What is it?

Problem Validation is the process of measuring the scale of and relationships between the defined business, user and process problems.

Why do we do it?

Problem Validation is separated from Problem Definition to force the assessment of problem size and frequency. Validating a problem means that another person or team can measure or analyze the problem and show that there is a "real" problem to be solved. This demonstrates "repeatability" of measurement and validates that the defined Problem is indeed worth solving. That the solving of the Problem can be measured. Defining and Validating Problems increases the probability of creating and measuring value.

What problems does this solve?

This step solves the problem of selecting an unmeasurable problem. Some problems are indeed very difficult to measure. This does not reduce their value. The problem, however, is that solving unmeasurable problems undermines value measurements, which in turn undermines ROI. Lack of ROI is an immediate red flag to every large business, and repeated lack of ROIs normally leads to negative consequences.

How do we do it?

To validate a problem, we must:

- Measure it (i.e., have proof that it is "real")
- Determine the benefit of solving it (i.e., know how "big" it is)

Measurement is very contextual. A problem may be experienced every day by field workers but not be measured by any current metric.

Impact is usually financial. There may be exceptions to this, but even safety and risk problems need to be budgeted to be solved, and the development of a budget is always better when justified by the potential benefits.

To validate a problem, I recommend this simple test:

- Who has it? (Use a name, not a job title. Name the person who has it, and their title / role. No hypotheticals here, say "Jim has it")
- How often do they have it?
- What do they do when it happens?
- How much time does it cost us?

If you can do this, nine out of ten times you can then calculate a cost, and assign potential benefits to solving this problem.

Recommendations

Users

There is no substitute for talking to users. Structured interviews with users you didn't interview in Definition is even better. Go find other people with the same problem, and ask them how it presents, how often it presents, what conditions create and coincide with it, and for examples of it. Same job, same problem, good validation.

If you can find the same jobs without the same problems, that's even better for downstream. Now you're finding patterns that narrow down on what causes or coincides with the problem, and that's starting the process of narrowing in.

Upstream and downstream consumers

Another source of good data is to interview people who are downstream of, or consumers of, the users who have the problem, and those who are upstream of, or customers to, users who have the problem. These people are often in different teams and may present different problems or consequences from Users. This can be extremely validating, however, as the consumers of people with problems may (should) experience their own issues as a result of the problem, if the user problem creates a large enough business problem. Remember, you are looking for relationships between problems, and consequences of siloed / team problems very often create larger impacts than siloed problems alone (i.e., the business problem may be larger than the silo thinks, or the consequences may not even present in their silo).

Find the numbers

Find the numbers. Where are the metrics that measure the problem, and what are the numbers that change when the problem occurs. We talk a lot about leading and lagging indicators, but ultimately, we are talking about the change of numbers having meaning in the real world. For ROI, financial numbers or financial proxies are required. This can be very difficult for some problems. Difficult does not mean impossible, and difficulty can also indicate that many others have walked past it and it's even more valuable to solve.

Where financial numbers cannot be found, approximations must be created. Engage with the business problem owners and financial managers to agree / negotiate how this number X translates into that number Y. It may be wrong, but it's a start, and the difficulty you have in creating the approximation directly determines the difficulty you will have proving ROI. Invented metrics move the validation problem from measurement to "proof," which itself is a measure of "belief in this number causing that number." Remember, all metrics were invented, and all of them were disbelieved at one time, or still are today, but imperfect measures can still be better than no measures, especially if you have validated that users have real problems and that the business has real problems. This measurement then becomes the *abstraction of validated problems*, rather than just an aggregation of other / random metrics. You will find that validating the problem increases confidence in the metric, which in turn reduces the coefficient of disbelief (ok yeah, I made that one up).

Is this perfect? No. Is it good engineering? Maybe. Is it scientific? Heck yes. Validating problems and creating hypotheses are what good problem solvers do. We are not seeking to create a proof that completely removes risk from the creation process. That would likely result in never addressing problems that need solving, and there are very deep pools of knowledge about the limitations of creating highly engineered solutions for humans to use.

Search for the numbers that provide your north star and keep them firmly in your mind as you twist and turn your way through execution.

The struggle is the way

Experiencing difficulty validating problems is a sign that validation is extremely necessary. This is the kind of thing that can confuse teams who are inexperienced with problem validation. When you push into validation and realize that you are invalidating some of the original definition, you are doing high value work. Every assumption that you demolish saves 10x or 20x or 100x the time spent in execution and opportunity cost. The key here is to not walk past the "hard bits." Gird your loins and push into the struggle. I guarantee that you will find new problems and that you will see your problem in a new light. The users you work with will respect you more for wanting to truly understand why the problem exists, and why someone else hasn't just "solved it."

What does great look like?

A well validated Problem has three elements:

- A clear and specific Problem Definition that provides measurement and context on the business, user and process challenges
- Evidence to support the business, user and process metrics, including the impact and frequency of the problems (numbers, including $$$), and examples of common, unusual and edge cases where possible
- Evidence to support connection of user problems and business problems

What are the minimum outcomes required to enable downstream success?

Nil. Some problems that are defined are already well validated. Where validation is performed, it increases the probability of solving real problems, and often increases the ability of solution teams to measure ROI.

When do we stop at this step?

Validation is a check. If a problem is invalidated, then go back to Definition. This is a strong check point for solution teams. In most cases, what will come out of validation is narrowed down areas of uncertainty around user-business causality. This is very normal and I consider this to be a good sign. Teams that understand the areas they don't know, usually choose to invest more in those areas. Most critically, if the problem proceeds into Feasibility without a measure of the approximate benefit that is possible, then this must be called out. Proceeding without any potential Return and then forcing the solution team to justify Return later, during delivery, wastes time and can often lead the solution team to attempt to reverse engineer ad hoc new uses. In other words, building an idea in search of a new, measurable, problem, half way through delivery.

How does this step fail?

This step fails when it is ignored, or more correctly when it is assumed that it is not required or valuable. Allowing non-problems to proceed into feasibility wastes time and costs money.

The other failure mode is when validation becomes solutioneering. This occurs when solution teams who have not had any training or experience in discovery start to dig into problems and immediately begin creating solutions with users. The excitement of "solving" problems can overshadow the hard work of understanding the problem.

Who should be involved?

Problem validation should be done by a team other than the solution / delivery team. It is often that the solution team is the only team with time available. In this case, I recommend bringing in an external player from the team that experiences the problem. Have them involved in reviewing the problem definition and the proof points of how much, when and who the problem impacts.

Expected effort / duration

Validation for a small problem may only be days, or it could be weeks of calendar time. For a problem that cannot be easily validated, the decision must be made on how long to continue trying to validate. This is always a function of the budget / business case requirements.

Stage 1 output

- A clear and specific description of a real Problem
- A maximum benefit that could be obtained by the organization if the Problem was solved

End of Stage 1

Stage 2: Feasible Ecosystem Change

Ensures proposed changes are practical in both real and virtual worlds by identifying measures of success, desired changes, actions, decisions, capabilities, and data needed to solve validated problems effectively.

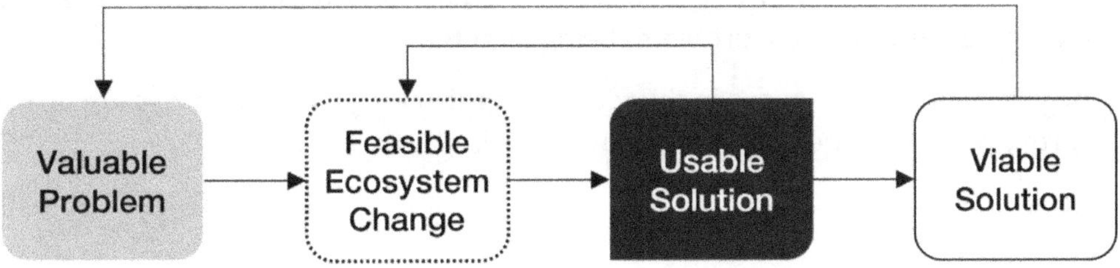

Purpose: Ensure that proposed changes are feasible in the real and virtual worlds.

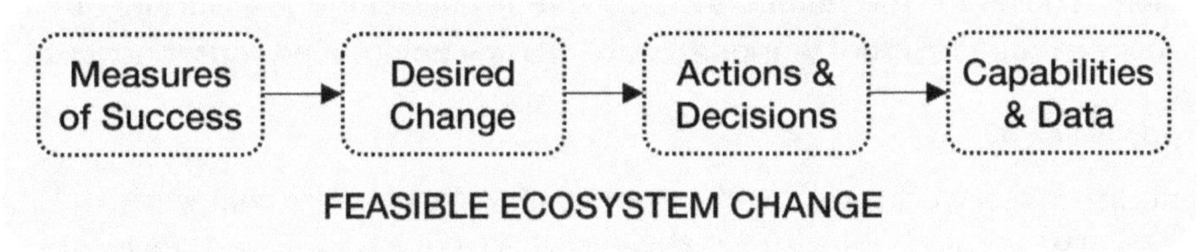

In the Feasible Ecosystem Change stage, we have four steps:

- Measures of Success
- Desired Change
- Actions and Decisions
- Capability and Data

When we produce Connected Action Maps, we break this out further to six steps.

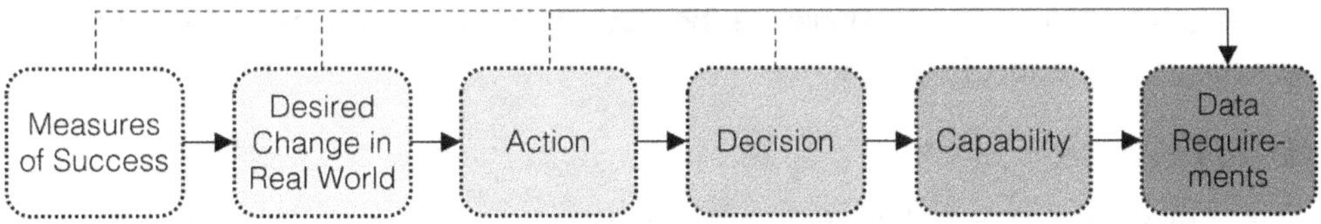

Stage 2, Step 1: Measures of success

Summary

What: Measures of Success give the solution team clear metrics or numbers in the real world to target for change. What are we going to change?

Why: Digital twins and applied AI as products or projects are frequently unbounded by real-world Measures of Success. Software measures – such as testing and user acceptance and model accuracy – frequently do not cause success in the real world. Twins require clear Measures of Success in the real world, to show how the changes they create are solving the problems being targeted.

How: Develop clear changes in the real world that can be measured and are direct or proxy proof that the Problem is being solved.

Detail

What is it?

Measures of Success is where we select the real-world measures that represent our Problem. These are the numbers that move if our solution is working, or move because our solution is not working, or are causing unintended consequences.

Why do we do it?

Events in the real world are our anchor on reality. We measure changes in the status of the real world as our closest possible proxies to the "outcomes." We select a mix of measures across time frames, from as close to real time as possible, out to "long term," in order to understand and be able to trade off short and long-term benefits.

What problems does this solve?

Selecting real-world events as the anchor for measurement removes the typical software ambiguity of building capabilities and hoping that they will be used to solve "a" problem or siloing ourselves to only user behavior in the system. By defining change in the real world as our measure of solution success, we can work backwards to designing the changes that create the desired change, and we can close the loop with measurements of that change.

How do we do it?

From our validated Problem, we know what parts of the ecosystem the Problem impacts. We select multiple measures, preferably lagging and leading, and designate these as our Measures of Success. We assign baselines to them, preferably from when the Problem is present and when it is not (some periodic / episodic problems require this nuance), and we set our targets to achieve. Typical targets are 5% or 10% improvement over baseline. This is not the "final" improvement we want to achieve – this is our thermometer. Are the changes we make pushing the measures in the right direction? If so, how do we do more? If not, what do we need to change?

We also designate expected frequency. This is important for the selection of changes later, and also for determining how we measure occurrence. If the Problem occurs within 30 seconds of a particular other measure exceeding a threshold (e.g., 20 sec after Temp > 85 deg), and only occurs when the threshold is exceeded, then we know that Temperature is a key measure. We also know that we have less than one minute to intervene, if mitigation (as well as avoidance) is part of our solution. If this has historically occurred at least 10 times a month, then we know that the frequency of the event is 10 times per month, or perhaps 3-4 times per week.

Selecting multiple Measures of Success sets the solution team up to consider multiple ways of solving this problem. It doesn't mean they need to impact all of the selected measures – these are "just" the measures of the Problem. But by using the domain expertise of the problem owner, the solution team is being given the best chance to solve this Problem.

On successive Iterations of the product, we can reset Baselines, Targets and Frequencies.

Measure 1 – Temperature
Type: Leading

Iteration	**1**	**2**	**3**
Baseline Value	80 deg C	80 deg C	80 deg C
Target	<85 deg C	<83 deg C	<82 deg C
Frequency	60 sec	30 sec	15 sec

Measure 2 – Occurrence
Type: Lagging

Iteration	**1**	**2**	**3**
Baseline Value	10 / mth	8 / mth	5 / mth
Target	8 / mth	5 / mth	3 / mth

Measure 3 – Cumulative Downtime
etc.

The key here is to understand what changes when someone does something. Change, When and Thing. You need to understand all three, and beginning with multiple measures of change in the real world will anchor you in the place and time you're most interested in.

Recommendations

Multiple bites create patterns

Give yourself multiple ways to measure success and spread them across time. You should always strive for lagging / cumulative and leading / near real time as close to the problem in the real world as possible, and then abstracted measures of output / outcome / impact on your key business measures (Downtime, Production, Cost, Energy etc.). If you only do the abstracted, you'll hit the usual problem of not knowing if your Problem caused that metric to move or some other problem did, and when it does move the right way, was it your solution or some other solution or just luck. Measure twice, high and low, before and after, to develop patterns that are amenable to further analysis.

User knowledge

Have you ever worked with a really gifted mechanic, or electrician, or fitter? Decades of experience and genuine love of their craft has given them gifts. They know when things are going wrong. They know leading indicators that you would never think of. Rattles, smells, temperature, things "not looking right." Soak this up. You might find it hard to connect that with how to solve the problem, now, but if you can get them to tell you all the ways they know things are going wrong, you are a massive jump ahead on solving this Problem.

What does great look like?

Great real-world Measures of Success are:

- specific
- spread across time (before / during / after)
- measurable
- as close to the Problem as possible and abstracted / output that underpins the ROI

What are the minimum outcomes required to enable downstream success?

At the minimum, we need to be able to measure success, in the form of change to the key Measures of Success that underpin the ROI.

When do we stop at this step?

We rarely stop at this step, as problems that get to this stage are real Problems and there is always some metric or measurement impacted by the Problem.

How does this step fail?

This step fails when the measures in the real world are too high level, or too aggregated with other problems, to be able to tell us if the solution is working. If Problem Definition has been done correctly, there should be little chance that the measures selected are not related to the problem. But it is still possible. Selecting single financial metrics like "revenue," is almost certainly going to cause difficulties downstream.

Who should be involved?

The users of the system, and people who experience the Problem, or who are expected to mitigate / overcome the problem every day – are the most useful. Going to where the problem occurs, or is seen / detected (not always same thing), is the most useful way to do this.

Expected effort / duration

Measures of Success should only take a day or two, if business problem owners / users are accessible, and validated Problems are being targeted. Select a spread of measures, and validate with people who are involved in that area of work. More measures can always be added later.

Stage 2, Step 2: Desired change in the real world

Summary

What: Desired Change in the Real World is the hypothesis of what changes can be made, that will move the Measures of Success in the right direction.

Why: Anchoring on change in the real world, forces practical thinking about what could and would need to change, in order for the Problem to be solved.

How: Ideate changes in the real world that domain experts believe could impact the Measures of Success favorably.

Detail

What is it?

This is where we select the changes that we believe will move the Measures from Baseline to Target and beyond. This is the step where we decide what we're going to attempt to change in the real world.

Why do we do it?

We focus the solution team on changes in the real world, to create the changes in the Measures we desire. This step is deliberately divergent. This is a design term, meaning to go wide – exploring many possibilities, without limiting options on the basis of whether they have been done, or not done before, or are difficult, or easy, or costly, or... We use this step to explore many possibilities, before we test the feasibility of each possibility, to try and find the best possible ways to create our desired change.

What problems does this solve?

This step focuses the team's efforts on real change, without the distraction of abstract financial metrics. Using validated Problems and real-world Measures, the team is now free to explore ways to create change, knowing that the follow-on steps of Action-Decision-Capability-Data, will ensure that only feasible (that is, executable) changes will progress to delivery.

How do we do it?

We know what Problem we're trying to solve.

We know what Measures we need to move.

Now we need to come up with some ideas on how to solve them.

First, we diverge, then we converge.

Divergence

I suggest four methods at this stage:

- Workshops with users
- Mind mapping
- SCAMPER
- Chat it up

Workshops

The best way to capture ideas is to run a series of workshops with a good cross section of people. Get users, technology people, business problem owners, and well-wishers into a room. If you've never run a workshop before, don't panic, there's a ton of resources online on how to do it – face to face and hybrid. I always suggest doing face to face – when possible – but sometimes it's just not possible, or you'd have to wait months to get the right people into one room. In this case, run multiple workshops, keep them small, and synthesize and playback your findings to everyone who participated.

Mind mapping

Mind mapping has a bad name in some circles, but this is often because it doesn't start with a solid foundation, or it's done without a clear guidance. Using workshop inputs, and similar solutions for similar problems, team members can explore connections to, or alternatives to, existing inputs.

SCAMPER

SCAMPER is an acronym standing for:

- Substitute
- Combine
- Adapt
- Modify
- Put to another use
- Eliminate
- Reverse

SCAMPER can be used in workshops or after workshops, to help prompt exploration of connected actions, or alternate courses. SCAMPER is a good human prompting tool.

Chat

We should never overlook LLMs such as ChatGPT, Claude, Perplexity etc. as tools to develop potential changes and to explore alternatives. I highly recommend feeding workshop inputs into your LLMs of choice, preferably multiple LLMs, and using a variety of prompts to explore many options.

Convergence

When the divergent processes are over, or exhausted, as is sometimes the case, we need to prioritize and narrow down. We need to converge on likely or preferred options. We typically do this in a two-step process:

- Clustering
- Prioritizing

Clustering

We bring together similar solutions to reduce the sheer number of options, and to be able to identify the key clusters of options. You will often find many similar changes by multiple people. If you don't, it's possible that your Problem is ill defined.

Prioritizing

With clustered changes, prioritization can be accomplished in a number of ways. Voting in workshops is a very good way of getting inputs, and equally voting on infeasible options is also a great way of getting feedback on things that might fail downstream.

Recommendations

Diverge before converging

Divergent thinking is hard for technical people. I should know, I'm an engineer, and we're some of the worst. We love to jump to the answer. We trust our instincts. We argue our point. All of that is ok – as long as we don't treat this as "the decision" workshop. It's not. We're going wide to get inputs from multiple different people, with different points of view and experience. It's not a free-for-all – the validated Problem and the Measures are the aim points. But don't try and "solve" the problem in a workshop. The solution team is there to learn.

Don't stress about people jumping "ahead"

Straight after I say don't solutionize, I recommend not worrying if people jump to solutions... I say this because you, the workshop leader, need to control yourself, and create the environment for people to want to give their all. When they do, they'll go too far, and that's cool. Your domain experts will very likely skate forward to the Action-Decision loops, your tech heads will jump to Capabilities, and your data scientists will jump to models and acquisition and training. It's all good gear. Encourage it. Let them get it all out in the open... you're about to learn a LOT.

Be a great host

When you run a workshop, people have agreed to invites received via their work emails, and arrive at a work meeting room to do work. You're not just the meeting organizer, you're their host. Be a great host. Have water ready, organize food breaks, organize so people can get coffee or tea. Give people merchandise... I know this sounds crazy. Give them something to remember the workshop. Stand out from your peers. When you come calling again for help, and validation, and adoption – they'll remember you.

What does great look like?

Great – in this case – has two components:

- A list of potential real-world changes that the team believes could solve the Problem, and has been developed with input from people who have or deal with the Problem.
- A well-structured and searchable body of knowledge that can be referenced by the solution team later, and by future solutions teams (enable the organization to learn faster).

What are the minimum outcomes required to enable downstream success?

A list of potential real-world changes that the team believes could solve the Problem.

When do we stop at this step?

We rarely stop at this step, as there are always many potential changes that could be made, and the cross-functional teams always have many ideas.

How does this step fail?

This step rarely fails as a standalone. In my experience the only minor failure modes are too many potential changes and an inability to prioritize them well. This can lead to wasted time downstream.

Who should be involved?

The users of the system and people who experience the Problem, or who are expected to mitigate / overcome the Problem every day are the most useful.

Expected effort / duration

Given a number of workshops, it is likely to take two weeks to complete this stage.

Stage 2, Step 3: Actions and Decisions

Summary

What: Actions are the literal physical actions that humans (users and non-users) or machines (agents and control systems and automated tools) need to take to create the Desired Change. Decisions are the precursor to Action. We do not limit these to what we think will be "inside" the twin. These are ALL the Actions and Decisions that would be required to create the Desired Change, regardless of who / where. Existing systems and people will likely make up 90% of humans and machines. We will cover later how "tech" outputs (Capabilities and Data) go into the solution design, and "non-tech" outputs (Actions and Decisions) go into the change plan.

Why: The first true test of feasibility is – can you convince a cross-functional group of people that these Actions and Decisions are possible? Bonus points if they are possible in the timeframe required to create the Desired Change.

How: Use the Connected Action Map to develop Actions that would be required to create the Desired Change, and the Decisions required to take the Action. Some changes are already Actions, and some Actions may seem trivial ("press a button"), but they provide valuable insights to the solution team. Note as many Actions and Decisions as are required, to create the Desired Change. Detail the multi-step interconnected Actions if required.

Detail

What is it?

In this step, we define Actions and Decisions that could create the desired Changes. The Actions and Decisions are not limited to what we believe will be "inside" the twin. We are developing the Actions and Decision inside the *ecosystem* that would be required to create the Desired Changes.

This point needs to be emphasized... work backwards from the Desired Changes. Do not suddenly flip to working forwards from what you think a "digital twin" should look like.

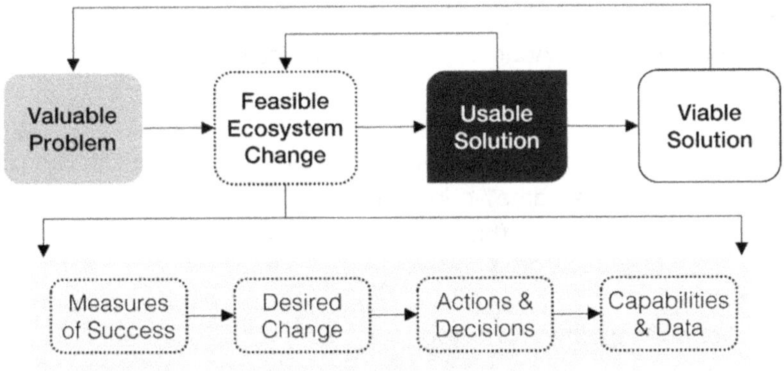

Breaking this out more, we can see that there are six steps to produce a "Connected Action Map."

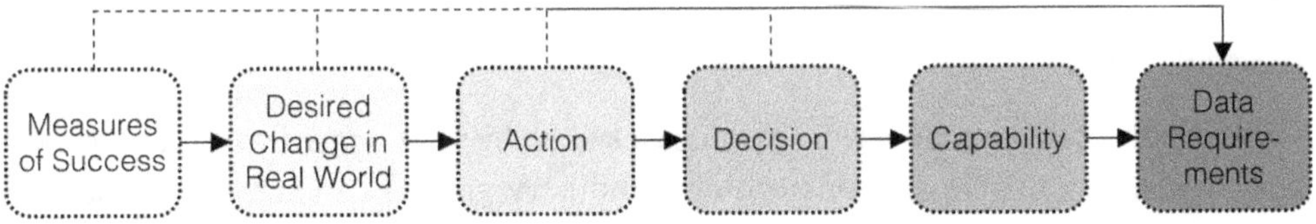

Why do we do it?

We work backwards from the Desired Changes to explicitly link what people and machines do to create the change. We do this to prevent technology led insertion of shiny things.

We bundle Actions and Decisions together to again force the thinking on feasibility. If someone needs to make a Decision to "change the way the business works" before an Action can be taken, then either the way the business works needs to change to make the Action feasible, or the Action will be infeasible. Either way, once it's on paper, the team can then assess feasibility, before anything is built, or changes are made in the real world.

What problems does this solve?

This step solves the problem of abstracting real-world changes without regard to measurable ecosystem change. Both "real-world" and "technology-led" solution design concepts tend to skip over this step because it's hard without defining specific changes in the real world.

How do we do it?

With the provided Desirable Changes in hand, the team can work backwards to develop potential chains of Actions-Decisions, and to then discard infeasible chains.

The steps are:

- Use the Connected Action Map to develop potential Action-Decision chains
- Cluster similar chains (same Actions or same Decisions)
- Prioritize the "best" chains (but don't discard the others yet)

Develop

Connected Action Mapping Workshop

In a practical sense, the Desired Change workshop runs on into the Action-Decision step, and often into the Capability-Data step. We call this end-to-end feasibility "Connected Action Mapping." We'll discuss this more when we go through how we iterate through the DTDP.

Process Mapping

A good exercise is to map existing processes used by your organization, and similar organizations, to solve similar problems. Industry groups can sometimes be very valuable here too, and will often have consulting / advisory arms, that can bring best practices to your team. Starting with the As-Is helps level set everyone. In some cases, the As-Is will solve the Problem if a new / improved Capability is deployed to e.g., deliver predictions for Decisions one day before the fault occurs. In these lucky cases, we don't need to invent "new" Actions in the real world. We just need to improve when, or how often, they occur.

Chat

We should never overlook LLMs such as ChatGPT, Claude, Perplexity etc. as tools to develop potential changes and to explore alternatives. I highly recommend feeding workshop inputs into your LLMs of choice, preferably multiple LLMs, and using a variety of prompts to explore many options.

Cluster

We bring together similar solutions, to reduce the sheer number of options, and to be able to identify the key clusters of options. You will often find many similar changes by multiple people. If you don't, it's possible that your Problem is ill defined.

Prioritize

With the remaining Action-Decision chains, prioritization can be accomplished in a number of ways. Voting in workshops is a very good way of getting inputs, and equally, voting on infeasible options is also a great way of getting feedback on things that might fail downstream.

The "infeasible" step is fraught with risk. This is the step where overly conservative team members can prematurely eliminate novel and potentially valuable solutions. My recommendation is to err on the side of exploring potentials, rather than reducing workload. The DTDP is a front-end loading investment. We are investing a small amount of thinking now, to save a huge amount of ineffective building later. AND we are also investing a small amount of thinking now, to try and unlock massive benefits later. "Outside the box" ideas that could be feasible, should be included in the connected action plan.

Recommendations

Leverage outside experts if possible

Sometimes, the biggest issue is that a single subject matter expert dominates the discussions, and insists that "we can't do that here." I find that the Action-Decision step is where this occurs the most. A great antidote to this, is to bring in an outside expert who can talk about how similar changes are made in other places. The use of a third party can not only help with softening the "expert silo," but it can also introduce diversity of thinking into the team. I have leveraged experts from other parts of the lifecycle paradigm too – e.g., for an asset owner, I bring in someone from a service provider who works with many asset owners. For a service provider, I bring in an asset owner or operator who has many service providers. Diversity of thought from outside your peer group, but inside your lifecycle (i.e., they have credibility but aren't involved in your politics) can be very beneficial. Customers and Suppliers are also potential contributors, with the usual cost / benefit considerations.

Not in the "solution" box

Reinforce in your briefing, and during the workshop, that we are not trying to find Action-Decision chains from inside the notional "digital twin" or "AI." I use " ", because we don't have a twin yet. We just have a Problem and some Desired Changes to solve that Problem. We WANT Actions and Decisions from outside the twin. We want the Actions and Decisions that solve the Problem! Then we will figure out which ones are feasible, and put the non-twin ones into the change "box", and the twin ones into the Solution "box". Then, we'll have our ecosystem design.

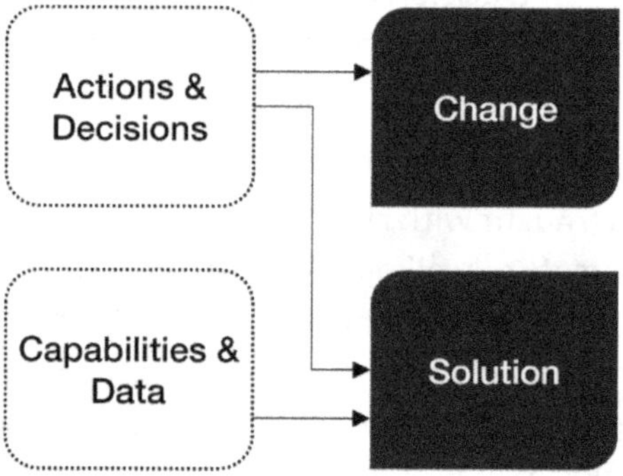

What does great look like?

Great Action-Decision outputs are:

- A list of Action-Decision chains that are assessed as "not infeasible."
- Action-Decision chains that genuinely change how work is done in "not infeasible" ways, and would provide significant benefit to the Problem.

What are the minimum outcomes required to enable downstream success?

A list of potential Actions and Decisions that the team believes could create the Desired Change.

When do we stop at this step?

We only stop at this step if there are truly no feasible ways of creating the Desired Change.

How does this step fail?

This step rarely fails as a standalone. In my experience, the only minor failure modes are elimination of valuable but novel Action-Decision chains (this is an opportunity cost).

Who should be involved?

The users of the system, and people who experience the Problem, or who are expected to mitigate / overcome the Problem every day, are the most useful.

Expected effort / duration

One week, with two workshops and synthesis / playback time.

Stage 2, Step 4: Capabilities and Data

Summary

What: Capabilities are the features or technology that utilize Data to enable or create the Decisions and Actions from the previous step.

Data comprises three forms:

1. Inputs required by the Capabilities.
2. Activity measurement of:
    - Measures of Success
    - Desired Changes
    - Actions and Decisions
    - Capabilities and Data
3. Emergent response related to Activity Measurement.

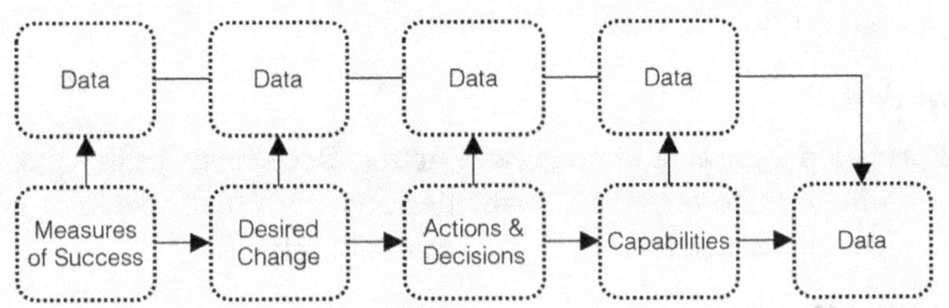

Why: Data is the lifeblood of digital twins and AI, and powers the Capabilities. Additionally, measuring what is happening and what isn't, what Actions were taken, and what weren't, provides the genuine measurement of "is this working?", that enables improvements in successive iterations.

How: Develop the Capabilities and Data required to enable or perform the Actions and Decisions. Develop activity measures for all preceding steps.

Detail

What is it?

In this step, we define the Capabilities and Data that are needed to create the Actions and Decisions, and measure the Ecosystem Changes. The Capabilities and Data are not limited to what we believe will be "inside" the digital twin. Much of what is needed, may already be present inside the existing virtual world.

Why do we do it?

We work backwards from the Action-Decision chains, to explicitly link what Capabilities and Data are needed, to enable or create the Actions and Decisions. We do this to ~~prevent~~ limit technology-led insertion of shiny things. We do this to link the real and virtual worlds together.

We bundle Capabilities and Data together, to again force the thinking on feasibility. A Capability without the required Data is... not really a Capability? At best it's a feature. A feature that won't be used much.

We drive measurements from the connected chain of change in the real world explicitly, so that it doesn't get lost, or forgotten, or deprioritized.

What problems does this solve?

This step explicitly links the real and virtual worlds. Regardless of which "world" is driving the design – both are represented, and both must be considered in full, to create the change required to solve the Problem.

How do we do it?

With the provided Desirable Changes and Action-Decision maps in hand, the team can work backwards, to develop Capabilities and Data that enable or create the Actions and Decisions, and to then discard infeasible chains.

The two steps are:

- Develop potential Action-Decision-Capability-Data chains
- Cluster similar chains

- Prioritize the "best" chains

Develop

Connected Action Mapping Workshop

In a practical sense, this is the Desired Change-Action-Decision-Capability-Data workshop. We call this end-to-end feasibility "Connected Action Mapping." We'll discuss this more when we go through how we iterate through the DTDP.

In this step, we face the major challenge of ecosystem design head on: virtual world people must convince real-world people that Capability A + Data B will enable or create Action X or Decision Y. *This is a crucial and potentially contentious phase.*

"Real world" people are rarely invited into the domain of technology ideation. They are excellent, however, at criticizing technology that hasn't helped them in the past.

"Virtual world" people are rarely asked to explicitly link Capabilities to real-world change. They are excellent, however, at creating plausible-but-not-quite-thought-through-to-the-fine-details-because-I've-never-done-that-work-in-the-real-world hypotheses.

However, we have arrived together at this point in the journey with a map. With a number of maps: Connected Action Maps. These maps were drawn together, debated together, and parsed to this point together. Now, together, real and virtual world team members can collaborate to create connected change.

Workshop

A good warm up exercise is to:

- Select one or two simple As-IS Action-Decision chains that are supported by existing Capabilities, and map them out.
- Then, for these ones, map the Data required to enable that Capability.
- Then, work back from Desired Change, to Actions, to Decisions, to map the Data required to measure these activities.
- Lastly, determine which Data is not currently available.

Working through "easy" connected action maps warms the team up to how to work together, and often gets both "sides" interacting, and suggesting known quantities, and gets all used to the new language of the DTDP.

A key leading indicator of success is tech people making calls on the real world, and vice versa. When you see this happening, it's a good indicator that this is a safe space for everyone to contribute, regardless of their "expertise."

Then move onto progressively more difficult chains, or prioritize the highest perceived value chains. This is a judgement call. Whichever way you go, don't leave the best but hardest ones until last People will often start flagging on energy and attention levels. Get into the ones the team thinks could make the biggest impact, while every still has energy and intent.

If you get stuck, just put it in the parking lot. Again, don't let people spend too long hitting the same wall.

Deprioritize

In the case of completed chains, I recommend deprioritizing before attempting to determine which full chains are the "best." At this stage, at the end of the connected mapping, so much information has been exchanged, that people are saturated. Vote the ones down that people think won't "move the needle" (create real or large Desired Change), and leave it at that.

Recommendations

Three kinds of data

1. Inputs required by the Capabilities
2. Activity measurement
3. Emergent response related to Activity Measurement

The first is obvious, and the primary data that is collected in any solution. Capabilities need Data.

The second, measurement of Activity, is common to SaaS products, but usually limited to the user who is taking action in the product. In the DTDP, we extend this to the other humans who are involved in making Decisions and taking Actions – as far as possible. I say as far as possible, because many Decisions are hard to "collect," and many Actions are taken in isolation. The key here is to think about how and when structured data can be collected. The Decision to use a prediction, to take Action, to create a new work order, may only be "collectable," if we can Measure that the existing work order was cancelled, and the prediction was used to create a new work order. There can be major benefits to digitalization in this context, to capture changes to workflows, or selection of alternate workflows, especially when piloting new Capabilities in parallel with existing ways of working.

The third type of data is the most difficult, and the least thought of - capturing changes to the ecosystem, to provide feedback to the solution & change designers. I usually make a strong case for including some form of this in every twin, because I have seen the benefits of this so often. But of course, many others haven't, mostly because they have never tried to collect it, nor have a process for using it. My preferred way to do this is by building a knowledge graph of the portion of the ecosystem that we are interested in. The first order relationships alone, provide a wealth of information, and will track the impact of many changes. For the data scientists who are aware of how large and formidable a task this could be if taken to the extreme, I counsel that this cannot distract from the main event. We are seeking feedback to improve our solution and change, not causal analysis of all the higher-order impacts of the change we create. Focus on what data can be obtained relatively easily, that will help the solution and change designers improve their work.

No magic wands

I also have a rule in this phase of the workshop: no one is allowed to say "AI." The acronym AI is replaced by "Magic wand." Every time someone says "AI" as the Capability, I change it to "magic wand."

The ~~AI~~ magic wand will tell the operator when to turn off the machine...

No.

Let's try it again.

The existing fault prediction model, trained inhouse, and currently in production with a model accuracy of approximately 75%, will pass a notification to the operator, via the "operator dashboard," and an alert via visual notification, and vibration to the operator's mobile device, alerting the operator that a fault is potentially imminent, and they need to make a Decision on whether or not to take the Action of turning off the machine.

Less pithy. Nil wands.

Decoupled Capabilities

Many Capabilities will be proposed that are used currently, or have been used by someone at another organization, to solve a similar problem. The question is not "will this work?" but, "what exactly is output by this Capability to enable the Decision or

Action?" Anchoring the output from the Capability to the input of a Decision is critical, as it forces the thinking through the real-world events required to create the Desired Change.

I suggest flagging that the Capability is "decoupled," and scheduling time to repeat the Action and Decision cycle. Then, if this chain seems feasible, doing the check on Desired Change-Action-Decision-Capability when you are reviewing the solution and change (next step).

We'll cover the scenario where a Capability is mandated a bit later.

New Capabilities

Perhaps the most uncertain area is when a new Capability is proposed to solve the Problem. This is the time to intervene and challenge, gently, how the Capability enables the Decisions and Actions that are being reviewed to occur. I find that very often, the Capability is a high-level idea, or someone has heard it was used elsewhere, but that they don't know how exactly it would help *us* solve the Problem. Don't stomp on the idea – it may well be a great idea. It may well enable an existing or new Action-Decision chain to create the Desired Change. The key is to draw out what exactly (and often when, exactly), the output from this new Capability would be. Treating an output as a requirement can help people focus down onto what is required, rather than what needs to be built. Later on, you can then examine the feasibility of building / buying said Capability, but only if the output could feasibly create the Decisions and Actions and Desired Changes to solve the Problem.

New Decisions and Actions

Another common challenge is that people have been thinking about how to create the Desired Change, but those thoughts didn't make it onto the Actions and Decisions boards, or the thoughts only solidified afterwards. In this case, people will often bring up new Decisions and Actions that are enabled by the Capability. They are "working forwards" from a Capability, towards the Desired Change. This is all good. I suggest adding the Action and Decision back in, and then if this chain seems feasible, doing the check on Desired Change-Action-Decision-Capability when you are reviewing the solution and change (next step).

Note that I don't advocate "working forwards" with a blank canvas. I'm saying that after you've anchored everyone on the Desired Change, and people's creativity is primed by the Action-Decision workshop, they will be in a good head space to work forwards.

Actions without Decisions and other Missing Steps

Very commonly, in a workshop environment, interim steps are missed. E.g., "the User needs to press the button to send the notification." Don't stress about this. In the actual detail design and building of the solution, you will find many missing steps and enabling actions are required. The Connected Action Map is designed to massively reduce the probability of infeasible and unviable solutions and changes being invested into. It is not designed to provide a step-by-step guide to every little thing you need to do and build. I guarantee you will find many missing steps. However, you will have a Connected Action Map that these steps can be added back into, and the feasibility challenged, and you can remain confident that the overall design of change remains sound.

You will never get all the data you want

I can't say it enough: it's not all there. But, and here's the but – we're defining what we need, and the potential payoff, to justify getting what is needed. The DTDP is the path to getting budget to improving data that benefits more than just this twin. Don't kill the chain just because you don't have the data, but note that the Data needs to be acquired, so either find the work around or the proxy/abstracted data or put that chain in the parking lot until you can get the Data.

Please don't try and collect all the data

On the other hand... please don't try and get "all the things." Please don't try and add data that you think is "needed" but isn't linked to Decisions and Actions or measuring activity. Why? Because see the point above. You will inadvertently undermine the ROI of the twin and create an overly complex solution.

Get the Data you need to produce measurable value, fast, and then connect more data to more value later.

Some measurement is better than no measurement

We are not trying to imply causality with measurements. We are playing the correlation game, for further analysis, to then create causality connections, to improve the twin in follow on iterations. Measurement across ecosystem is a very immature science. With teams who are feeling a bit overwhelmed at this point, I often dial back the measurement data to some key areas of focus:

- Did the user know the Problem was happening?
- Did the user try and do anything about it?

- If they did, did it work?

With these three pieces of information, you have a rich vein of golden goodness to look at during the Adoption and Support step.

Don't worry if your twin starts looking very boring

I should not laugh, but this is the point where I have seen some tech teams have their first little panic. The Desired Change-Action-Decision-Capability-Data chain of sticky notes suddenly looks really... easy. And simple. And not twin-like at all. On the other side of the room, the person who has this Problem has a big grin on their face.

Long ago in this book I said that two key traits for creating great products are:

- Wanting to solve real problems, not create shiny things.
- Wanting to create great outcomes for your actual user, including making their life better, not just solving the business problem they're responsible for.

Take that deep breath, hold firm, trust that we're on a good path, and, your user (your customer) is looking happy.

Also, we haven't finished yet. We still have to actually solve the Problem. Trust me, more pain will come to us all down the track.

Don't panic if you have 120 post-it notes on the wall.

We are mapping potential chains of Desired Change-Action-Decision-Capability-Data... POTENTIAL. In the follow-on step of solution, we take very few chains through to Delivery. Some of these chains will stay on the wall for a future iteration. Many will be eliminated.

Record all the notes!

What does great look like?

Remember, this is the direct follow on to the Action-Decision work.

Great Action-Decision-Capability-Data outputs are:

- A list of Action-Decision-Capability-Data chains that genuinely look like they could create the Desired Change, and have been bought into by technology and domain experts.
- Lists of Data measurements that correspond to key (and very often common) activities.

What are the minimum outcomes required to enable downstream success?

A list of potential Capabilities and Data that are connected to Actions and Decisions that the team believes could create the Desired Change.

When do we stop at this step?

We only stop at this step if there are truly no feasible ways of creating the Actions and Decisions.

How does this step fail?

This step rarely fails as a standalone. In my experience, the only minor failure modes are elimination of valuable but novel chains (this is an opportunity cost), or the insertion of capabilities that are unrelated to the Action-Decision chains (inefficiency / complexity cost).

Who should be involved?

The users of the system, and people who experience the Problem, or who are expected to mitigate / overcome the Problem every day, are the most useful.

Expected effort / duration

Two weeks, with two workshops and synthesis and playback time.

Stage 2 Execution – Connected Action Maps

In practice, we put the Feasible Ecosystem Change steps together into Connected Action Maps.

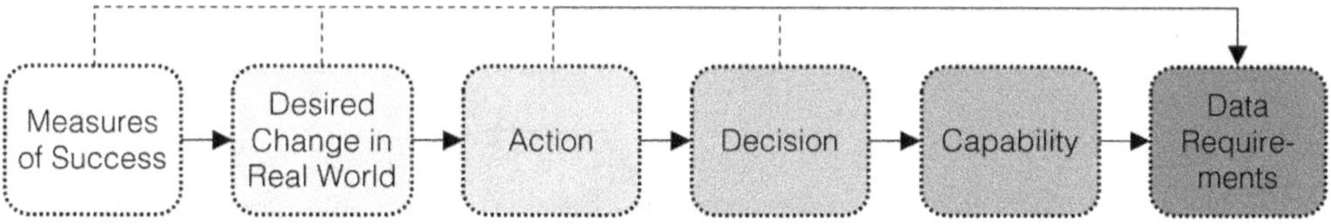

Why "Maps"? Despite appearances, this process is not *mentally* linear. It's not precise, it has a lot of dead ends and one-way streets, and neighborhoods where maybe you just don't want to go until you're a bit better prepared or supported. The maps produced are the "terrain" of the *solution space (fancy term for the set of possible solutions to a given problem)*. Producing these maps requires exploration of this space. The cross-functional team uses their experience to ideate possible ways to create the Desired Change. Humans "jump" forwards and back, from changes to capabilities, to data to actions to decisions to change to actions... It feels chaotic when you watch it happening, but that's how you, yourself, work internally, and then you smooth it all out and tell a story that sounds plausible... but may in fact be totally made up.

Why "Connected"? The working backwards part is a forcing function. It doesn't require you to work backwards, but it demands that whatever you come up with, is coherent and plausible, to you, and peers. It might be too expensive, or require more or better data than any real organization has, but that's a later problem (viability), and that is not a direct cost alone problem anyway. It's probable value versus probable cost. And you can't assign value without a real problem, and you can't assign probability without having a reasonable peer group consensus that something is both doable and likely to be done. Hence, we map, we explore, we put our best feet forwards, and then we analyze and discard.

Why "Action"? We are designing our twin or our applied AI to create change in the real world. That can only be done through actions. All the other parts of the DTDP support this goal - designing the actions that are feasible, viable and usable inside the organization / industry / situation we find ourselves, in order to repeatably create high-ROI outcomes. "Applied" people are action-oriented techy people.

Mapping Advice

Many "chains"

I like to refer to any single set of measures-changes-actions-decisions-capabilities-data as a "chain." It sounds cool, but also it creates the right mental image. The chain is continuous, made of links that must be connected together, and it is strong, but only as strong as its weakest link.

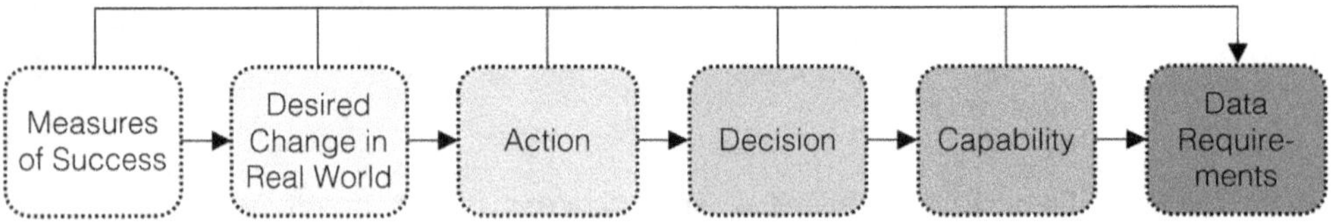

Measure driven chains

A common path is to identify a chain or chains for each Measure. It makes perfect sense, as the Measure is the starting point, and you can ensure each Measure has at least one chain.

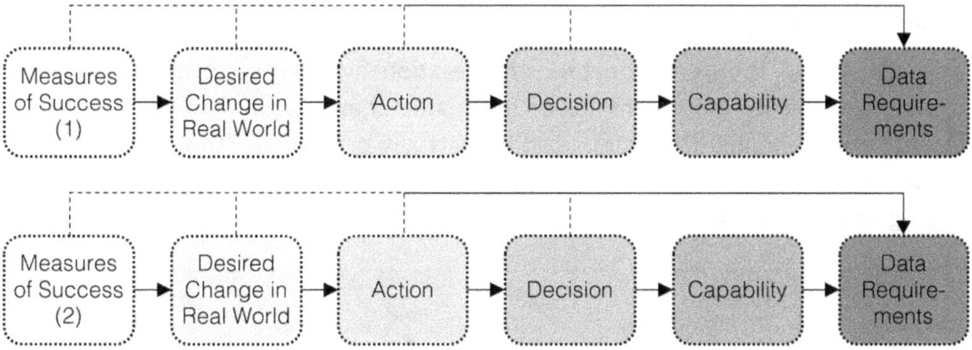

One change / Many actions

Often, there's more than one way to skin a defenseless creature... I find identifying multiple Actions for each Desired Change is a very effective way to get real-world buy-in from experts, and it drives *action coherence*. It's also great for the techy people, as it starts to show them the various ways that action can be taken in this solution space. I find that Actions defined in this way, often get brought back later in new ways by the non-experts. Sometimes without all the context, but it gets people thinking of the kinds of actions that could create this change. It also makes it easier later, to prune some Action-Decision-Capability-Data portions of chains, leaving just the best chains.

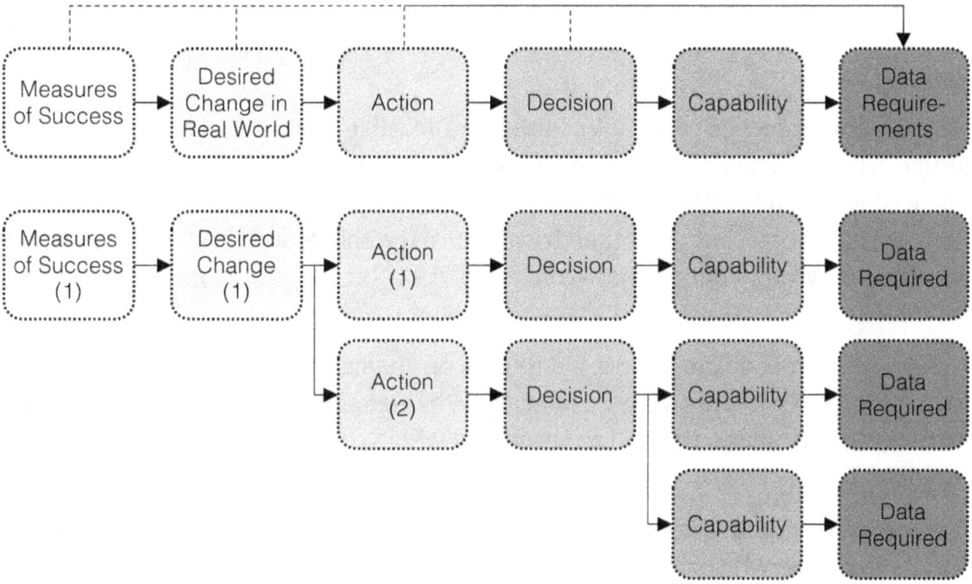

Changes that create changes

The real world is interconnected, and relationships between changes can be exploited to create more complex or multi-step changes. Similarly for Actions, or Decisions, or Capabilities – steps can be partially ordered as “this before that” to show the causality of Actions, which in turn often drives Data, and in turn often highlights Decisions as bottlenecks.

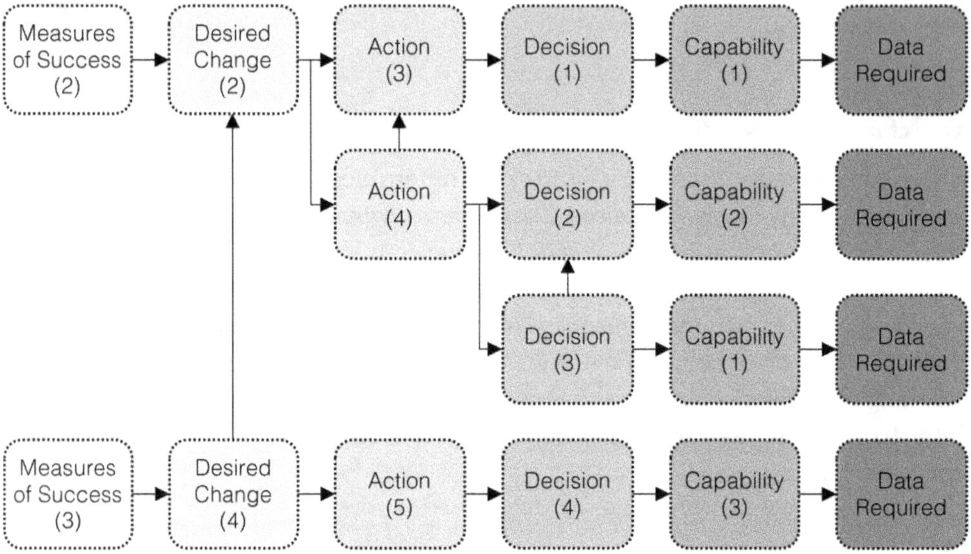

Pruning

Pruning the branches of a chain, leaves the feasible chains intact. I prefer to not prune in public, because sometimes the act of destruction in a group setting can have the wrong dynamic. It’s not quite the opposite of creation. Set the workshops up to inspire and diverge, but don’t then try and turn the ship around and destroy parts of it... it’s the wrong energy, the wrong vibe, it’s a bit ick, and it goes political and cultural, fast.

What I recommend is to get people to vote on chains. Put green stickers on “good” chains, and red stickers on “bad” elements. Why elements? Because if you ask people to identify bad chains, they often throw the whole chain out for just one infeasible element. Upvote chains, downvote elements.

Then, in private, with the decision-making group, begin analysis and synthesis of the inputs to decide which chains to prune. Remember we said that we may not throw them away? We don't. We prune, to exclude the chains from this upcoming iteration of Delivery, but we keep the chains so that when we repeat these exercises, we have templates to work from, and examples of chains or elements which have been thought of before and rendered infeasible.

Bundling

Bundling is the right form of group convergence. Chains that survived pruning are gathered together into bundles that are coherent, and have a very high probability of creating the Desired Change, and moving the measure of success in the desired direction to create real returns.

Coherent Desired Changes can reinforce each other.

Coherent Actions can involve multiple teams / departments and can be sequenced in time and space.

Coherent Decisions can be bundled into single changes to governance / business process in order to minimize cognitive cost of these changes.

Coherent Capabilities can often leverage existing Capabilities or teams who support these to make the required changes.

Coherent Data can often be owned or managed or improved by a single team to ensure completeness and reduce the chances of one small data product holding everything up.

Stage 2 outputs

- Completed Connected Action Maps with Bundled chains
- Incomplete and infeasible Connected Action Maps (don't throw them away yet)

End of Stage 2

Stage 3: Usable Solution

Focuses on delivering usable solutions and implementing real-world changes to address validated problems, emphasizing adoption, support, and measurable benefits for sustained value creation.

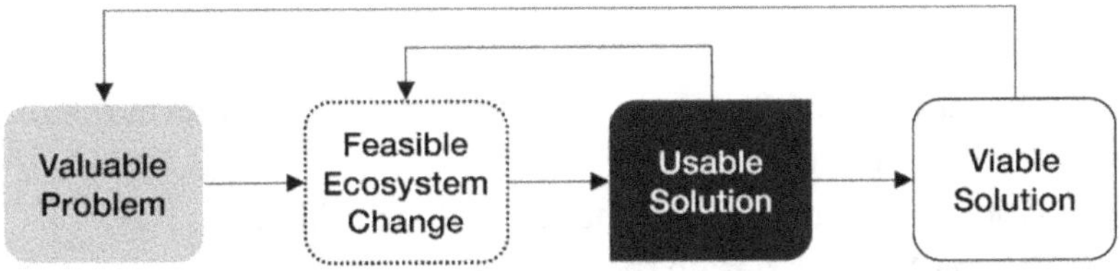

Purpose: Deliver the solution and change to Users and Measure Benefits

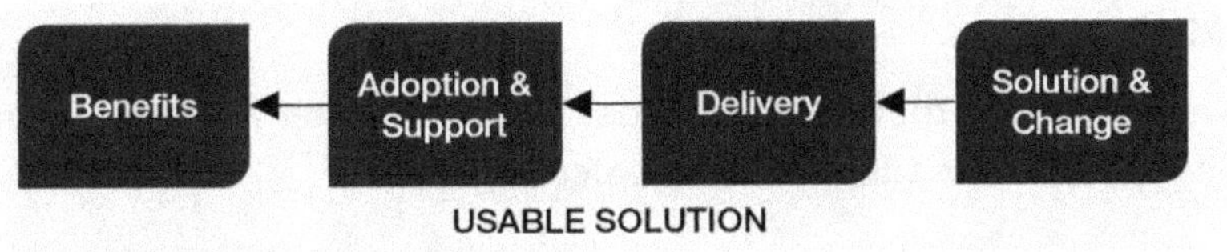

In the Usable Solution stage, we have four steps:

1. Solution and Change
2. Delivery
3. Adoption and Support
4. Benefits

Stage 3, Step 1: Solution and Change

Summary

What: The solution is the overarching name for the design of the technology (Capabilities and Data and Actions in software land) and the Change describes the design and requirements for real-world changes (Actions and Decisions outside software land).

Together, they describe the change to the design of the ecosystem to solve the Problem, which vary in detail depending on the maturity of the iteration:

- Early = Description of proposed solution and changes
- Middle = Solution design and change design
- Late = Design of the solution and design of the change

Why: The key output of the Digital Twin Design Process is the design of the Digital Twin. The amount of "design" required is dependent on what iteration / cycle you're in.

How:

- Select coherent sets of Connected Action Map chains to form the basis of the solution and the change in the real world
- Develop the solution design and change design package
- Design the solution and design the change

Detail

What is it?

Solution and change is the overarching description of what and how we propose to create Desired Changes to solve the Problem.

Why do we do it?

Holistically designing change massively increases the probability of a high positive ROI outcome.

What problems does this solve?

This step solves the inherent problem of designing technology solutions without, or in spite of, the real-world changes required to make that technology solution valuable.

How do we do it?

This step involves five major steps:

1. Bundling Connected Action Maps together to form a coherent plan to achieve the Desired Change.
2. Selection of the "go-forward" Connected Action Map.
3. Decomposing bundled maps into the proposed "Solution" and "Change" artefacts.

4. Returning to the Feasible Ecosystem Change steps when problems / missing steps are found.
5. Iterating through solutions and change processes and artefacts as the project / product is further approved / invested into.

We will return to Iterations in Delivery. If this is your first run through, the descriptions below should suffice to follow the thread.

BIG NOTE: I have never yet seen an organization where the team that designs the technology solution is also the team that designs, or even proposes, changes to real-world business processes. This step is collaborative. It requires a team or teams that can, and are, authorized to do both. It does not need to be done simultaneously. I recommend the solution/product team goes first, and then the changes required in the solution are incorporated in the change management of the change design. BUT, I highly recommend that the solution team be involved in the change design. It's critical that the elements from the Connected Action Mapping aren't discarded, changed, or watered down without review and approval to make these changes. The Change design isn't just "change management," in the sense of "making it easier for people to swallow change." The change design is where we lock in the changes we'll make in the world. If Actions and Decisions are modified here, you need to return to your Connected Action Map, and assess the impact. Is the chain where the element was altered still feasible? If not, is the "loss" of this chain critical to the overall bundled solution? You may need to redo the chain and the map to re-establish feasibility. You may also be able to discard chains, as there is no point building Capabilities when the real-world actions have been removed...

Remember – we're not building shiny things.

Bundling connected action maps to create a coherent plan to achieve the Desired Change

With a set of feasible Connected Action Maps in hand, we must now bundle chains of actions to create an effective and feasible solution. Effectiveness often comes from coherence – multiple small and supporting changes that systemically avoid or mitigate or solve the Problem, by giving us the best possible chance of creating the Desired Changes, where, and when, we need them.

To do this, lay out the not-infeasible chains in parallel (either digitally in something like Miro or physically on a wall). You may have dozens of them. If this is the case, I suggest clustering by different dimensions, such as:

- Common Capabilities
- Common Action types

Common Capabilities

Capabilities related to a common defined Problem are, unsurprisingly, quite common. Perhaps 80% of the Capabilities will be common and 90% of the 20% remaining will be new. Anchoring on common Capabilities gives a point to expand out into the real world from.

- Bundle the Connected Action Maps that include that common Capability first
- Prioritize chains that are "coherent" (i.e., remove ones that aren't coherent or seem infeasible or are repeated / redundant)
- Review the bundled Connected Action Map on a single board / page

Common Action types

Actions always fall into a few basic categories inside any particular organization. A factory has actions related to production schedules, downtime for maintenance, quality control, turnarounds etc. Hospitals are remarkably similar to factories, though we don't like to think about them that way. The type of organization and industry you're in sets the types of Actions that create change in the real world. Clustering "actions that stop production before faults," or "actions that prevent unplanned downtime," will give your team a focal point to then consider "how can we best enable these actions?" The clustered connected maps will almost always share many cross overs in Decisions (e.g., who can authorize production stoppages), as well as Capabilities (because the same people often use the same systems of record), and data (e.g., production and maintenance data).

- Bundle the Connected Action Maps by Action-type
- Prioritize chains that are "coherent" (i.e., remove ones that aren't coherent or seem infeasible or are repeated / redundant)
- Review the bundled Connected Action Map on a single board / page

Whatever method you use, the key here is to get to a single Connected Action Map, with multiple chains that all contribute to creating the Desired Change.

You will often find multiples of the same Actions, fed by very different Capabilities, or the same Capabilities, that lead to very different Actions. That's ok. This is why we have cross-functional teams. Let the teams have their inputs, and prioritize the chains down to sensible, and at least semi-feasible groupings.

Decision Point – Selection of the "go-forward" connected action map

This is perhaps the largest crux in the DTDP. We have lots of ideas and inputs from multiple parties.

Firstly, this is not a workshop. At least, I don't recommend this should be attempted in a group setting. Why? Because this requires some analysis, and some thinking time, and ultimately, some tradeoffs.

With the prioritized Connected Action Maps in hand, all of which are (in theory) feasible (i.e., they can be done), the product team must now select a coherent set of chains that they believe will create the Desired Changes, and hence solve the Problem.

This is where Effectiveness versus Efficiency, and Budget, and Wide versus Narrow, and product leadership, and ultimately culture, all come into play.

Sidebar: Courage

There's no playbook for this. I have included recommendations a bit further on, but here I will tell you the plain and challenging truth: depending on the Problem selected, and the culture and willingness to change at your organization, and the mandate / support you have from your boss, you will either have a very clear-cut run at trying to create meaningful change, or you will have an awful tangle of "maybes," and quite a bit of negative feedback about why nothing you do will change the way things are.

Here's my unfiltered advice: Courage is a real thing that we don't talk about at work anymore. The courage to try and do what is right. The courage to try new things. The courage to try something five, six or seven times, even when you keep failing. The courage to set bars higher than your employer does. The courage to be transparent. The courage to admit mistakes.

You can choose to be courageous. You can choose to aim high and not let little things get in your way.

You can also choose to help others be courageous. You can encourage them. You can tell them when you don't know if something will work, but why you want to try it anyway. You can be respectful and tenacious at the same time.

Like any aspect of culture, courage is contagious. Modelling positive and courageous behavior isn't easy, but I guarantee you'll attract others of a like mind. There are people in your organization right now who want to make a difference, but feel trapped in the system. If you're responsible for creating a new way of solving an old Problem, then courage is your friend. Find it. Build it. Fake it. Make it. Do what you need to do. But keep that Problem

> fixed firmly in your mind, and keep caring about the people you're trying to help.
>
> Courage is a lot easier when you're doing things that matter for people you care about.

Begin by analyzing your Connected Action Maps to identify recurring patterns and shared touchpoints across different use cases. Look for actions, decisions, or data flows that appear in multiple maps. These common elements, often represent critical areas, where your solution can have the most significant impact.

Based on the patterns you've identified, prioritize the Capabilities and Actions that will have the most impact on the Desired Change. Focus on those Actions and Decisions that will feasibly create substantial change in the real world. Focus on those Capabilities and Data that enable these Actions and Decisions. Converge, converge, converge onto a use case that is technically feasible and usable.

Decomposing bundled maps into the proposed "Solution" and "Change" artefacts

Solution Design – the New Virtual World

Map Capabilities to Existing and New Virtual Systems

For each prioritized Capability, determine whether it can be addressed by existing virtual systems, or if new functionality needs to be developed. This step helps you leverage your current technology investments, while identifying gaps that need to be filled. Be mindful of the ecosystem you're working within – your solution should complement and enhance existing processes, rather than creating unnecessary disruption.

New Capabilities

For new Capabilities, or modification of existing Capabilities, you need to branch here to domain expertise, and technical evaluation. The outputs required to create the Decisions and Actions should be clear. These are your requirements. Dig into your new Capability, and evaluate the feasibility of creating it. Then, test it against your requirements.

If you have started with this new Capability, and are anchoring it to an existing Problem, then this is the last pass of outputs versus requirements. Will it feasibly enable the Decisions and Actions to create the Desired Change?

Design Data Flows and Interconnections

With your Capabilities mapped out, map the Data measurements (Measures / Changes / Actions / Decisions) and enabling Data for your Capabilities, and design the data flows and interconnections that will bring your solution to life. Pay close attention to both the Real-to-Virtual (R-V) and Virtual-to-Real (V-R) connections. Ensure that your design accounts for the appropriate frequency and fidelity of data synchronization required to support your prioritized Capabilities.

Remember, we want three groups of Data:

1. Data required to Enable Actions, Decisions and Capabilities.
2. Data required to Measure activity and outputs of our Measures of Success, Desired Changes, Actions, Decisions and Capabilities.
3. Data from elements Related to our chains, that we believe provide lagging or leading indicators of risk or unintended change.

Consider Scalability and Extensibility

While your initial focus will be on solving specific Problems, design your solution with scalability and extensibility in mind. Create a modular architecture that allows for easy addition of new Capabilities, or expansion to adjacent problem spaces. This approach may not future-proof your solution, but it will set you up for maximizing long-term value by reducing the cost of solving adjacent problems.

Write the Solution Design artefact

In some organizations, a solution design is a small and mostly technical document that references other technical documents. In others, it is a book. Given the vast variety of documents and requirements and processes across the globe, I can only advise that you need to do what you need to do to satisfy your organization's requirements. My recommendation remains: get to what and how you'll create real change that solves real problems before you concern yourself with the ISO standard for flowcharting.

Change Design – the Altered Real World

Identify Critical Actions

Begin by pinpointing the specific, critical Actions, that need to occur in the real world, to directly create the Desired Change. These Actions should be concrete and observable, not abstract concepts. These Actions are non-negotiable and immutable i.e., they must be baked into business processes and people must be trained and empowered to take them, when required.

Define Decision Points

Map out the critical Decision points that lead to the critical Actions. These are the moments where data and insights from the virtual world will inform choices made by humans or automated systems. For instance:

- Determining when to schedule preventive maintenance.
- Choosing between multiple repair options based on cost and downtime implications.
- Deciding to alter production schedules based on equipment health predictions.

Specify Measurement and Feedback Mechanisms

For each real-world change, define how its impact will be measured and fed back into the Capabilities. This creates the crucial feedback loop that allows for identification of change and future continuous improvement.

Consider:

- Installing sensors to monitor equipment performance post-maintenance.
- Implementing quality control checks to verify the effectiveness of process adjustments.
- Collecting user feedback on the outcomes of dispatched work orders.

Consider Physical Infrastructure

Some real-world changes may require modifications to the physical environment or infrastructure. Capturing specific data or measurements is a common challenge. Getting messages to the right person at the right time or enabling remote collaboration is another one, especially in traditional work environments where mobile devices are typically large tablets or only used by supervisors etc. Remember that in these cases, there are additional Actions and Decisions such as a supervisor receiving and reading a message, choosing to act upon it, walking to find the relevant person, communicating the instruction etc. All of these chains of Decisions and Actions should be part of the Connected Actions Map, as they are the necessary steps to create the Desired Change.

Examples include:

- Installing new sensors or IoT devices to capture required data.
- Upgrading network infrastructure to support real-time data transmission.

- Modifying equipment to enable remote control or automated adjustments.

Business Process Change

Where real-world changes require changes to existing business processes, you will definitely need approvals, and there will be review processes and potentially risk assessments. Consider how the experts you leveraged in the Feasible Change stage can help in this. I usually recommend development of a single change design artefact before engaging in approval processes, so that the proposed changes are placed in the context of why and what.

Remember that many real-world changes will involve direct change of human behavior. Consider the training and skills required for people to effectively implement the Actions suggested or prescribed by the twin. Revised Standard Operating Procedures, new training courses, altered incentives or KPIs, are all enablers of change, or blockers of it, if ignored.

Plan for Scalability

As you map out real-world changes, consider how they can be scaled across multiple assets, locations, or processes. This forward-thinking approach ensures that your solution can grow with the organization, or can be applied across it without extensive bespoke alterations.

Write the Change Design artefact

Unlike solution designs, many organizations do not have any change design template. They have many change management plans and processes, but these are usually aimed at helping people cope with change, as opposed to deliberately creating change, and citing the why and how, and how benefits will be measured. I highly recommend you create a design for your real-world changes. Off the back of this, there may be some or many artefacts and approvals required to enter into the process of changing processes in the real world.

Validate with Domain Experts

Before finalizing your solution design and change design, validate them with domain experts from both the real and virtual worlds. Their insights can help refine your approach and identify potential challenges or opportunities you may have overlooked. Remember, the success of your digital twin or applied AI solution depends on its ability to create meaningful change in the real world – and domain experts are your best allies in ensuring that change is both feasible and impactful.

By following these steps, you'll create a solution design that is deeply rooted in the real-world Problems you're trying to solve, while leveraging the power of digital Capabilities to drive meaningful changes in the real world. This approach ensures that your digital twin or applied AI solution is not just technologically advanced, but truly fit-for-purpose in addressing the complex challenges of your ecosystem.

Returning to the feasible ecosystem Change steps

The detailed DTDP shows feedback loops from the "end" of the Usable Solution stage. In reality though, when driving into the detail of a solution, you identify missing steps and problems, and infeasible assumptions. Never fear, just return to your Connected Action Map and address the issue head on. If you need to make different changes in the real world, propose some changes (and remember you will have a plethora of examples from Connected Action Maps), and return to the relevant real-world subject matter experts to test these out. If required, re-run small and quick workshops of altered changes and adjust your Connected Action Maps, and return to this stage.

Iterations

Along with the iterations of steps, we also typically build new products in stages. If you're fully and properly agile, with full approvals to execute, you can ignore this section. If, like 99% of the world, you're bound by stages of conceptual and detailed design and cost estimates, and progressive budget and change approvals, then you'll be familiar with the below.

Iteration 1 – Concept

The first time you iterate through on a given Problem, you are in the Concept phase. You have:

- A set of Connected Action Maps, and
- A firm belief that there are ways and means of creating the Desired Change, and
- Sufficient reason to believe that these Changes will alter your Measures of Success, and
- Validated the Problem that these Measures of Success represent

You don't have:

- THE connected action maps that you'll Deliver
- Budget and Approval to try and solve this Problem
- Users or User Feedback
- Production Data on Measures of Success or Activities

You need to:

- Select which Connected Action Maps will be included in the Business Case
- Produce sufficient solution and change design documentation to support your organizations internal Business Case / Approvals (very likely you need to estimate cost and time)

Iteration 2 – Delivery

When you have made the decision to start building the solution and making changes, you are in the Delivery phase. You have:

- The Connected Action Maps that will form the basis of the solution and the change, and
- A firm belief that there are ways and means of creating the Desired Change, and
- Sufficient reason to believe that these Changes will alter your Measures of Success, and
- Validated the Problem that these Measures of Success represent, and
- Budget and approval

You don't have:

- A solution designed
- Users or User Feedback
- Production Data on Measures of Success or Activities

You need to:

- Produce Concept / Wireframe / Preliminary designs to enable the Delivery team to build the solution
- Develop and deliver a complete solution design package, including the technical specifications required by your organization
- Develop and deliver a complete change proposal, including business process changes and change management considerations

Iterations 3 / 4 / n – Improvements

When you have made the decision to invest further to improve the solution, you are in the Improvement phase. You have:

- The Connected Action Maps that are being used in the solution and the change, and
- Evidence that these ways and means create the Desired Change, and

- Sufficient reason to believe that additional or altered Desired Changes will alter your Measures of Success, and
- Evidence of how much of the Problem can be solved, and
- You have budget and approval, and
- Users and User Feedback, and
- Production Data on Measures of Success and Activities

You don't have:

- Any illusions left

You need to:

- Do whichever steps from above are required to make the Improvements needed, and get approval to deliver them

At all iterations you may need to:

- Conduct risk assessments
- Use company templates and processes
- Develop presentations and gain buy-in from others
- Produce roadmaps or forward-looking plans far beyond where you think you're ready to commit to (more on this later)
- Back your process and explain why you did it this way

Emergence and Improvements

Iterative improvements are the lifeblood of solving problems in ecosystems. They are so critical because deliberate changes *always* create unintended consequences, and because other elements of the ecosystem always change, deliberately and otherwise. Emergence is a property of multiple changes to elements that are highly interconnected. The only questions are where, and what, and how often.

Continuous improvement is the secret sauce that allows us to harness the power of emergence in complex ecosystems. By iterating product designs and ecosystem measurements, we create deliberate feedback loops that reveal unexpected patterns and behaviors. These emergent phenomena, which arise from the intricate interactions within the system, can be leveraged to our advantage. As we measure, tweak, and refine, we're not just optimizing individual components – we're tuning the entire ecosystem. This iterative process allows us to adapt to unforeseen challenges, capitalize on serendipitous discoveries, and ultimately create more robust, efficient, and innovative solutions, that evolve alongside the ever-changing real world, they're designed to improve.

To enable Ecosystem improvements, we need to commit to improving how our ecosystem operates, and this means we need to measure more than just the elements in your Connected Action Map. By including *related elements of the ecosystem*, you are narrowing your focus to the processes of interest, without myopically focusing only on inputs and outputs, or abstracted financial metrics.

Recommendations

Whew, ok. Strap in.

Usability

For the love of all the heavens above and below... make sure the proposed changes to the ecosystem are usable. As in, the humans that Act and Decide can actually *do* these Actions and *make* these Decisions in their place of work. It's amazing how many times this gets forgotten. The person designing the shiny thing is probably not the user. Hopefully, by now, the DTDP has sufficiently embedded an ethos of working for the user, to help the user, but it needs to be said again.

Here's a little diagram I like to show solution/product teams when we talk about making things usable.

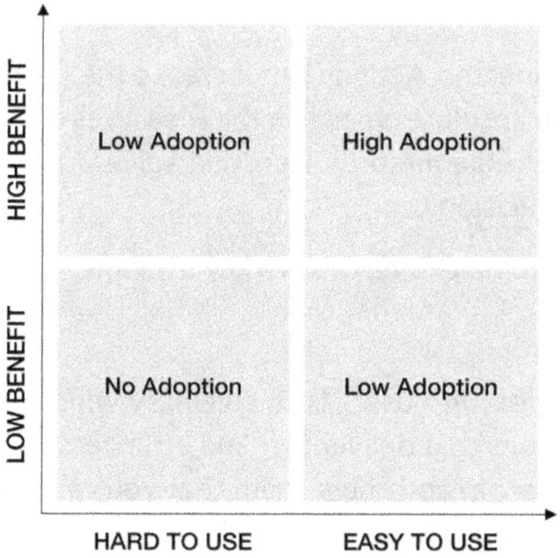

It's not hard to explain – unless it's of benefit and easy to use, it won't be adopted widely or used frequently. If it's not widely adopted, you won't get the Benefits you desire. If it's adopted slowly, you'll get benefits slowly, creating an opportunity cost. If it's neither, you'll get nothing.

Complexity

Be cautious about designs where 20 things need to go right. Solutions that have many steps, in exact sequences, or that need very rapid Decisions to be made, or Decisions to be made under conditions of great uncertainty, end up looking "complex" to users. I don't mean complicated – I mean complex: the myriad of possible interactions between steps in a game, combined with the inherent uncertainty of what a human will do in any given situation, leads to seldom-repeated outcomes.

Start simple, iterate up. Complexity is best tackled through emergence. Create small experiments, measure what happens, make bets on the next round of changes – measure, measure, measure, repeat.

Rate of change of real world

In situations where the Problem has elements that move or change very quickly, the frequency of this change needs to be explicitly considered in the proposed solution. Highly dynamic situations degrade situation awareness and reduce the efficacy of human decision making. Try not to create solutions that require lightning reflexes to enact. They might be on their phone when the moment arises.

Coherency

Selecting multiple Connected Actions can increase the probability of creating the Desired Change, or the absolute change in the Measures of Success. In other words, we try and solve the Problem more often, *and* solve it better through the use of coherent actions and decisions.

See above for note on complexity... this is a key tradeoff.

Time to First Value

The best way to get wins with users is to give easy wins, quickly. Actively seek to create Connected Actions that deliver fast and effortless value to the user, as early as possible. Get them a win and show them that you really listened and took into account the real-world issues they face.

Existential Change

Beware Changes that are existential or fundamental in nature. While they may get approved, getting a large workforce to adopt a complete 90-degree, or worse yet, 180-degree turn, is hard. Where Change is significant, involvement of key users during the DTDP is the start of the change management process. Buy-in trumps documentation, every day. But buy-in from workers may not create approval from executives. Validated Problems help a lot here because you can show the size of the prize. For my money, I avoid existential changes until I have wins under my belt.

Champion Designs

It is very normal for one subject matter expert to volunteer to be a part of the DTDP. Very often, this champion is not a "normal" worker in that role. They have an extra dose of passion or commitment or purpose, and they can inadvertently guide teams to creating designs that they (the champion) think are wonderful – but are almost unusable by the "average" worker faced with the same activity. Test and validate proposed solutions with non-champions, in the same situation.

Selecting the go-forward connected action maps

I left this until after I had planted some seeds above...

There's no way to sugar coat this. Selecting the coherent, sufficiently non-complex set of Connected Actions that are easy to use, deliver quick value, and don't create existential angst, is not a science. This is the very heart of product management. Budget is finite, change is bad, we need good results etc.

It's hard. It's very hard. But everything leading up to this point has been gaming the system. Ideating with the users. Challenging everyone to connect real-world change and virtual capabilities. Forcing ourselves to consider how and if one thing causes another. Demanding that we measure activity and consider data in the context of how capabilities are actually used. Banning magic wands.

All of it was to give you the best possible chance of creating a highly valuable and usable set of changes in your ecosystem.

I recommend:

- Selecting a set of no more than 3 coherent Connected Actions Maps where you believe every step in the entire chain is feasible
- If you have 10 great ones, great! Put 7 away for now. Come back to them in your Improvement iterations
- Write up a succinct description of how the Desired Change will move the Measures of Success, and what the potential Benefits are of solving this Problem (partially and completely)
- Explain how the Connected Action Maps will create the Desired Change

- Attach Connected Action Maps showing the chain of activities (Decisions & Actions) and Capabilities
- For each step, break out:
  - Who / What does it
  - When do they / it do it
  - How long will it take to do it
  - How often will they do it per day / week / month
  - What will it cost in time and money to do it each time
- Sum up the potential Cost and Benefits
- Do you still believe it? Test it with others. Test it with real-world people.
- Ok, you're good to go. You have your set of Connected Actions to base your solution and change off.

What does great look like?

A great solution and change design have to be aligned to the stage you're at – whether Concept or Delivery or Improvement.

Great here = everything the Delivery teams needs to build a great solution that will work and be highly usable. This includes sufficient context on the what, and the why, (Connected Action Maps), as well as approvals and budget, to make changes and acquire Capabilities and Data.

What are the minimum outcomes required to enable downstream success?

At the minimum, we need enough of a solution design and a change design to be able to estimate the potential Benefits and Costs to the business, and to enable the follow-on steps of Delivery when required.

When do we stop at this step?

We stop at this step when we can't create a coherent set of Actions and Capabilities that we believe have a reasonable chance of solving the Problem – at acceptable cost and risk. At times, we revisit the Connected Action Maps, or mapping process, based on feedback during approvals stages.

How does this step fail?

This step fails when we don't use the work that's been done to create a coherent set of changes, leaving the Delivery to be largely made up by the delivery team.

Who should be involved?

The solution and change management / business line teams need to develop and gain approval for the solution and the changes.

Expected effort / duration

This can be a very quick step early on, synthesizing clear maps and developing a business case.

A complex solution design can take three months to do if there is sufficient technical uncertainty or challenging approvals.

Stage 3, Step 2: Delivery

Summary

What: Software, Hardware and Business Process changes.

Why: We need to change the real and virtual worlds to create the Desired Change.

How: Build and Deploy the solution, and change the business processes and real world, as designed.

Detail

What is it?

Delivery is the act of bringing the approved solution and changes into existence. This encompasses all of the work required to create the Desired Change, the first time.

Why do we do it?

We need to create change in the real world to create value.

What problems does this solve?

This step, or rather, the many steps contained with this step, are the foundational plan / design, build and deploy steps of any new solution.

How do we do it?

This is perhaps the hardest step to describe in a book like this. It's also a step I had a lot of debate with reviewers about. I also had some quite negative feedback from one reviewer – who told me – she thought I was going to teach her *exactly* how to build digital twins.

First and foremost, I cannot tell you in a few paragraphs how to code, or how to develop applications. I can't explain to you how to create an API. Nor can I explain to you the processes of developing a change program.

My assumption is that you have these skills inside your organization, or you can acquire / hire / engage them.

The best that I can do is give you some tips to align how you already build software and roll out change with the DTDP.

Recommendations

Proof of concepts

I encourage Proof of Concepts (PoCs), and they have become a norm in many large organizations. For the DTDP, I encourage "Connected PoCs" – that is, *showing* that the Capabilities and Data can enable or create the Decisions and Actions that in turn, move our Measures of Success. Here again, the method behind the Measures of Success versus financial benefits comes into play. A PoC is, or should be, short and sweet. If your definition of success is long-term financial metrics, it's very difficult to prove anything from a PoC. If you have short and long and leading and lagging Measures of Success, you can show movement in the real world, quickly. Remember we also spoke of Time to First Value as a principle – it applies here first. Demonstrating proof of value, not just working software, in a PoC is probably the gold star of any technology deployment. With digital twins and applied AI, it also means demonstration of the real-world change – including business process changes if required. Doing "end to end" in the real world is the only real test for change.

With your Connected Action Map, you have multiple chains that are all assessed as feasible. PoC is just one chain, end to end. This forces you to work through the entire loop to acquire data from the real world and create change in the real world. Doing this also proves the concept of the Connected Action Mapping process, and validates the inputs of real-world and virtual-world experts. There's no tonic like success.

Be wary of being too agile in non-agile environments

A common issue occurring at this time is tech teams who have embraced agile or agile-like methods inside organizations that have no idea what agile is, or who want no part of it. Agile as a methodology is great, and has been an incredible boon to the tech industry. It has also had amazing impact in non-tech industries, when it is surrounded by an organization that embraces and supports it. When it's not supported, it can be very disruptive. My advice is to be agile and flexible.

Discovery

Ok so you're a real product person, and you haven't heard me say discovery once, but a lot of what I've talked about is familiar to you. Congrats, you cracked my secret. Hopefully, you can bring your talents to the DTDP, and the process I've outlined is loose enough for you to use what you know within this context. My only caution is to remember that the real-world processes and changes are every bit as important as the software. I have seen two instances now where the DTDP collaboration broke down once a key designer got involved in delivery. They threw out all the non-software learnings as went it alone in delivery, creating substantial gaps between the connected action maps and expectations of the real-world counterparts, which only came to light after deployment.

Prototyping

Prototyping, mockups and all forms of conceptual visualization and engagement with users are great tools. If you have a good design crew, and can swing it, you could do quick and dirty mockups and wireframes in or immediately after some of the workshops and do playback and validations sessions. The value of transforming the maps and words into visual context is very high, though many teams don't have the internal capability or capacity to do this, unfortunately.

Testing

I recommend including users and people who were involved in the workshops to be a part of user testing. I also recommend going a step further, and communicating well about what internal tests were done, and why. I find that a lot of non-tech people are very interested in testing, and how things are validated, and many "non-tech" people are, of course, highly technical in other fields. Testing with twins should also incorporate data model tests and verifications, even if these are done separately or by other teams. Data transformations can be even more of a dark art than software, so highlighting specific use cases and transformations, especially predictions, is a great way of getting people comfortable with "what's under the hood." It's also a great way to get developers talking to non-developers about real things.

Training

Where users need to use software and change their Actions or Decisions in the real world, I highly recommend training on both, together. Don't fall into the trap of the product team training on the software, and the change management or improvement team training the same person at a different time on the business process changes. Very often when this happens, the two look nothing alike. Each team has its own templates and ways of working and spin. If you can, bring them together, and run end to end training, and run it from start to finish – Data to Capability to Decisions to Actions to Desired Change. It's a tiny incremental investment for people to see what happens "under the hood" or "over the fence," but when one team gets to see what the other team does upstream of them to enable them to do their job, and vice versa, it sets up far better collaboration and context for everyone. Train how to create the change the way we designed the change – connected end-to-end.

What does great look like?

Great Delivery is normally judged on two main factors:

- Adherence to cost and time expectations / promises
- Passing testing

I would argue that for digital twins, and coming from a world of working backwards, great Delivery should be judged by:

- Adherence to cost and time expectations / promises
- Passing testing
- Successful PoC / rapid Time to First Value
- Rapid adoption
- Low bugs and complaints in first 90 days

What are the minimum outcomes required to enable downstream success?

Working software and trained workers.

When do we stop at this step?

We only stop at this step if the project is suddenly cancelled, or runs so over budget that it is cancelled, or some technical issue fundamentally prevents us from achieving the outcomes.

How does this step fail?

This step can fail as a project (cost and time), but the real failure is if this step doesn't create the desired change.

Who should be involved?

The solution and change teams own this step. Users are brought in for discovery, testing and training as required.

Expected effort / duration

How long is your piece of budgetary string?

I've seen twins take four weeks to design and deliver. Very good ones by the way. Super simple, smashed it in the field. Highest ROI I've ever seen.

I've seen twins that are at five years and USD25 million and still going. I'm sure you can appreciate I don't endorse giant shots in the dark.

So...

It'll take as long as it takes, but if you've validated your Problem and designed your Feasible changes, you'll have a good idea of the time and effort and potential payoff.

Stage 3, Step 3: Adoption and support

Summary

What: Creating and sustaining usage of technology and desired change in the real world.

Why: People need help to do things well, and things go wrong when we least expect.

How: Design for adoption and provide support to users and stakeholders.

Detail

What is it?

Adoption is the process of people changing their behaviors to use new technology and follow new business processes. Support is the process of helping people to change successfully, and with low effort and frustration.

Why do we do it?

We need to create change in the real world to create value. We need to help people create that change. We want to help people change well, and as easily as possible.

What problems does this solve?

This step is part of the solution, or mitigation, of one of the major challenges of complex technology-based improvements – lack of adoption.

How do we do it?

To maximize Adoption, we pull on four big levers:

1. High levels of inclusion in the lead up.
2. Deliberate focus on making the solution easy to use.
3. Good Support when required.
4. Proactive engagement.

The DTDP has Adoption maximisers baked into it at many steps:

- When we narrowed down to real problems, we made sure that users would know this change had some real purpose – it's not just a "shiny thing."
- When we included the people who do the work in the ideation of changes, we massively increased our chances of them being able to create that change (because they have very good ideas on what is not possible in the real world) – they know what's coming.
- When we included the people who do the work in how Capabilities and Data enable or create the Actions and Decisions they will need to make, we got buy-in from people with far more "credibility" than the solution / delivery team normally has – they understand better how the technology will help them.
- When we stressed simplicity and rapid time to first value we were forcing ourselves to consider how to make it easier for the user to use the solution and make the changes – "usable" solutions are always, always, always more adopted than hard to use solutions.
- When we involved users in prototyping, testing, training and change management during Delivery, we demonstrated that what they had input into is being created for them and with them – we demonstrated our commitment to helping them.

All of these steps are precursors to the main event – deploying into the wild.

Let's look now at how we can help drive Adoption and the role Support plays in this.

Support

Support is often seen as the "front line" of helping users. The Support team needs to help users with how to use software, how to troubleshoot, and how to overcome simple or complex problems. Support also is often the first to encounter reports of bugs, and very often they bear the brunt of user dissatisfaction. In the worst cases, Support people get yelled at, and blamed for things they did not create and have little power to change. Being a Support person is hard. It's a mostly thankless role. It's also critical to supporting Adoption.

It's beyond the purview of this book to describe how to create a Support function.

A key learning I have from digital twin support, however, is to try and ensure that Support team members are included in the DTDP if possible, and are educated in what the real-world Desired Changes, Actions and Decisions are intended to be. When Support people, who are usually "tech" people, talk to non-tech people, there is often a terminology gap. Non-tech people are often very judgy of people who don't know what they're talking about, or don't know what they're meant to be doing with the technology that the Support team supports. Education and training of the Support team in the real-world changes is high leverage work.

Proactive engagement

The last piece of the puzzle is proactively engaging with user and stakeholders who are impacted by use, or non-use, of the solution and change.

Support is generally seen as a reactive function – waiting for the ticket to arrive. Not all Support functions work like this, and if you have a Support team who can be proactive, read on. Many organizations now have a proactive user team called Customer Success – who work *with* Support – in a more benefits-driven and proactive manner.

Whatever you call it, it's important and valuable to have a small crew (even one person) that is going out and talking to users and those who are impacted by the changes, to find out what's working well, and what's not working well. Support is great, but studies show that the silent majority can sit quietly sometimes and just "not use it" without making a fuss. Or, in some cases, their complaints are suppressed or at least discouraged by the culture of their workplace. Whatever the case, you need to assume that things are happening that you need to know about, and you can't wait for the phone to ring.

Being effectively proactive can be as simple as going to where they work and talking to them when they're doing their jobs. Observing what and how they do it is much better than asking in an office later. Another good tactic is to set regular meetings with managers of those who use the solution, and ensure they know you are available and ready to help. Sometimes you have to make the offer five times before anyone takes you up. That's ok. Be polite but be persistent. Because when you get feedback and do something with it, the next time will be that much easier. Even if it's something small like helping them to reset a password – you can't believe how many times people are just too embarrassed to ask for help on little things. Remove the embarrassment and you remove a barrier to adoption.

Finally, don't forget the change management and improvement people who carried a lot of the weight on the change side. Meet with them regularly. Get feedback on what is and isn't working, and what could be better in the solution.

Recommendations

Get out there

You've heard the phrase "Walk a mile in their shoes." Do it. Walk a mile to get to where you can walk a mile beside them, in your own shoes. There is no, nil, zero substitute for face-to-face interaction with the person doing the job. It is by far the greatest, highest value, post-Deployment activity you can do.

Don't sell your shiny thing

The person you are visiting is busy. People are constantly coming in and out, the phone is ringing, they're triple-booked on meetings and going to none of them. Their team isn't using the solution properly, or well, or often enough.

DO NOT GO INTO SALES MODE.

Ask how you can help. Be a trusted advisor, not a salesperson. Find a way to help. Find a way to help that fits in with that team and those personalities. Ask them how you could help them. Suggest ideas, remind them how much you want to spend time with their people doing the job. Polite but persistent, on their turf, walking beside them. It works but it's not easy – trust me on this.

On the spot help without training

When you're talking to users, and you see or hear something that you know was covered in the training – do NOT say "Remember we covered that in the training?"

Just... don't. It's not helpful. Instead, just help them. Show them, preferably, and maybe explain the "why" and "how" behind it. But just be cool and help. Training is not the panacea for all problems. Understanding is. Sometimes it takes three or four goes before someone "gets it," for whatever reason. Getting them to "getting it" is the goal, not getting them to do more training.

Discovery

Ok this is the main course for product people. We talked about user feedback – that's gold for product people. And if you know Discovery, then performing continuous discovery post deployment is where we first actually learn how people use the solution. This is literally the Start of learning about how people use it and how well it works and how often they use it. Everything up until now was theoretical or in controlled conditions. Now it's in the wild. They're using it (kind of), and it's working (kind of), and by watching how and when they do (and don't) use it, and what happens next (and you're lucky you get to combine these first-hand observations with data from your Measurements), you get a whole truckload of insights, qualitative and quantitative, to identify what's preventing the Desired Change.

What does great look like?

Great Adoption in highly connected solutions is (in order of increasingly "good" Adoption):

- People use the solution as and when intended.
- People use it easily and quickly.
- People tell their peers they like using it.
- People ask for more like it.
- People fight to stop it being taken away from them.

Great Support enables great adoption.

What are the minimum outcomes required to enable downstream success?

Efficient reactive Support and effective proactive engagement.

When do we stop at this step?

Never!

Actually, I think quite a few teams are told to stop here. By stop, I mean they are given no budget or time to support the things they've built and deployed. They often do support their users in an ad hoc way, but it's not structured or resourced and it's very unlikely to be successful. If you ever get stuck in this unfortunate situation, I suggest using the Measurement data as supporting evidence that people need help, and showing what Actions are being prevented. Try and use data as your lever to get budget to support your users.

How does this step fail?

This step can fail if it's not done at all, and it can never succeed if the solution is hard to use or doesn't create the Desired Change. In the longer term, if the Benefits aren't measured, the adoption won't matter.

We need both Adoption to create Benefits, and we need Benefits to continue investing our people's time in Adoption.

Who should be involved?

The solution and change teams own this step, but other teams such as Support and Success may be the primary participants with users.

Expected effort / duration

From day 0 to retirement of the solution.

While the solution is live – you're never off the court.

Critically, this means that if you have a program to deliver 10 things in the next two years, and you've delivered 10 in the last two years, you should be allocating budget for supporting 20 things… with who knows how many users and ideated outcomes.

Support is a big deal – especially if it's invisible or just "expected."

Stage 3, Step 4: Benefits

Summary

What: Measuring the positive Benefits and identifying negative consequences and risks.

Why: We invested to achieve a Return on Investment, now we need to measure the Return.

How: Classic measurement and validation of Benefits methods.

Detail

What is it?

Benefits are why we invested in a digital twin and applied AI in the first place.

Why do we do it?

We need Benefits to justify the decision to invest, but we also need to measure ongoing Benefits to measure if ongoing Improvements are creating more Benefits.

What problems does this solve?

Measuring Benefits solves the problem of twins that can't be justified.

How do we do it?

Here we close the loop, in two places:

- Connected Action Activity
- Measures of Success

Connected action activity

We defined Data requirements as including the data required to measure activity across our Connected Action steps:

- Desired Change
- Actions
- Decisions
- Capabilities

In this step, we analyze that data, and we are searching for patterns. Patterns in what humans did, how well and often Actions were taken, how much and how often and how well our Capabilities were used.

Defining these patterns is difficult because they are very often use-case specific. The twin that is predicting failure modes in a turbine has different patterns than the twin that identifies changes to stockpile volumes and road conditions and updates production forecasts.

In practice, at this step I work with the subject matter experts and the solution team to start to develop models of what "good" looks like.

At the very least, you should try and determine if the right people are using the solution to create the Desired Change, and how much of the Desired Change is occurring.

Measures of success and benefits

We also defined Measures of Success. These of course are what we judge success on. But, and it's a big but, we don't yet know how well we've solved the Problem. What we do know is how to sum up the Measures of Success to give us the Benefit we've created.

Benefits = The Actual Values of our Measures of Success.

Why the layers of abstraction?

The reason evolved over many seasons. It came initially from the observations that when we set out to create change in the real world with technology, there is a gulf between what a user does and what happens in the real world, and then what is measured as "success" is usually financial in nature, but very often is actually sentiment driven. We abstract user actions into pseudo-financial outcomes. You can see this in action very easily by adding up all the benefits from your all your SaaS vendors; it may well be multiple times your orgs entire revenue.

I finally worked out that the user-only level is too low, the financial metrics are too high, and the things that happen in the real world are what links them all together. We measure at all three levels, and we measure along the chains of Connected Actions, and causality becomes much easier to find than abstracted correlation.

That being said – no, it's not easy. But it's a goal to shoot for.

Recommendations

Activity before outcomes

Did you notice I put Activity before Benefits? Did you think that was odd? I swapped it three times, for the record. I put activity measurements before success because success is an output – we can't control it. The activities, the use of the solution, the changed Actions, the Decisions taken or not taken – these are levers. Spend 90% of your time on what did and didn't happen versus what you had hoped would be the outcome.

Find the unintended consequences

Interesting things happen when you start working across functions, across teams, and across the real and virtual worlds in a coherent and designed way. Odd things happen. Some are good, some are not good. Unexpected things always happen, and these are the things that teach us more about our ecosystem, and about our solution and change.

Identify the new problems

A key learning is that when we start to solve one Problem, we very often find new problems. This is great news. The path to creating more value is solving more Problems. Identify these problems and push them back into your Problem definition process, to make sure they're valuable Problems. See more in the Chapter on recommendations where we discuss the Problem Bank.

What does great look like?

Great Benefits are:

- Actual values of our Measures of Success that exceed our Targets
- Learnings from our Activities that inform Improvements in the solution and change
- Newly identified problems that are adjacent to our Validated Problem

What are the minimum outcomes required to enable downstream success?

Actual values of our Measures of Success.

When do we stop at this step?

Perhaps for a mature solution that is well bedded in, with no real new Improvements on the horizon, this step would be downgraded to just "is it still working?"

These days though technology and the ecosystem are changing so fast that it's hard to imagine a digital twin getting "stale" if it's providing value. Users will demand more because they have something that actually helps them do their jobs.

How does this step fail?

This step can fail if it's not done at all, and therefore no Benefits can be shown, and therefore there is no ROI.

A minor failure mode is ignoring Activity and believing that there is nothing new to lean from the changes we have created. This is a large opportunity cost.

Who should be involved?

The solution/product and change teams own this step.

Expected effort / duration

From day 0 to retirement of the solution.

Stage 3 outputs

- Solution (Concept / Design / Designed)
- Change (Plan / Management)
- Working Software
- Implemented Change
- Adoption and Support
- Benefits measurement

End of Stage 3

Stage 4: Viable Solution

Ensures that the solution's total cost, benefits, and ROI are measured and evaluated, confirming the investment's effectiveness and informing decisions on future improvements.

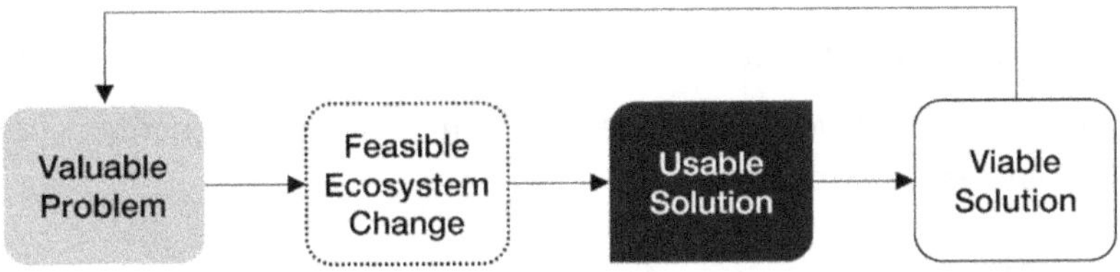

Purpose: Ensure the Benefits and Change are worth continuing.

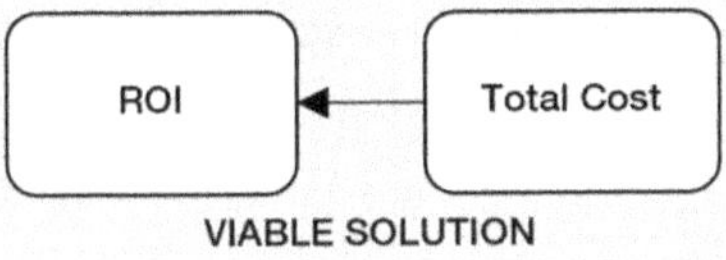

In the Viable Solution stage, we have two steps:

1. Total Cost
2. ROI

Stage 4, Step 1: Total cost

Summary

What: The Total Cost of our solution and change.

Why: We invested to achieve a Return on Investment, now we need to measure the Investment.

How: Measurement and calculation of total costs.

Detail

What is it?

The Total Cost is the sum of all costs associated with the creation and Support of the solution and change.

Why do we do it?

We need to know the Total Cost to be able to assess if the digital twin has created any net benefits (positive ROI), and to help determine if further Improvements are likely to be worth the additional cost.

What problems does this solve?

Measuring Total Cost solves the problem of twins that can't be justified, because we have already measured Benefits.

How do we do it?

As with all organizational activities, we should be tracking costs of the entire process and all direct costs (e.g., travel to where users are).

Don't forget, we have already established the possible Benefits, in the form of the size of our Validated Problem, so we have some idea of how much can be spent.

Recommendations

Don't forget the people not in your team

The real-world people spent time with you that was supposed to be spent on their own Problems. Make sure you include these costs.

What does great look like?

Great Total Costs are:

- Genuine costs
- Within Budget

What are the minimum outcomes required to enable downstream success?

Actual costs and time tracking with reasonable assumptions applied to generate a Total Cost.

When do we stop at this step?

It's too late to stop now...

How does this step fail?

This step can fail if it's not done at all, and therefore no Total cost can be shown, and therefore there is no ROI.

Who should be involved?

The solution and change teams own this step.

Expected effort / duration

Should be fairly easy to track. In most organizations you would be tracking costs every month anyway.

Stage 4, Step 2: Return on investment (ROI)

Summary

What: The calculated Return on Investment for our solution and change.

Why: We invested to achieve a Return on Investment, now we need to calculate it.

How: ROI calculation using Total Costs and Total Benefits.

Detail

What is it?

ROI is a calculation to show how "successful" an investment is. It is expressed as a percentage. A positive ROI is good, a negative is bad (spent more than the benefit gained).

The formula for ROI is:

ROI = (Total Benefits – Total Cost) / Toal Cost x 100%

In reality, investments are expected to have a certain level of return. "Break even," or Benefits equaling to the Total Cost, is often considered a failure. The reason for this is that the same investment could have been used elsewhere, to create a greater return.

Why do we do it?

We need to know the ROI to determine if our investment has provided tangible benefit to the business. Where the Problem had a well-defined financial value to the business, this is the final step in determining whether / how viable the solution & change have been.

What problems does this solve?

Measuring ROI solves the problem of ongoing twin investments that can't be justified, especially Iterations. Demonstrating ROI, iteratively, also helps to train businesses to invest to solve Problems AND to learn more about Problems.

How do we do it?

With direct and total cost tracking in hand, and benefits measurements, ROI calculations are straightforward. For wide twins or twins with ill-defined Problems, ROI can be very complex.

In the worst cases, ROI cannot be measured, only benefits can.

Recommendations

Don't forget the non-financial benefits

While ROI is a "hard" number, you should also ensure that non-financial benefits are highlighted and tracked. If you can measure both, and invest to grow both, you are providing a genuinely viable solution.

What does great look like?

Great ROI is measurable and auditable. In other words, a 3rd party can derive the ROI independently of your team and get a similar answer.

What are the minimum outcomes required to enable downstream success?

ROI as measured against the Total Cost.

When do we stop at this step?

If ROI is low, or too low, or indeterminate, this can be the final stop for a solution. It may prevent further iterations or force a return to earlier stages. See more in the section on low and No-ROI situations.

How does this step fail?

This step can fail if it's not done at all, and therefore no ROI can be shown.

Who should be involved?

The solution and change teams own this step, but usually finance sets the standards and is the internal customer.

Expected effort / duration

Perhaps 5-10 hours of effort once a quarter would be normal.

Stage 4 outputs

- Estimated Cost (Solution)
- Total Cost (Estimated)
- Total Cost (Actual) – after Iteration 1,2, n
- ROI (Estimated)
- ROI (Actual) – after Iteration 1,2, n

End of Stage 4

Part 5: Digital Twin Design Process (DTDP) summary

Summarizes the DTDP's structured stages, guiding the design of digital twins and applied AI through solving valuable problems, implementing coherent changes, and iterating solutions to sustain measurable benefits and ROI.

The DTDP has multiple stages, and there is a flow to the order of these, but this flow must be tempered by the situation you find yourself in.

At its highest level, the DTDP seeks to maximize the probability of repeatably achieving positive ROI outcomes. It does this by:

- Focusing efforts on valuable Problems (which have high potential to create returns)
- Designing feasible and coherent changes in the real and virtual worlds
- Developing solutions that are usable and viable

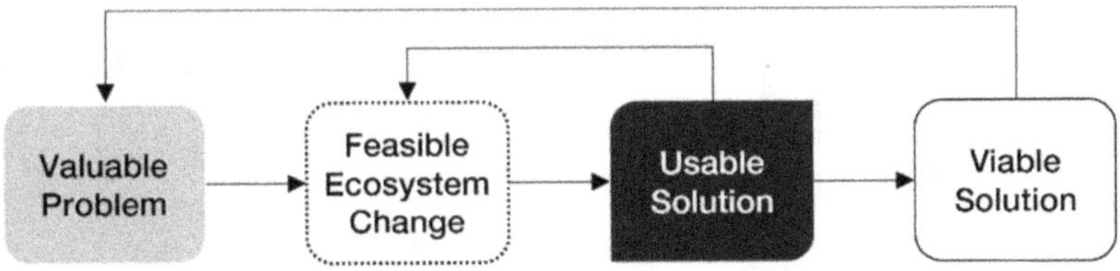

Within this flow, there are multiple recommended steps to achieve progressive outcomes. These steps are malleable and provide a guide, but are not mandated. Why only a guide? Because as players we find ourselves in so many different situations, and coping with so many different constraints, that any rigid process is doomed to failure. Or more likely, doomed to be shortcut in ways that undermine the desired outcomes.

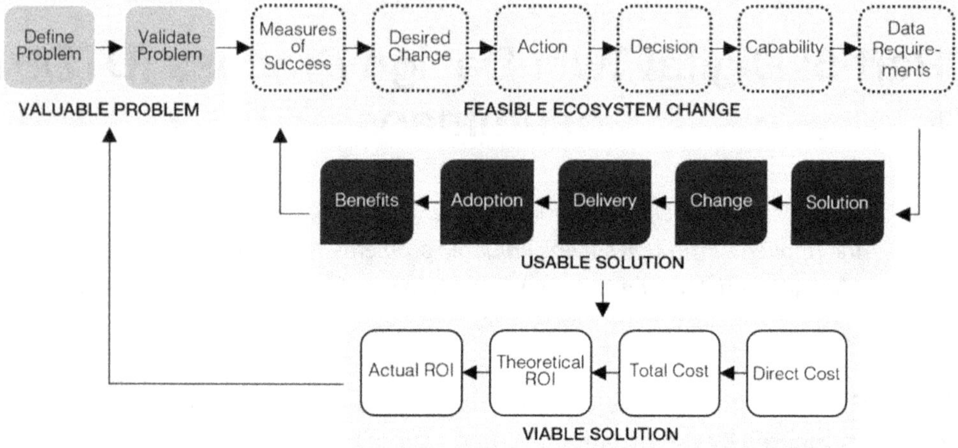

I present the "full" DTDP above. My hope is that the preceding, very detailed chapter gives you enough information to make this process work for you. Or perhaps more likely, for you to massage your existing processes to achieve better outcomes.

The only "rigid" process within the DTDP is the Connected Action Map exercise.

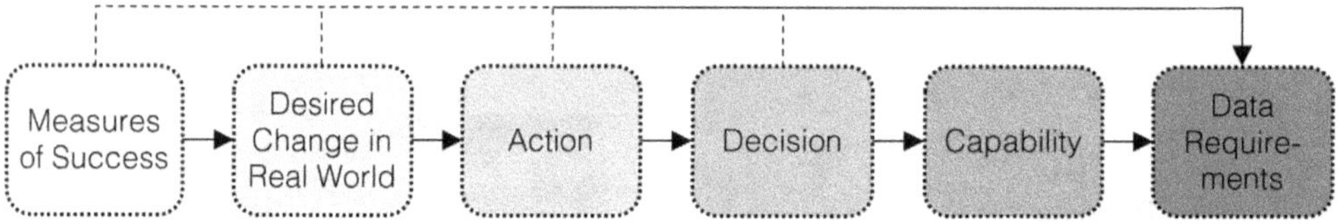

We map to explore the solution space with cross-functional teams.

We ideate chains of connected, real and virtual world activities that are linked together logically and pass the peer group assessment.

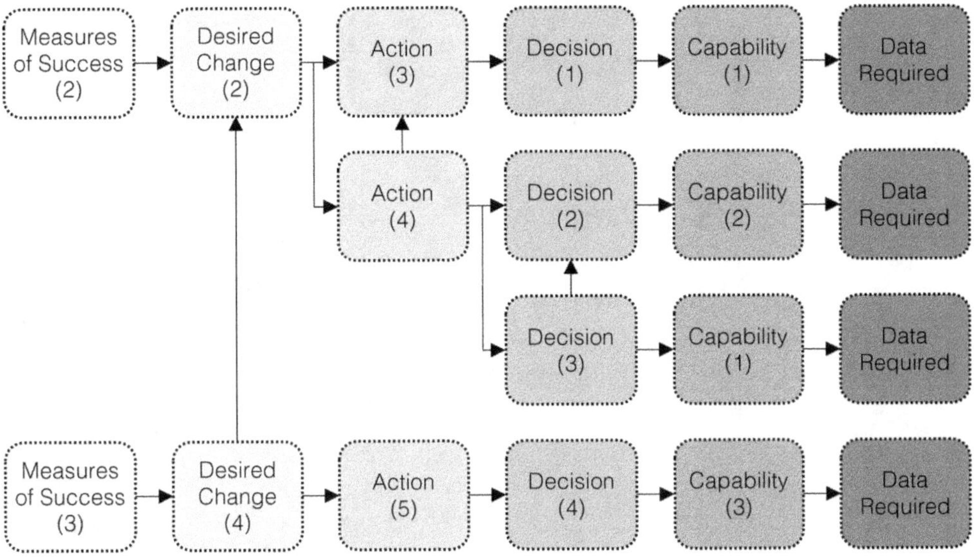

We prune non-feasible chains and bundle the chains together to create coherent changes. We seek to create coherence in chains to give us multiple chances to achieve the Desired Change, and / or to make multiple incremental improvements in Measures of Success.

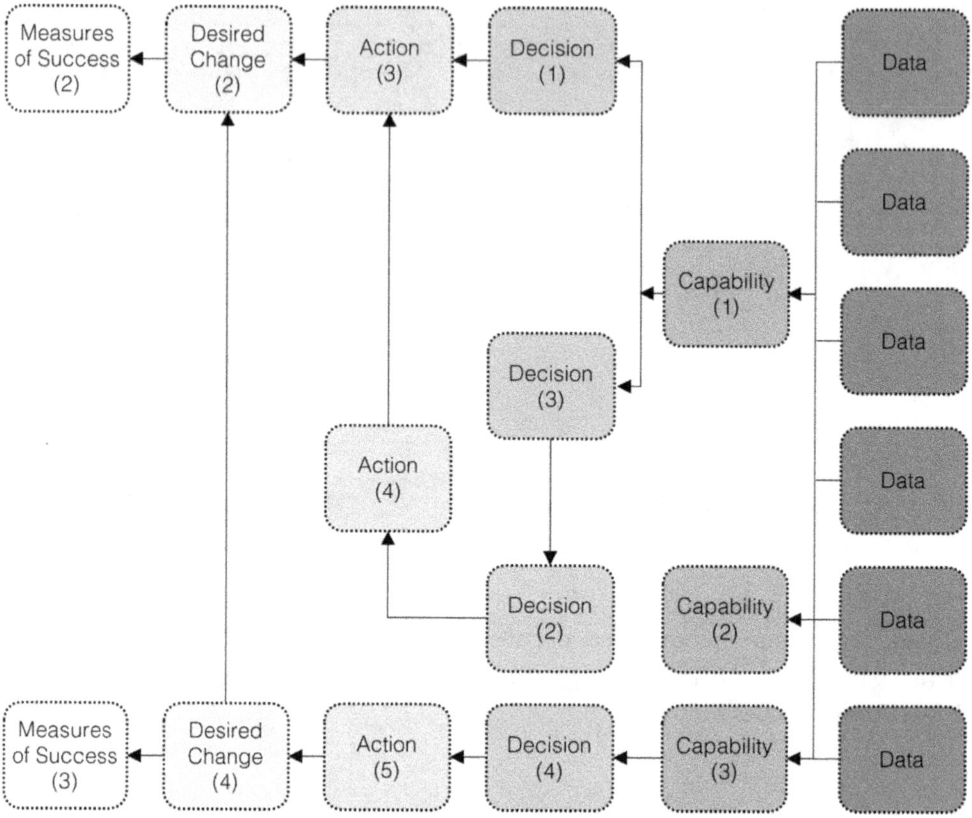

The bundled chains form the basis of our solution and our change.

Pruned chains are retained as they may be needed in future, for iterations or alternate solutions.

Some of the processes seem a little arbitrary, or even pedantic, like specifying a separate "Solution" and "Change" design. We do this to reinforce that we are not *just* designing a software solution, and that the design of change in the real world is more than *just change management.*

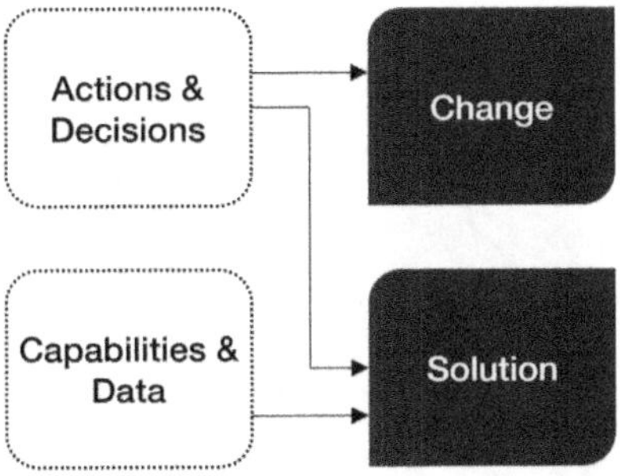

In Concept / Scoping, we iterate Feasible Ecosystem Change until we have a bundled set of chains that conceptually solves the Problem. High-level estimating of solution and change may be enough to support the business case - otherwise we execute Usable and Viable steps to develop a complete design and plan.

If Procuring, we use our Concept as the basis of a Scope of Work to give vendors the clearest possible direction and requirements to solve our Problems in feasible, usable and viable ways.

If Delivering, we use our Concept to verify Feasibility, and then we dive into detailed Usability and Viability to design, build and deploy our solution and create our changes. Detailed design and solution design may force changes to our feasible chains. So be it. Refer to the Connected Action Maps to assess impacts or repeat the exercise to identify alternate feasible ways of creating the Desired Change.

When Iterating, take feedback from the field and revisit the Connected Action Maps to modify or develop new chains to deepen value or widen capability. Concept - Procure / Deliver and repeat.

We use the DTDP to maximize the desired changes to the real world. We Measure systemically because we know that new problems and blockers will emerge from our changes no matter how well we design and execute. We seek to identify and iterate improvements to overcome these blockers and achieve our Desired Change, at acceptable cost and risk. We iterate because we know there will be unintended consequences - positive and negative. We seek to leverage the former and mitigate the latter in order to maximize the probability of repeatably delivering positive ROI outcomes.

Part 6: Advice to players

Explores managing validated problems through problem banks and roadmaps, emphasizing their role in prioritizing impactful solutions and driving cultural change across interconnected ecosystems.

Managing Problems – Banks, roadmaps and emergence

There is a huge congress of information on managing projects, portfolios, solutions and products. 99% of it centers on "better ways to do what you want to do."

I shall not repeat or even attempt to summarize that here. Do as thou wilt shall be the whole of the law when it comes to building your solutions.

The antithesis of the solution is the problem. The other side of the coin, so to speak. And yet we only ever look at the coin "right side up."

We have shown that *starting* with problems provides us with benefits. Let us now consider how to *manage* problems.

The Problem Bank and the Problem Roadmap

A Problem Bank and Problem Roadmap provide a method of prioritizing real and validated Problems that could deliver value to the business over a reasonable time (e.g., the next year or two). Longer-term problems need to be broken down into smaller problems, or pushed off to the indefinite future. There is every likelihood that the problem you see today will be different – changed by the time many years have passed. It may wear the same name, but the details will have changed and the partial solutions will have changed and thus it is not the same problem.

A Problem Bank is a backlog of validated Problems.

A Problem Roadmap is a time-phased sequencing of validated Problems from the Problem Bank.

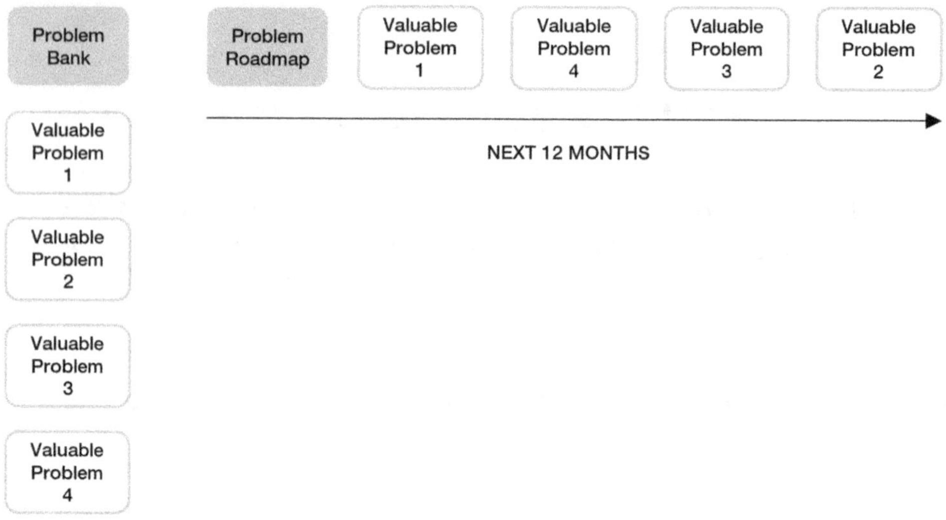

Why create a Problem Bank and Problem Roadmaps?

For internal tool teams, any single tool or project is but one of many possible areas that time and money could be invested into. Every business of any meaningful size has many problems. Selecting the first and next problem to solve becomes a challenge in itself. This is particularly the case now where virtually every business has a technology roadmap, and is committed to building lots of capabilities and lots of solutions.

As discussed previously, the Problems that are validated can sometimes be thought of as opportunities and risks. Opportunities to create more value usually come about by solving existing problems, even if the problem is that the capability or capacity to achieve higher value are not present or are not usable by the organization. Risks are future potential problems. If the problem is present now and has been present historically – it's a problem – not a risk. Moving an opportunity or a risk into Feasible Ecosystem Change should not affect the downstream steps if the opportunity or risk can be thought of as desired change in the real world that can be measured now, or in the reasonable near future.

Where does this fit into the DTDP?

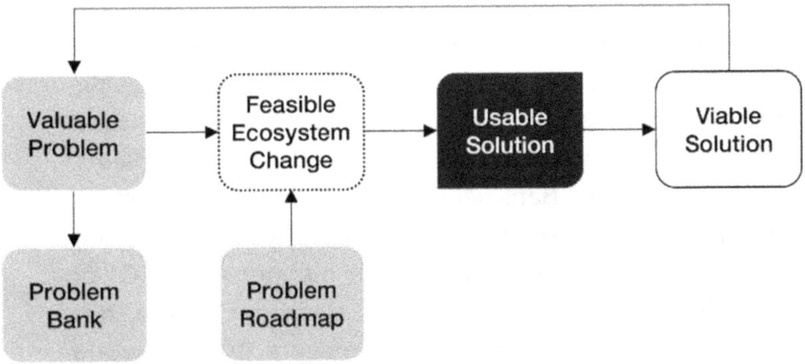

The Problem Bank is the "hopper" into which Valuable Problems are loaded, and the Problem Roadmap sets the proposed order in which they are extracted to enter Feasible Ecosystem Change.

Validated Problems are pushed into the Problem Bank, and decisions are made about the priority and desired order to solve these Problems. The Problem Roadmap then becomes the primary artefact to make decisions on when a Problem is intended to be solved, and the groupings of Problems that if solved collectively, provide genuine and coherent benefits to the organization.

Note that in both cases, the approval to solve a Problem should not / will not come until some indication of ROI has been established. While the magnitude of the Problem has been estimated, the cost to solve the Problem and the likelihood of being able to solve the Problem (at all, and at the estimated cost) have not yet been established.

The Problem Bank

The purpose of the Problem Bank is not to decide which Problems to solve nor to guarantee that these Problems can and will be solved. It is to ensure that Valuable Problems are available for solving. Importantly, the intended benefit of this is that non-valuable problems are prioritized less often over real and validated Problems. In other words, the Problem Bank helps to reduce the chasing of shiny things, which in turn increases the probability of any one investment creating real value, which in the aggregate increases the ROI of improvement investments. The Problem Bank is thus a key mechanism in enabling systemic improvements to real-world problems through digital twin investments.

Within the context of a digital transformation, which all large businesses are undergoing all the time now, the Problem Bank can be applied to a department, function or major technology purchase / change out. For example, an ERP upgrade and embrace (or rip and replace) will often create significant business process and data changes. Targeting problem validation exercises in the areas being impacted by the ERP change will result in the creation of multiple Valuable Problems that could come under the banner of that transformation initiative. Similarly, a large regulatory change, say to environmental requirements, may lead to a large body of work relating to required changes – which may create new problems that need to be solved – either as a result of changes or to be able to make the required changes.

The Problem Bank at its most simple is a single repository of Problems that have been validated. A SharePoint folder of Problem definitions or a wiki that lists and links Problem definitions is sufficient. There is no need to overcook it, nor to take the bank analogy too far (though I have had some interesting suggestions about Problems accumulating interest the longer they go unsolved).

More sophisticated expressions include analysis of each Problem to create a score of how "valuable" or "serious" or "urgent" a particular Problem is. Further metadata such as expected value in $, which users, departments, sites etc. are impacted, problem frequency and problem duration also provide filters upon which to analyze and compare Problems. The comparison of Problems relative to each other always leads to the discussion on prioritization – how do we choose the next Problem to solve?

Problem prioritization

Problem prioritization is the selection of the next Problems to be solved. Prioritization is a dark art in every business. Problems are like beauty – they exist differently in the eye of the beholder. And like all beauty contests, the selection of judges has as great or greater influence on the winner than the objective criteria. It is for this reason that executive decisions and whims frequently upset carefully-laid departmental plans.

There is no panacea to this problem of prioritizing Problems. The best that can be done is to keep the digital twin ethos uppermost. If the problem can't be measured objectively, it will be very difficult to determine the desired change in the real world. Thus, measuring and improving change will be more difficult, and thus, measuring and proving ROI will be almost impossible.

There are many ways to prioritize backlogs, and most businesses have some methodology in place. Stack rank, cost of delay, and even MoSCoW (must-should-could-would) all have their places.

Another way of prioritizing is to group, or select out types of problems. The first and most obvious selecting out is problems-without-measurement versus Problems-with-measurement.

Some ideas for grouping / selecting:

- Sub-problems: Problems that belong to a larger meta-problem
- Elapsed time: Problems that are have been problems for many years versus "new" problems
- Size: Large problems (large benefit if solved) versus small problems
- Urgency: Problems that "must" be solved ASAP versus all other problems

The above can be very helpful, but in a large organization, or with a team that is very excited about documenting all the problems, even the above can produce unwieldy lists. Another technique I apply in these situations is putting types of problem criteria in tension on X-Y graphs:

- Size versus Urgency
- Size versus Elapsed Time
- Measurable versus Unmeasurable

A final technique, especially when grouping problems, is to show the problems visually by department or function.

If the problems are measurable, sometimes you can allocate potential $ value to each department. A word of warning on this: the exact solution developed may deliver radically different value to different stakeholders. It's a good idea and many seem keen on it, but I've seen it go poorly when this becomes the jumping off point for deciding who should *pay* for the solving of this problem.

As always, choose a way and use it. Then measure what works and do more of that. I strongly suspect many of you will find that investment into user research changes how you think about problem prioritization – for the better.

The Problem Roadmap

With a set of prioritized Problems, a roadmap can be created. A roadmap is not meant to be a Gannt chart / program schedule. A roadmap is meant to be a current snapshot of the direction and sequencing of activities or outcomes. The key here is snapshot. Roadmaps are meant to be malleable because as things are learned, problems are solved, and priorities and initiatives change – so too should the roadmap change. The Problem roadmap in particular is not the technology, or capability, or solution roadmap. As Problems are defined and validated, so too should the priority of problems change, within reason. This last phrase, within reason, is overlooked by many practitioners. There must be a balance between flexibility and planning. Too much flexibility results in continuously re-planning, or in all plans being useless – which leads to feelings of chaos or hyperreactivity. Too little flexibility results in fixing last year's problem or not fixing an extreme problem that has suddenly appeared. Or in continuing to build solutions to things that have already changed or lessened in benefit.

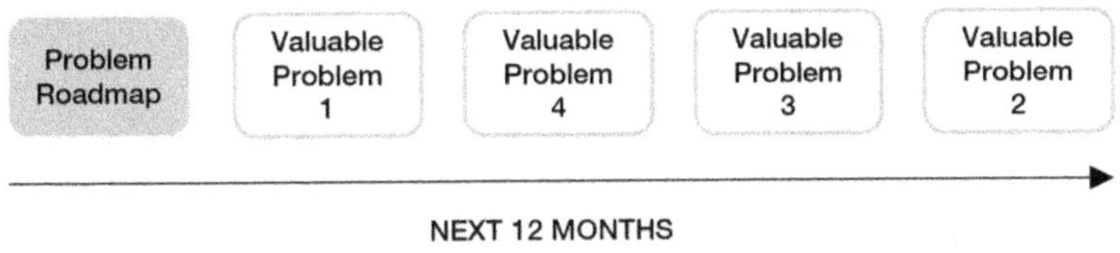

The Problem Roadmap helps with a number of key issues:

- Sequencing by Problem forces the prioritization (and de-prioritization) of Problems
- Sequencing by user type or user problem or area / initiative can reinforce transformation or revitalization cycles
- We are all capacity constrained and need to impose some order on the solving of Problems

The Problem Roadmap does NOT:

- Set the order in which solutions will be built
- Determine which Problem provides the highest ROI if solved.

The Problem Roadmap has three potential inputs:

- A Valuable Problem loop, OR
- The Problem Bank
- The technology / capability roadmap / program

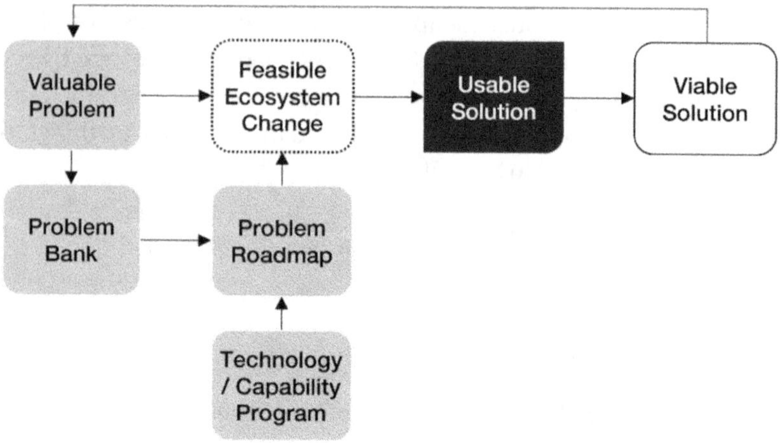

In most large businesses, the technology / capability program is strong and dominant. Large procurement initiatives will dominate the landscape of investment and upcoming rollouts. It need not however, dominate the selection of valuable Problems to solve. Juxtaposing multiple desired paths can be valuable, if the proper frame of mind is adopted. Yes, the business wants X, and yes, the business wants to solve problem Y, but the business also wants and has many other Xs and Ys. Probably 1000s of them in a large business. So don't be overly drawn by or apprehensive about any one X or Y. Solving Problems creates value, and the more Problems you solve, the more your ideas about solving Problems will be adopted.

In an ideal world, the Problem Roadmap and validated solutions would be inputs to the Technology roadmap, which in turn would feed back into prioritizing which problems to validate.

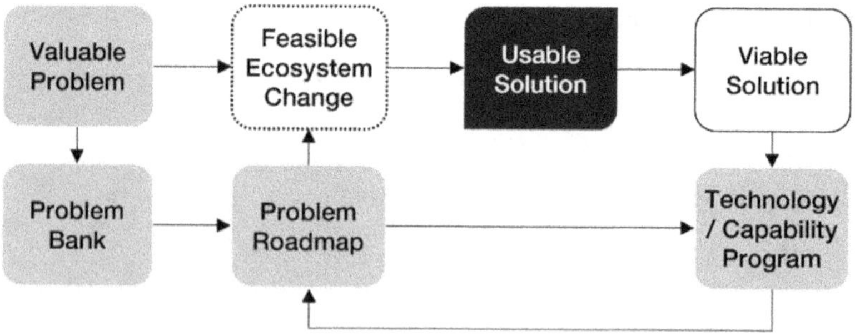

We would add validated solutions to our technology roadmap, and they would be allocated budget and co-exist with all the other changes being implemented across the organization. Similarly, the regular reviews of the Technology roadmap would feed back into prioritizing which problems to push into solution validation mode.

In the above diagram, I hope this captures the true essence of a roadmap – it's a tool for deciding where to spend money, time and energy. It's not the road that we *will* drive down – it is a map of many roads we *may* drive down one day. We look at the roadmap to understand which roads are available to us and this helps us choose which road to drive down next. *It's not the road.*

How to create the Problem Bank and Problem Roadmap

The challenge to creating Problem "anythings" isn't technical – it's justifying the time investment. In other words – it's the business case. Or in other words – it's applied politics.

If you are creating solutions or own a product team, then the first deposit into the Problem Bank will likely need to come from you. Even if you only have one Problem to solve (as in you have orders to solve that problem and no other), you have the beginning of a Problem Bank. I know for sure that as part of your work, you have spoken to end users who have more and related problems. The effort to document these problems and arrange them as potential problems to be solved, with a single validated Problem, provides the context for an initial and valuable Problem Bank.

Remember, there is no tonic like victory. Before embarking on a crusade to find many more problems, I strongly suggest solving one Problem well. Use the example of ROI from Problem 1 to explain the ethos of validating problems and solutions before building.

There are some unexpected (they were to me, anyway) outcomes of an explicit problem focus. Beyond the "higher probability of measuring ROI" advantage, there are other benefits to cultivating an explicit problem focus.

Cultural change

Digital twins as a tool of digital transformation are often seen as one of the levers to changing culture. We are "transforming" how we work, and we know that culture / people / process is a key part of transformation, and digital twins require behavior / action / decision change, ergo digital twins as part of cultural change.

The interesting part occurs when, in the midst of a giant multi-year enterprise program, people on the ground actually get to be involved in crafting a solution to specific problems that also benefits the business. This can be quite a revelation, and in some cases a shock – workers were involved in designing the change they are expected to deliver.

"No problems here"

In other places, as we have discussed, it is not acceptable to talk about problems. Problems are bad. Complaining about them is bad. Talking about problems means you're complaining.

I can't offer much advice here except to say: if you're running a complex industrial organization, with thousands of moving parts, and you hire technical people to manage technical processes and equipment, you have problems. And your people are by and large, trained to identify and solve problems. They might not actually be very good at "problem focus" (because they have been trained to have a "solution focus"), but they sure do have to overcome problems every day, and they know it. Creating rules to say "you can't talk about problems" is akin to tying one hand behind the back of some of your best people. I can only state that the DTDP, even when modified to convert problems to opportunities, will highlight and focus on solving real problems. You should expect that at least some of your team will point to the process and say: see, this ROI only exists because of the problem we're trying to solve!

Collective problems

Many (most?) problems that come from the real-world, impact more than one function / department. Organizational boundaries are often arbitrary and driven by personal experience: the real-world changes, new equipment new processes, and new functions are added (e.g., data science) but the existing silos remain. We add organizational complexity and rename silos to cope with additional real-world complexity.

Speaking to real-world problems before assigning responsibility for solutions can bring teams of people across multiple silos together to focus on these "collective problems." The collective, of course, is that artificial grouping of silos that may need to be involved in the solution. By putting the problem before the assigning of responsibility, many more voices can feel freer to engage in defining and validating the problem. And as we've seen, "good" problem definition and validation sets up so many downstream processes. This might seem overly subtle, but any reduction of silo / politics and fear of "upsetting" other silos is to be encouraged. Politics reduction through collective problem definition is subtle but high-leverage work.

Narrow versus Wide

One of the most useful concepts as a practitioner or advisor on twins is breadth: narrow versus wide. We touched on this earlier but it's a critical tool that has provided me with many insights and ideas about digital twins.

A summary of Narrow versus Wide twins is shown below.

Aspect	**Narrow Digital Twins**	**Wide Digital Twins**
Design Focus	Designed to solve specific problems	Designed for non-specific problems or classes of problems
Problem-Capability Coupling	Strongly coupled problem-change-capability-data loops	Loosely coupled problem, capability, and data
Data Requirements	Need "strong and complete" data directly enabling capabilities and change	Often start from data related to a problem type or known beneficial capabilities
Data Coupling	Strongly coupled to specific data needs	May have looser data coupling or incomplete / unknown coupling between capability and problem
Benefit Measurement	Easier to measure benefits due to clearly defined problem and change	More challenging to measure success and ROI
Approach	Work backwards from the real-world problem	Work forwards to the real world, often technology-led
Extensibility	May require modification and additional cost to solve other problems	Can potentially address a wide variety of purposes
Example	Digital twin of an HVAC system to optimize energy consumption versus. occupant comfort	Digital twin with multiple capabilities for addressing various "risk" or "improvement" scenarios
Problem Specificity	High	Low
Capability Focus	Specific capabilities tailored to the problem	Multiple, often advanced / untried capabilities

Aspect	Narrow Digital Twins	Wide Digital Twins
Value Definition	Clearer definition of value and user journey	May struggle with attributing user behavior and defining value

The first key message, once you know and understand this table, is that it's completely arbitrary, and neither is "better" or "worse" than the other. There are plenty of narrow twins with incomplete data, and plenty of strongly coupled wide twins. There are way more twins that provide no measurable ROI than ROI, and they are often the most popular.

The point is that for new twins, I see teams very often mixing and matching narrow and wide concepts into a single new thing. They do this because they don't have a strong frame of reference. A "bitsa" twin is very often a twin that's reverse engineered to what's available, without a strong connection to the real world, or is a mix up of all the favorite capabilities the team thinks are beneficial, in the sense that it must be of benefit to us because it is beneficial to others.

Why even bother?

The value of a frame of reference is that you can quickly pattern match your situation to a situation, and from a given situation, there are known patterns to work with that have worked before. Frames of reference don't "tell" you what to do – they narrow down your focus to a particular direction. If (IF!) your frame of reference is close enough to the actual real-world situation, then it provides fast and effective ways of thinking through next steps. If the real world is radically different to the frame you select, you'll extrapolate non-sensical next steps and get very confused and frustrated. This is good. It's good because you should be able to tell quick if the frame of reference is useful. If it is useful – use it. If not – discard and go at it a different way.

Narrow Twins

Ok so you're building a narrow twin. It's problem specific. Your Capability is tied to the Decisions and Actions you need to create in the real world. You need all the Data required but no more than that. You are planning to build a specific product to solve a specific valuable Problem.

Here's the narrow twin framing.

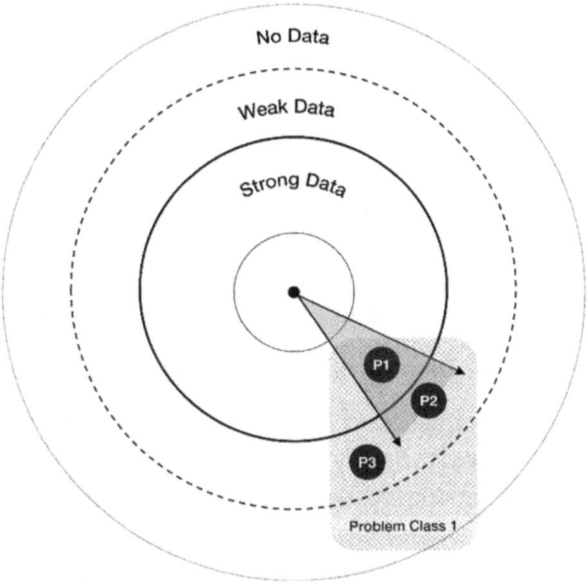

The first two things to notice are:

- Problem classes
- Data strength

Problem classes

All problems are members of a problem class. There is no "single" problem. No problem that lives on its own or is isolated form other problems. Problems are connected because problems are manifestations of the real world, and the real world is highly connected. We also very often target problems that are aggregations of many smaller problems. When we solve a problem, we often open up the possibility of solving a follow-on problem that wasn't solvable or perhaps even visible until we solved the first.

All problems are members of a problem class, and many problems can be said to live in many problem classes. The predictive maintenance problem belongs to the maintenance class, and the financial class, and the asset management class. How you define classes of problems says more about you than the problem. Practitioner note: I like to ask people how they group problems and then have people compare notes publicly. None out of ten times the persons job title will correlate with their class definitions. It can be a good little ice breaker for cross-functional teams.

Data strength

I labored over this a bit and I'm still not happy. It's not data quality that we seek to show here, nor the presence of data, nor the necessity of data for the solution. It's all three. And hence none of them. And hence data "strength" ... which only makes sense in the context of the data required to solve the problem.

Strong data: we have "all" the Data we need to solve the problem.

Weak data: we have "some" of the Data we need to solve the problem.

No data: we don't have the Data we need to solve the problem.

Data strength determines the distance from the center of any problem. If you have all the data related to the problem, it's nice and tight. If you have very little, it's loose and further out. Mapping the problem against the available data (rather than mapping data against capabilities) instantly gives you a qualitative measure of how ready you are, from a data point of view, to solve this problem.

Interestingly, problems in the same class can often be spread far apart from a data strength point of view. When we speak in generalities ("we need all the data related to energy use") we set ourselves up for many problems during execution (solving unknown data problems on the fly), and / or many excuses to never start ("we don't have all the data").

Starting point

Ok so you have some number of problems, you can map them against data strength, and you can group them into a class.

Your narrow twin is aimed at a problem. You show this by drawing the "solution ray" from the center to encompass that problem.

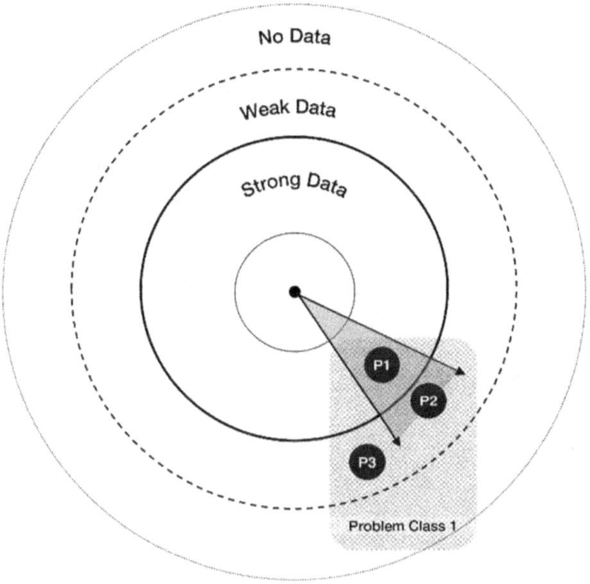

Narrow twins - Deepen capability and data

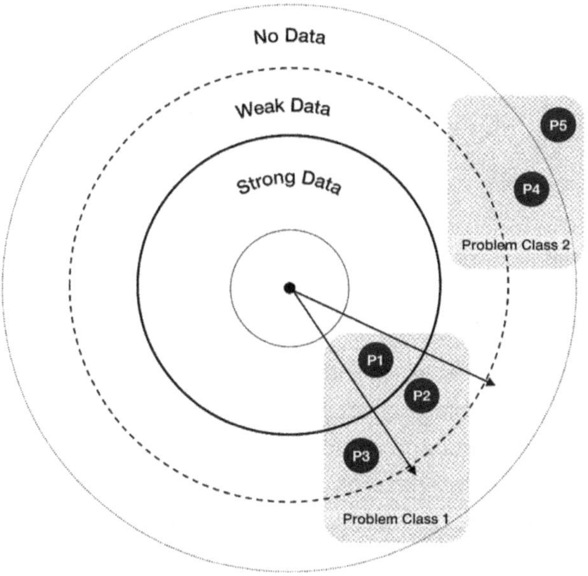

Deepening a narrow twin by adding more Capabilities and Data enables the solving of problems that couldn't be solved before, or to solve the same problem more deeply (more completely). For example, if your narrow twin reduces energy usage by

17%, and we want to reduce by 25%, we will almost certainly need additional Capabilities, Data or Desired Changes in the real world to achieve this. I often like to assign this new Desired Change as a "new" problem. I find that when teams continue to extend or change scope on a very dynamic (as hoc) basis, the fundamental investment cost and return get diluted across changes. Assigning a "deeper" problem or target as a new problem helps to force the process back to step 1 – valuable problem, feasible ecosystem-change etc. It's very easy for teams to get caught up in adding more features without any clear view of how those features solve the problem more completely.

Narrow Twins – Adjacent problem

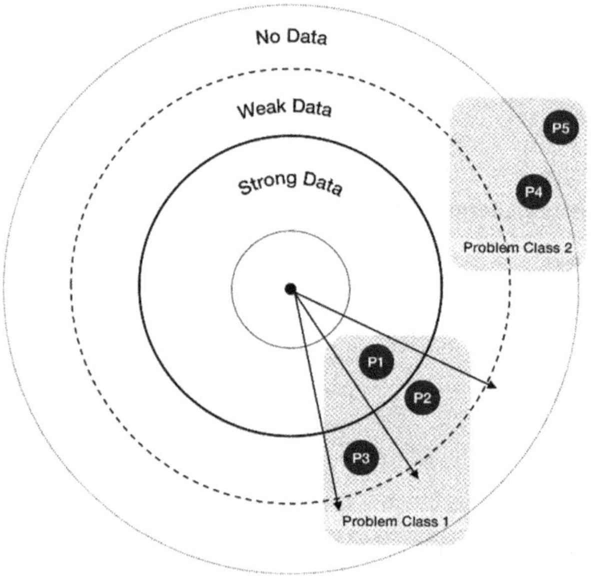

The other "direction" is to move around to an adjacent problem. An adjacent problem belongs to the same problem class, but may require different (sometimes very different) Capabilities, Data and Actions to solve. Adjacent problems are another form of increasing completeness of problem classes. We solve more problems related to a key theme that is constraining the business.

For Narrow twins:

- Go deeper with more Data and Capabilities to solve a Problem more completely
- Go adjacent with different Data and Capabilities to solve more of a problem class

Wide twins

Now we're building a wide twin. It's capability specific. Your problem(s) are related to the Capabilities, and potentially many problem classes could be addressed. You need Data to support the Capability. You are planning to build a specific product to enable specific Capabilities.

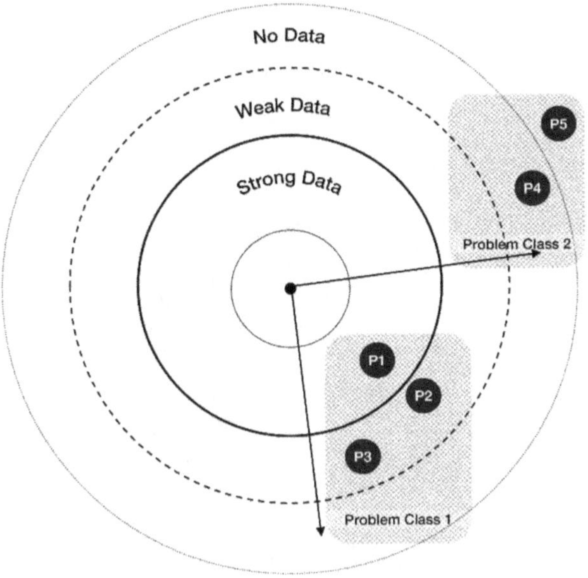

Similarly to narrow twins, we can widen our Capability or deepen our Capability (or both).

Widen capability

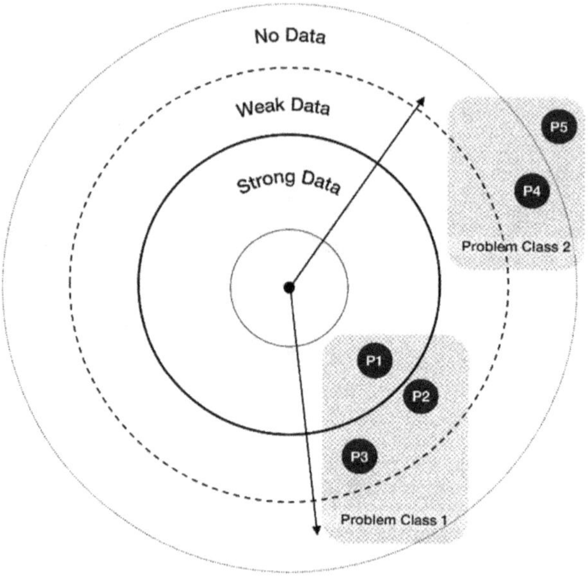

Widening a wide twin means adding capabilities, data or actions that increase the variety of changes that could be made in the real world. Widening generally accompanies new capabilities (e.g., adding simulation or predictive tools). When increasing capabilities alone it's very tempting to show that "all" the problems can be addressed now by this new twin configuration. But if we factor in having the right data, then you will find it's difficult to pull problems into the strong, or even the weak category.

Deepen capability

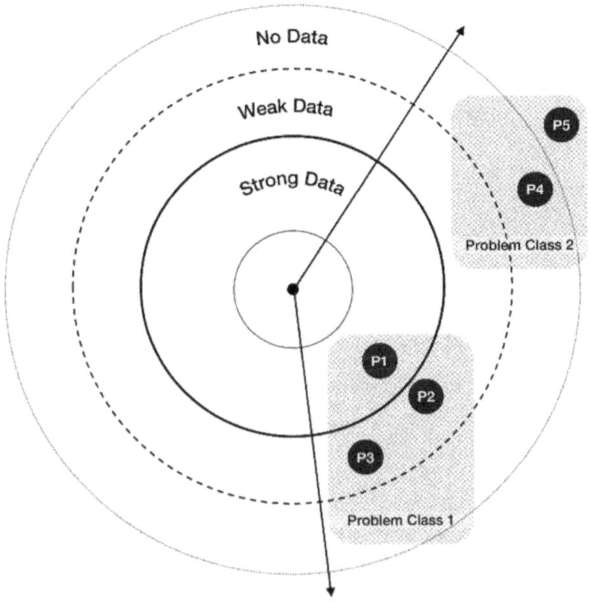

The obvious other motion is to add more data, deepening the Capability. A similar motion is to improve the validity and accuracy of data models. Deepening a data model may involve improved algorithms, improved training, greater variety of features etc.

Deeping a wide twin is intended to move more problems into the strong zone, where they can be solved or at least the Capability and Data is present to enable solving (if we have the right Capabilities and Data to solve the Problem).

Again, when looked at problem by problem, additional data may move some problems in, while others remain weak and some will have no data. A classic problem for many complex problems is not knowing what data is even needed. I always advise that unless you can explicitly match data to problem, leave the problem at weak or no data, to force the exercise to determine what data is required.

Wide + (n) Narrow

The obvious question I often get asked is: how do we design a twin that solves many problems?

The solution to this is to think of the wide twin as the capability / data foundation, and narrow twins as the use cases that requires specific Capability and Data.

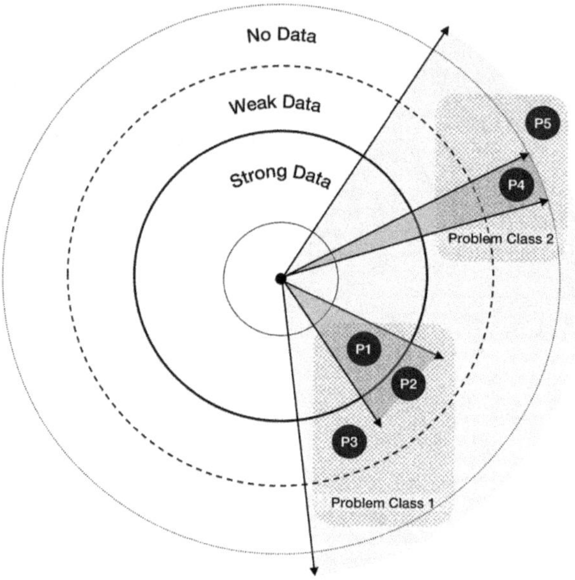

A wide + many narrow twins bring together wide capability foundations with narrow, targeted use cases aimed at solving specific problems. Critically, while capabilities are wide, data requirements are narrow. Narrowing your data down to only what is required to solve specific problems, i.e., deepening by problem, not by capability, saves huge time and effort costs. When more money is spent on the right data, we increase ROI and decrease time to first value. This is "right-sizing" data. We still need data to support wide capabilities but this data need not be anywhere near the fidelity or even synchronization of the narrow data.

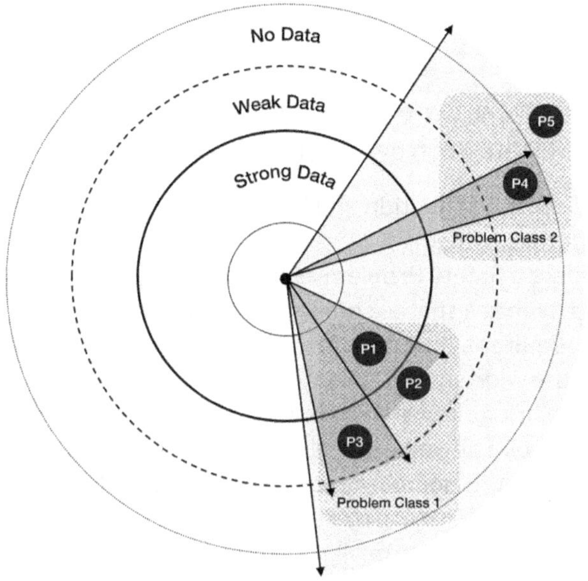

Wide + Narrow twins also benefit from problem adjacency. With common foundations, growing sideways to solve more problems in the same class is easier, and we don't suffer from scope or change creep. New problem, measured separately, leveraging existing Capabilities and Data. The incremental change versus the new problem benefits creates recurring high-ROI growth that is measurable.

We grow twins by growing Capabilities and Data, but we only grow value by solving more or deeper problems. I posit that you should use Problems to guide growth, and invest to change the Capabilities, Data and Actions to solve these new Problems.

Visualization twin redux

Let us revisit our old friend, the visualization twin, as a wide + (n)narrow twin.

I find that in order to maximize adoption (use) across an organization, a "horizontal" problem class (i.e., is a problem for many) is better to start with than a vertical (i.e., is a problem for just one team / group / department). An ideal staring point in industrial organizations is Safety.

Safety is everyone's problem, has a dedicated team, and leaders of every team have safety responsibilities. This is great for theoretical adoption and risky for actual adoption. Many strong opinions and usually matrix-style RACI, and subtle nuances of actual work done (especially office versus field).

In a wide + narrow world, I like to proceed like this:

1. Iteration 1
   (a) Use the DTDP and work backwards from a horizontal problem class [Safety] to create a narrow [Safety-related] use case
      a. Work with Production and Safety to identify and define multiple potential problems
      b. Validate a Safety Problem as the starting point use case, preferably one that has a spatial component (i.e., location of people / plant / risk) and requires siloed data from another existing system. This ensures that the wide spatial data is included in solving the Problem and that we are bridging systems (making an existing system more valuable). Bonus points if you can include a new Capability such as a third-party AI tool, but remember that giving a third-party tool a reason to live is not what we're trying to do here
      c. Follow the DTDP to design Connected Action Maps to solve this Problem
   (b) Start from the narrow Capabilities identified in the DTDP, and work forwards towards the problem class to create greater context
      a. With the Capabilities for Use Case 1, work forward to identify other potential problems that could be solved with the Capabilities needed to solve the Problem in Use Case 1. Don't add new Capabilities!
   (c) Bank potential adjacent problems.
2. Iteration 2 / 4 / 6
   (a) Take operational feedback to extract an adjacent problem that likely needs existing Capabilities
   (b) Use the DTDP and work backwards from the adjacent Problem to create a new narrow use case
   (c) Start from the combined narrow Capabilities and work forwards towards the Problem class to create greater context
   (d) Deliver new change and solution
3. Iteration 3 / 5 / 7
   (a) Take operational feedback on how an existing narrow use case could potentially be more complete (deepened)
   (b) Review the Connected Action Maps to modify Change or improve the solution

(c) Deliver modified changes and solution

Note the Even / Odd iteration focus:

- Even iterations: Identify adjacent problems to existing ones and seek to solve them
- Odd Iterations: Identify improvements to existing Problems

By moving sideways to widen the twin, but constraining to adjacent problems that have shared Capabilities, you limit the potential of Featuritis, and maximize the value of existing Capabilities and Data.

By moving down existing Problems, you show that you are focused on taking user feedback onboard to solve real Problems more completely.

In this manner, a visualization twin will have narrow Safety-related use cases that are highly measurable, and have involved a cross-functional team of people who do work in the real world. Upon successive iterations, it will widen the problems we solve and deepen how well we solve those problems.

The Wide + Narrow can be the foundation for organic, bottom up (problem-driven) transformation of classes of problems, such as Safety, that require wide Capabilities and cross-functional collaboration.

Failure modes

We have mentioned a few already, but let's turn our attention to the ways in which we fail, so that we can explicitly mitigate the most common causes.

The common connected solution failure modes we'll cover are:

- No ROI
- Low ROI
- Setting up to fail

No ROI

The cardinal sin today, in my opinion, is starting no-ROI twins and promising explicit Benefits. Explicit Benefits imply measurable change. Measurable change implies measurable gains. Many wide twins and many, many AI tools are flaming out one to two years after creation because they promised ROI, not because they don't deliver Benefits.

Advice:

- If it's your first twin, or the first twin in your organization, or if you have the choice:
    - Build a narrow twin on a small validated problem and deliver ROI, then
    - Build an adjacent narrow twin on an adjacent problem that requires only incremental investment (e.g., uses 80% of data from first twin and / or the same data model and / or an additional data set to retrain your existing model) and deliver subsequent very high incremental ROI, then
    - Build a wide twin around your narrow twins that provides a foundational Capability aimed at the same problem class, that requires successive wide and deep changes to overcome, and use that to find out what you need to create a genuine interconnected applied AI solution that substantially solves the problem class
- If you are instructed to build a wide twin:
    - Attempt to remove ROI from the outcome, and focus on change in the real world as your measure of success
    - Seek to validate known and valuable problems within range of your desired capability, and prioritize your feasible ecosystem changes on that narrow use case
    - Use your narrow use case as the proof of success but don't fool yourself that you can reliably reuse that to solve other problems
    - Prepare your roadmap with the next or adjacent or deeper problems that can be solved with incremental changes to your wide twin, or additional narrow use cases, and seek to achieve a second iteration of ROI

Low ROI

Low ROI is different than No ROI. It is not a degree of change, but rather the difference between 0 and 1. Low ROI means you have measurable benefits that can be enhanced. No ROI means you can't measure anything. Twice of nothing is still nothing.

Low ROI is common in twins. The following are some specific issues I have seen:

- ROI measurement was never agreed before design or build, and is reverse engineered 1-2 yrs after deployment.
- The twin is wide and ROI is reverse engineered from multiple sort-of-solved use cases.
- The twin was only adopted by a select few, e.g., 1 of 3 teams.

- The twin was adopted by enough people who made Decisions, but organizational processes and / or KPIs weren't changed to allow the change in behaviors, and Actions were rarely taken (this is usually where a separate team would have to accept pain for the twin users to achieve their goals, and they have successfully blocked action).

The last one is the most common. It's also often inadvertent: the other team / blockers are confused as to why the issue is even brought up, because they were never involved with these proposed changes or they heard about it once but nothing else changed etc. The usual transformation and bureaucracy-type problems.

There are other reasons, including some academic ones that are postulated often in theory or used in Lessons Learned, but not backed up by data and I have rarely seen in practice. Examples include:

- Poor data quality / garbage in garbage out
- Data pipelines are manual / clunky
- Changes to the real word have not been reflected in the twin (i.e., lack of synchronization / interconnection)
- Insufficient spatial fidelity

I find that these are rare because while they seem vital and obvious, twins that are flailing or failing often, do so long before and in different ways to that which is spoken of in theory. This was also a driver for me to write this book – the things people think will kill the twin, are in fact not the reasons they fail. Practitioners are often focusing on and investing in things that don't matter, or will only matter if you get past the things that matter first.

Advice on low or falling ROI:

- Whatever the outcome from iteration 1, invest to learn:
    - Dive into your data measurements and seek the cause of missed opportunities. Decisions that weren't Actioned, Data that was present and served to the user but no Decision was made. Often, the data will point the way, but you won't be able to determine causality explicitly. You'll need to go ask, and learn.
    - Adoption. Are the right people using it at the right time? Even if they are, the feedback on what issues this causes, or why they do sometimes but not others, is the gold you need to improve your twin.

- If your twin ROI was high and is now falling:
  - Dive into your data measurements and confirm that your interconnections are still strong. Has there been a business process change, or re-organization, or even a change of department leader? Are your Real-to-Virtual (R2V) connection still valid and functioning?
  - Check what people have changed in what roles. Sometimes a champion will drive change, and then when they leave it reverts / changes. I have mapped adoption to roles before and shown names against roles on the timeline – there can be quite obvious correlations to investigate. Don't assume nefarious – maybe they weren't trained, maybe their boss is new, maybe they have other priorities you don't know about. Go make a new friend.

Above all, investigate with users before building complex data models. People and process must be the number one cause of low ROI and failure in all major transformations. Start by talking. Preferably on their turf. Assume they have the best intentions. Be open and friendly. You're there to help them, not to accuse them.

Setting up to fail

I often have to broach this topic gently when running workshops with large organizations.

Let's level set, again: Digital twins are new. They have many definitions. A thing can be good and not a digital twin. A thing can fail and be a digital twin. A digital twin can be built as a project. A product can be called a digital twin and all the value comes from connected capabilities, not internal features. Your boss may never know or care what a digital twin is.

With that little morale boost over – here are some classic ways to create poor outcomes:

- No details at all in the scope of work
- Far too many specific and incoherent capabilities in the scope of work
- Weak or missing interconnections
- Wide twins for ROI
- Narrow twins for Capability
- Overemphasis on data without direction
- Siloed approaches
- Inadequate change management
- Slow time to first value

No details at all in the scope of work

The classic "1 x digital twin" in the scope of work. The problem here of course, is that with so many definitions of a twin, the probability of a "good" outcome is low, and the probability of the desired outcome is much lower.

If you have a need for a twin and can articulate your Problem, roll into the DTDP. If you can validate your problem first, do so.

Far too many specific and incoherent details in the scope of work

The opposite problem to above. "The digital twin must contain: GenAI, predictive maintenance models, be able to handle MQTT and Kafka, LOD500 3D models, browser based, low latency, mobile ready, and here's 15 diagrams from our enterprise architects. Above all, must be easy to use and create absolutely no security or privacy risks."

I like to call this the "all-the-things" twin. I've seen twin scopes that are 10 pages long of requirements, and there's absolutely no mention of desired outcomes. Usually driven by technical IT people who want to ensure "their" features / capabilities / requirements are met, and the business / problem owner has no idea what all these things mean anyway. They trust the vendor does, and they all collectively assume the thing which contains all these things will solve the problem.

If you have "fixed" points in your spec, map them as Capabilities in your DTDP and see where you land on your problem. You may be able to incorporate some, while others you may be able to prove are not needed, any hence lower the cost / complexity while achieving the outcome. The least number of Capabilities and feasible Actions & Decisions to achieve the outcome.

Weak or missing interconnections

Below the two extremes above, the next one is a lack of interconnections. In a twin that needs to help people do actual work, there must be some interconnection back to the real world. Very often, there also needs to be synchronization loops in place for change in the real world to be reflected back into the twin. The lack of these is often an indicator that the full cycle of creating and measuring change hasn't been thought through.

The key to fixing this is the Action and Decision components of the DTDP. Working through this will naturally bring out the interconnections required, and often they will be implicit. Doing this also helps avoid inadvertent siloed twin design.

Wide twins for ROI

We've spoken at length about this. Where there's ROI demanded, but a wide spread of capabilities without details of use case and change… beware.

Narrow twins for capability

The opposite to the above is when a specific use case / solution is also called upon to provide a specific capability for other / many uses. The most common one I see nowadays is "simulation." For the sim buffs out there, the idea of logical / numerical tools being universally usable / flexible is laughable. But for many non-sim people they think / have been told they need "simulation capabilities" and they use procurement of a narrow solution to "get them started" in sim-ing. Tears generally follow when excited end users try to apply it to their specific problems.

Overemphasis on data without direction

The equivalent to "all the things," "all the data," is aimed at acquiring and improving data and making it available or visualized. The end result is nearly always a dashboard. In a classical twin sense, many of these are not twins, but that is often because the virtual to real is left vague, rather than there truly being no V-R. This vagueness however, is often relegated to being less important than specifying all the data required. Look for explicit data-to-change statements. If you see none, just long lists of data, and a vague / absent V-R loop, then it's really leaving the whole desired change part to after the thing is built. I.e., reverse engineering value after delivery.

Similar to the "fixed" Capabilities situation, map the data you're mandated to use into the DTDP and work backwards to see what you need, and what you don't. I guarantee there will be other data not specified that is required, and that some data specified is not related to the problems you're trying to solve. This gives you the ability to ensure you get what is needed, and the ability to negotiate on reducing data specified-but-not-needed if possible.

Siloed approaches

The siloed approach can be hard / impossible to tell from scope / specifications. It comes from the department with budget asking a vendor / tech team to solve a cross-functional problem, without involving the other function(s).

Very tough to see before it hits you, unless you involve those who have the Problem in your problem scoping, and those who make the Decisions and Actions in your design processes. Then it all comes out in the open, and you can involve the right people in the design of the twin.

Inadequate change management

Perhaps the most talked about "reason" for failed twins, yet very often misplaced in the hierarchy of effectiveness. Talking about how people *should* use a twin is not effective change management.

Involving the effected people in the design of the solution is the correct first step in effective change management.

Slow time to first value

An interesting one is when the solution takes longer than expected (and remember expectations are usually not well defined, and indeed are often in the eye of the beholder...) or when it rolls over a financial / planning year / horizon. Some problems have a long natural frequency and measures of success are (by definition) usually lagging. Losing budget or support half way through the cycle is a sure-fire way to create a fait accompli.

If you find yourself looking at two years to see if the twin is "working," then it's time to introduce leading measures of success - often defined as measurements of desired changes in the real world. If this change is the large lag, then move down the DTDP to Actions. Are the right Actions being done at the right time. If that's too long, move down to Decisions... you get the idea. Creating a chain of coherent measures will give you a much better idea of if the twin is working as designed, and if it's not, you can investigate and take action long before declaring failure. On a purely pragmatic note, it's worth mentioning that even if your boss / problem owner is agreeable to waiting a year to find out if this "works" – that's not a good idea. People deserve to see progress. Not just owners, but also users and those who have signed off on their people changing how they work for you. Find and provide interim and specific measures to show that this is a good idea and you're in it together.

Digital twins + AI – playing to your strengths

In amongst the designing of twins to solve problems, we should discuss the genuine strengths that are emerging from the combination of digital twins + AI.

Normalization & Connection

In large organizations where many siloed systems still exist, the majority of systems are still manually run by individual users, and the users abstract away and "fill in" the differences between systems, and between systems and processes. An easy example is a factory with many different cranes, by multiple OEMs, being used for slightly different purposes. The digital twin can connect each crane to a central system, where data can be normalized through central data models and shared with central functional tools such as predictive maintenance, which can in turn push notifications into the twin, which pushes alerts to operators via mobile devices or the work management tools.

Creating Systems of Systems

Taking the factory example further, "dumb" cranes can be made smart with modern Crane Management Systems and add-ons such as sway control, collision avoidance etc. The twin that connects the crane can easily enable complex data to flow from and to the crane, but it can also house complex routing and scheduling models that turn siloed cranes into integrated sub-systems in a plant wide throughput and maintenance system. Where different OEM management systems exist, the normalization function serves to ensure critical systems level functions are usable on all cranes, without disabling or dismissing the uniqueness of any individual crane. We use the twin and internal or external AI models to preserve the unique parts that increase value and direct the individual parts that need to operate as part of a larger whole.

Human Adoption

The most critical layer is the people who operate and maintain the cranes and supporting systems, who have decades of experience watching cranes move and work and fail. The more experienced the person, the more difficult adoption can be. Especially in the semi-autonomous regime where some decisions previously made by humans are now automated, some are just suggestions requiring the human to choose to accept or reject an input (in real time inside a crowded plant). Some are still the human's full responsibility but immediately preceded or succeeded by automated actions that impact the up or downstream decisions. Adoption isn't easy. Especially on the journey to autonomy, because the journey to autonomy is really the journey of human adoption and changes to organizational governance.

The twin helps here in three ways:

1. Providing malleable user interfaces that are specific to each role / person, and that adapt to changes in environment and systems.
2. Fusing data from multiple systems to increase data driven situation awareness, including awareness of current status, predictions, and plans.
3. Giving humans the ability to accept or reject predictions and suggestions, and to see the source / accuracy / confidence of AI outputs.

Organization Adaption

Across multiple other systems in the factory, and across multiple factories, the organization needs to repeat the process of connecting, normalizing, standardizing, systematizing and adopting AI and non-dumb machines in general (not all smartness is intelligence). The other side of the journey to autonomy is governance and rules. To successfully adopt AI, organizations need to adapt to the changing required by AI and humans. This requires changes to rules, especially rules that require human signoff for everything, and requires changes to governance to make clear what decisions belong to what intelligence, and how and when these decisions are checked / validated / approved / rejected. Digitalizing the governance for AI requires far finer and more granular detail, and machines are needed to check machines operating at machine speed. Building governance into the twin is the only truly feasible option, and using AI to assess conflicts and alert humans to areas to investigate is the only way we'll stay on top of very fast-moving decision and action cycles.

Technology and Capability first versus Problem first – adopt the gentle way

If your business is run by a large central IT function and you are fighting to get a single digital twin onto the map, then do not concern yourself with defending or justifying your Problem Roadmap. Your Problem Bank has valuable Problems that will provide value to your business. Prioritize Problems that you think align to the technology roadmap or (even better), do not require anything from new capabilities. Do not chase the new shiny things unless you have to.

If you are being forced to deploy a certain capability, you have a process for that – Working Forwards. We discuss this more in Part 7. Find your class of problems that the capability is likely to help with, work through your definition and validations, and prioritize 2-3 Problems that have a high probability of needing the new capability and provide real value to the business. Align your Problem Roadmap to the Technology and move forward to create value.

Grouping to maximize problem class impact

When defining problems of problems, it can be helpful to group multiple smaller problems in order to address the larger problem piecemeal. Remember that we can build multiple contiguous narrow use cases to create larger aggregated use cases.

Grouping to maximize user benefits

Grouping by user type and / or benefit type can provide a focusing lens to solve multiple user needs within a single problem class. This also has an added benefit of providing longer term communication, and hence expectation, to the same set of users. "We're going to work with you to solve these five needs, in order to solve this business Problem."

To really hit the mark with your users, slip some small direct user benefits in that don't necessarily solve the business Problem. What do I mean by this? Give them some small wins to needs that you've discovered but that aren't important enough for the business to solve. Make their life easier and they may not thank you for it, but they're much more likely to work with you to solve the bigger Problems.

Sequence to progressively solve a larger Problem

Sequencing to solve smaller and lower risk Problems within the same larger problem class provides a readymade and logical staging of solutions. Solve Problem 1a, then 1b, then 1c. By staging around Problems, rather than Capabilities, you can often prove value and sometimes ROI early, even if only solving "half" a problem, by solving a small but valuable Problem. Measurable positive change is the catalyst for more change. Solving smaller Problems is also the tonic to "big bang" solutions that miss 10 small user problems and truly only solve "half" the Problem, providing no measurable ROI and much change and pain for users.

Sequence to progressively grow Capabilities

Similarly to the sequencing of smaller Problems, sequencing around progressive use or deployment of new Capabilities can lead to progressive value creation at lower risk. Many twin-related capabilities today are highly uncertain and fast moving (AI) or very large and cumbersome (BIM), or so blank and composable as to require genuine directional vision to be valuable (game engine visualization).

Checking your own work

In parallel to the Problem Roadmap, I always build two other roadmaps as my check and balancer:

- Data and Capability roadmap
- Change roadmap

Before you become exhausted by all this roadmap advice, let me counsel some patience. Roadmaps are tools to help you prioritize work and sequence resource allocation and investment. That's it. This is a primary role of every leader, and if you are responsible for creating new products and tools, then you need to think about this a lot. If you are accountable for creating new products and tools, then you should be reviewing these variations on the theme regularly and pushing your teams to invest to contract and compare. There is no right path, but there are many paths that create value and many dead ends that provide learnings.

Data and Capability Roadmap

The data and capability coupling comes from Connected Action mapping exercises. As you progress through connected action exercises, you will generate many similar couplings of data and capability. Start mapping out the common couplings to better understand where the same Capability and / or Data sets will be required.

Take the order of sequence from the Problem Roadmap, and chart what Capability and Data couplings are required. Large clusters of many Capabilities and significant new Data will be large bubbles.

Take the order of sequence from the Technology roadmap, and chart what Capability and Data couplings are required. Large clusters of many Capabilities and significant new Data will be large bubbles.

Juxtapose the two and look at where changing the sequence of the Problem Roadmap better aligns to technology investments.

With a few mappings under your belt, you will get a much better feel for data and capabilities versus problems, but a word of warning: don't fall into the "high-level problem" trap, and don't fall into the "high-level capability and data trap." Data in particular can become a "we need all-the-data" exercise for any sufficiently large problem. Meanwhile a capability can become so ill-defined at the high level that it can apply to every "problem." Hence why we have the DTDP. When you juxtapose

Problems, Capabilities and Data while executing the DTDP iteratively, you'll learn a lot more about efficient use of resources.

Change Roadmap

Similarly, as you start to design and deploy solutions, you will accumulate lists of changes that need to be made in the real world. Tag these with location, user type, department or function, and you will start to see patterns of change that are required by user. This is very important, as it can provide the catalyst to longer-range and more user-centric communication about change. User-centric communication doesn't mean emailing everyone in maintenance to tell them we are going to make changes. User-centric communication, as part of change management, should talk about user and business problems, and reference the good discovery work that has already occurred with those users, and the ways in which we believe these changes will present to those users (Actions and Decisions). The development of change management communications is beyond the scope of this book, but if you have experience in this space, think on what you can do with feedback and buy-in from future users, and with a map of the changes that will impact them, and the problems that we intend to solve together.

Part 7: Delivery

Focuses on iteratively delivering outputs that create the desired changes.

The great leveler. Let's talk pragmatic stuff: delivery.

General delivery advice

We are proposing that we will design and deliver changes to the real and virtual worlds, through closely connected data models and associated capabilities.

We are proposing that we will deliberately budget and plan to iterate, because we know that deliberate change in ecosystems creates unintended consequences, no matter how well designed / intentioned / analyzed / executed our work.

We are proposing that we will seek to maximize the Desired Changes and minimize the unintended changes, over a period of time, in order to deeply solve specific Problems or to maximize the value of specific designated Capabilities.

How do we use the DTDP to create great interconnected solutions?

Quick recap on DTDP

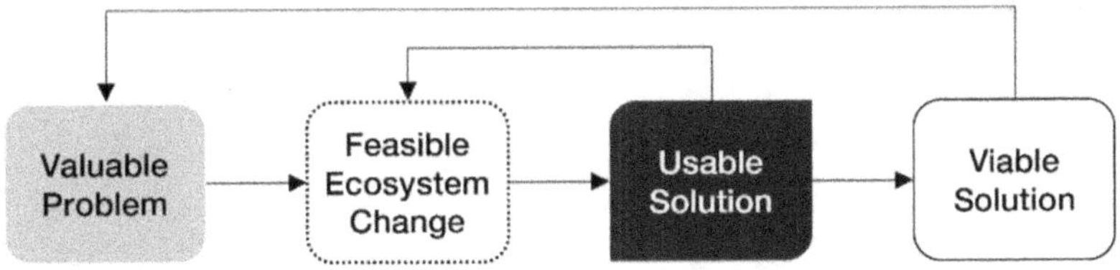

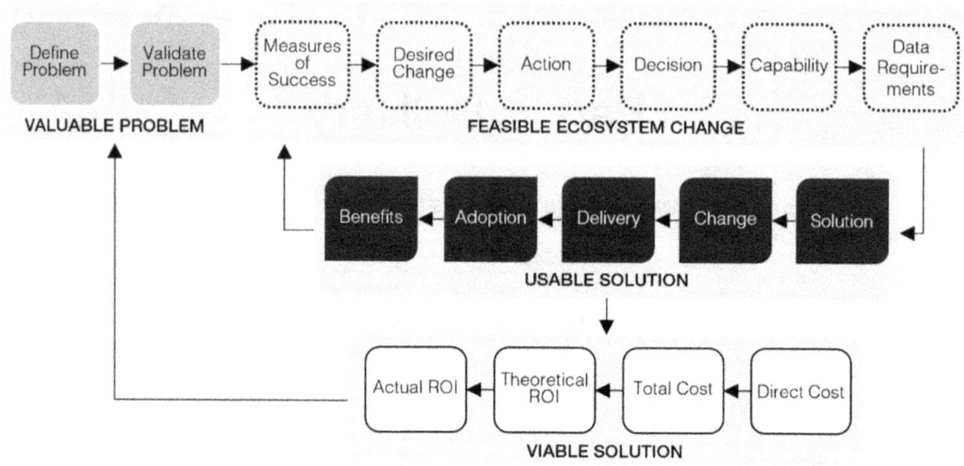

The stages and steps are:

Valuable Problem

- Define Problem
- Validate Problem

Feasible Ecosystem Change

- Measures of Success
- Desired Change
- Actions and Decisions
- Capabilities and Data

Usable Solution

- Solution
- Change
- Delivery
- Adoption and Support
- Benefits

Viable Solution

- Total Cost
- ROI

We iterate the portions of the DTDP based on the situation and stage of development.

Hippos in chat rooms

I consider there to be three large quadrupeds in the room for delivery:

- Starting points: We rarely start from a problem, we start from a solution concept or capability
- Internal versus External: Building for one group versus building to attract and retain as many groups
- Product versus Project: Project and product organizations can be very different in culture and process

Starting point patterns

Let's hit the first elephant in the room. Starting point patterns. If you are THE decision maker in your organization, perhaps you can change how your organization approaches technology. It's far more likely that you are inside an organization and you do what you're told, and for any given situation you seek to make the best of it and not break the (or too many) rules.

There are four likely places you will start in any digital twin journey:

- Problem (less likely)
- Metrics
- Existing solutions
- Capabilities (more likely)

For each starting point, we'll cover a motion for how to approach this.

For reference, I have encountered all of these. In some cases, I've had a mix of two or three in a single product where multiple stakeholders want different but related things, or existing capabilities must be incorporated into new solutions. Don't panic. The point here is to exercise your brain on how to think through how to connect the real world with Capabilities and Data.

The four motions are:

- Problems: Work backwards from Problems
- Metrics: Work backwards from Metrics
- Solutions: Work forwards from Solutions
- Capabilities: Work forwards from Capabilities

Problems: Work backwards from Problem

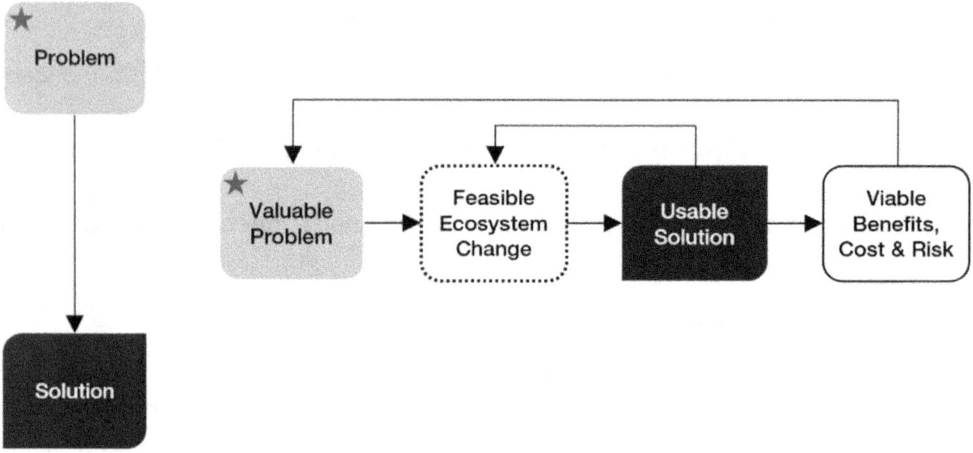

The design of a twin to solve a problem, or group of related problems, is perhaps the traditional view that most people have of digital twins. I would argue that there are very few twins in existence today that have actually been crafted to solve a specific problem. Working backwards generally creates narrow solutions, and many product creators and customers do not want narrow solutions, because they have not defined the problem. Therefore, they perceive that narrow solutions are less valuable (and / or less sellable), and thus they seek to expand the remit of the twin through increased but uncoupled capabilities (more features). We will address this explicitly by defining problems that are measurable, and measure the solving of those problems. Working backwards should give you strongly coupled change and measurable ROI. It's actually harder to create a wide twin when working backwards from a well-defined problem, because you keep getting pulled towards the problem.

Metrics: Work backwards from Metrics

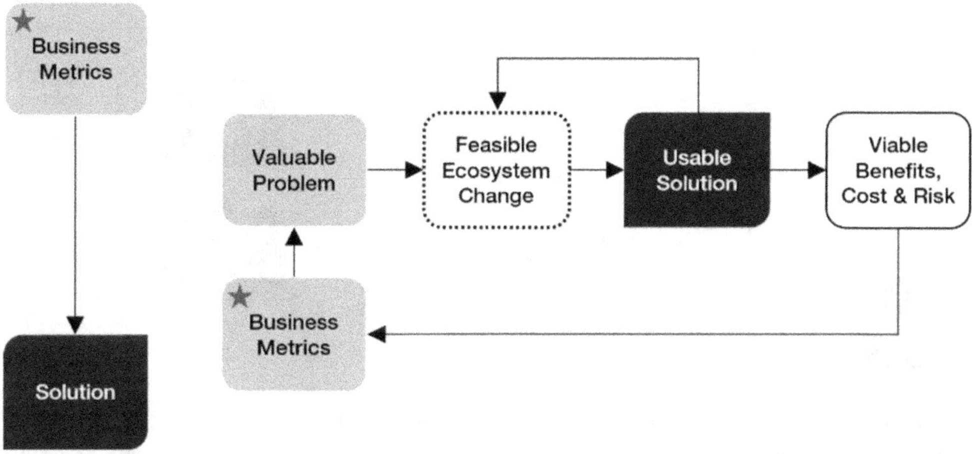

Closely related to starting with a problem, is starting with a Desired Change in a Metric. Lower downtime per operating hour. Lower energy costs per annum. Higher production per hour. The challenge with Metrics is that they are typically aggregations of many problems and actions. There might be a hundred ways of "lowering energy use," and a scope of brief may point towards "improved energy efficiency" as the desired outcome... this is not helpful.

Treat metrics as Measures of Success, and move into Problem definition to identify specific and validated Problems related to changes in the real world that could reduce energy use or improve energy efficiency etc. Treat Metrics as starting points for problem validation, then continue back through the DTDP, with the Metrics as your Measures of Success.

Work forwards from existing solution to adjacent problems

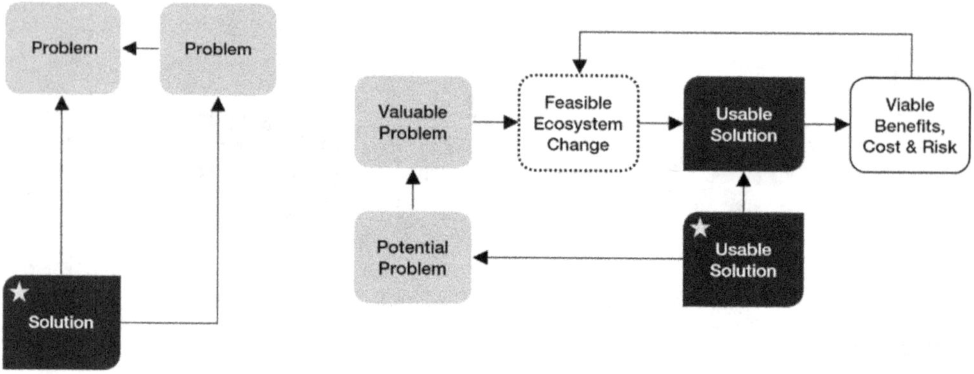

Usually, our twin is not solving a net new problem, but rather an existing and long-term problem, or there is a desire to increase the efficacy or breadth of the solution. In this case, there is always an existing solution, whether a technology or business process or even cultural / "that's how we do it here" solution, and this solution may have key attributes that *must* be maintained in any new solution. In this case, ignoring the exiting solution is a big mistake.

I show that the problem the existing solution creates is still a "potential problem," because there are always good and valid reason why an existing solution is being replaced. Besides solving the same problem as well or better, there will very likely be deeper problems that need solving or adjacent problems that prevent ROI. Many existing solutions solve "half a problem," but we use them because that's still better then not solving the problem at all, or solving it completely manually.

For both narrow and wide twins, there is a motion of working forwards to find adjacent problems that can be solved at low incremental cost / high ROI by adding data or models or specific capabilities to an existing twin. The concept of composability or configurability is important here, but more so the emphasis on finding more problems to solve or solving existing problems more deeply. A problem-first attitude is the foundation for ensuring that adjacency is ROI accretive – not just the addition of more capabilities for the sake of it. The adjacency motion is also common in digital transformation programs, and there is scope to align twin roadmaps to adjacent problems, to anchor development to incremental ROI.

Work forwards from new capabilities to problem class and then backwards to new solution(s)

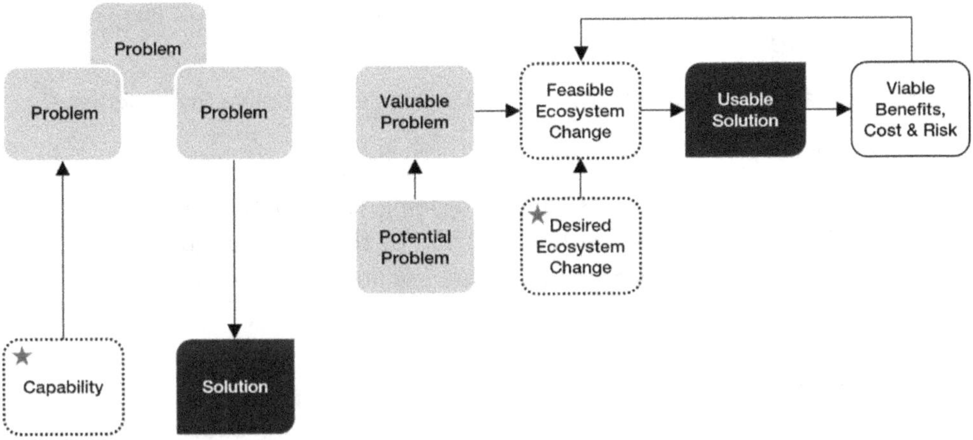

The design of twins that encompass specific capabilities is the most common twin pattern by far. The bolting together of real-time data (capability) with 3D visualization (capability) to create a twin is very often the first twin a customer buys or builds, and very often the first twin an IT vendor builds. Working forwards in this way often creates wide twins with many features, and this can seem an easier sell to all. Wide twins often suffer from lack of ROI, but that usually only appears after they have been built. We will address this by working forwards from ideated capabilities to classes of problems that these capabilities are likely to address, and then backwards to solutions. I say solutions because very often a wide twin will contain multiple narrow solutions to multiple problems.

Internal versus External

Internal teams build tools and products for their co-workers.

External teams build tools and products to sell to customers.

Both teams need to justify and sell future value in order to get budget allocated.

Internal teams can have as long or longer "sales cycles" than external teas, especially in large / fragmented organizations.

External teams can get "cheap money" from capital raises and madly build things that no one ever uses.

Both teams have users, or seek to acquire users, and both teams can build many things that no one ever uses.

Both teams can successfully deliver (budget and schedule) a project and deliver no measurable ROI.

Both teams can fail on delivery (budget and schedule) and deliver huge benefits.

Yeah... it's not simple.

There are massive commercial benefits to being focused on value creation and problem solving. I actually cut a huge section of this book on go to market and positioning and utilizing adjacency to drive upselling and retention... maybe book two.

Project versus Product

Both teams can be asked to deliver in a project mindset or a product mindset.

Project mindsets have fixed and firm cost estimates and schedules, and often detailed scopes of work (outputs), usually promised in advance to customers (internal or external). Often projects are stacked up in a roadmap or program and the team may have months or years of fixed dates ahead of them.

Product mindsets seek to deliver outcomes via targeted outputs, and seek flexibility in schedule and investment in order to iterate on outputs, with the outcome for users being uppermost in mind when measuring "success."

Many "product" teams live in project worlds. Many, many. Even when the product team is product-y (it's a word), they may live in an organization where everything must be pre-approved, fixed and firm, two-year lookaheads for resource planning etc. It is what it is.

I have met project teams who iterate and measure outcomes and reinvest with follow on projects to improve outcomes.

In 2025 I would say this whole project versus product debate is really messy and just saying "product" or "project" is potentially very misleading. Many teams now live in a hybrid world, and multiple teams in the same organization live in slightly different versions of this world, depending on the personality and seniority of their immediate leaders.

In this book, I generally take the view that you live in a project world but seek to improve outcomes iteratively.

It is my hope that if you are in a true product world, the concepts and processes described will be very familiar, though you will likely be surprised that I have extended them beyond software to change in the real world.

It is my hope that if you are in a true project world, the concepts and processes described will seem reasonable and within range of your current political capital.

Deliver to learn

You often cannot change the situation you find yourself in. Even if you do, you may find yourself in a different situation with unintended consequences. The grass is not always greener. Even if it is, there's brown patches and divots.

In all situations, it is my hope that you can see the necessity to measure outcomes and iterate investments when creating change in ecosystems. Things you designed will not happen, and things you never intended will happen, and patterns will emerge that help you learn what investments to make next.

Iterations

One of the key methods to maximizing the probability of and then the amount of value created is to iterate. Don't try and "one shot" solving complex problems that have resisted being solved for many years. Plan and budget to deliver change in successive iterations, and plan to make changes based on what you learn.

There are no hard and fast rules to iterating, but I do find many product experts are very wishy washy on what exactly we should do in these iterations, and overuse of the word agile abounds. To overcome this, here's my playbook for iterations.

Iteration 1 – Concept

The first time you iterate through on a given problem, you are in the Concept phase. You have:

- A set of Connected Action Maps, and
- A firm belief that there are ways and means of creating the Desired Change, and
- Sufficient reason to believe that these Changes will alter your Measures of Success, and
- Validated the Problem that these Measures of Success represent

You don't have:

- THE connected action maps that you'll Deliver

- Budget and Approval to try and solve this Problem
- Users or User Feedback
- Production Data on Measures of Success or Activities

You need to:

- Select which Connected Action Maps will be included in the Business Case
- Produce sufficient solution and change design documentation to support your organizations internal Business Case / Approvals (very likely you need to estimate cost and time)

Iteration 2 - Delivery

When you have made the decision to start building the solution and making Changes, you are in the Delivery phase. You have:

- The Connected Action Maps that will form the basis of the solution and the Change, and
- A firm belief that there are ways and means of creating the Desired Change, and
- Sufficient reason to believe that these Changes will alter your Measures of Success, and
- Validated the Problem that these Measures of Success represent, and
- Budget and approval

You don't have:

- Users or User Feedback
- Production Data on Measures of Success or Activities

You need to:

- Produce Concept / Wireframe / Preliminary designs to enable the Delivery team to build the solution
- Develop and deliver a complete solution design package, including the technical specifications required by your organization
- Develop and deliver a complete change proposal, including business process changes and change management considerations

Iterations 3 / 4 / n - Improvement

When you have made the decision to invest further to improve the solution, you are in the Improvement phase.

You have:

- The Connected Action Maps that are being used in the solution and the change, and
- Evidence that these ways and means create the Desired Change, and
- Sufficient reason to believe that additional or altered Desired Changes will alter your Measures of Success, and
- Evidence of how much of the Problem can be solved, and
- You have budget and approval, and
- Users and User Feedback, and
- Production Data on Measures of Success and Activities

You don't have:

- Any illusions left

You need to:

- Do whichever steps from above are required to make the Improvements needed and get approval to deliver them.

If the above doesn't suit, adopt your own ways of working. The DTDP is an iterative process itself, so iterating in ways that suits your organization is far more important than trying to strictly follow the above.

Situations

You will find yourself in many different situations across any delivery lifecycle.

The situations we'll cover:

1. Developing a scope / budget / concept for a twin
   (a) Internal tool / project
   (b) External product
   (c) Procuring a twin
2. Designing and building a new twin
   (a) Fresh canvas
   (b) Designated capability
   (c) Designated data

3. Iterating on an existing twin
    (a) Deepen
    (b) Widen

4. Problem Banking / Roadmapping.

Developing a scope / budget / concept for a twin

The starting point for the majority of twin work today is developing the concept for a twin which may never be built. This isn't a commentary on how well we develop scopes / concepts, but rather that many more innovative projects are conceived of than delivered. That's natural and proper. Ideas that shouldn't be built, or shouldn't be built right now, or that we cannot sufficiently demonstrate feasibility of, shouldn't be built.

However, it's important to recognize that there's two very different ways to enter this phase. If you're an internal tech team building what you've been told to build, you're in a quite different place to an external product team trying to build what *many* clients want. There's a lot of overlap, and the DTDP covers both, but your mindset and focus are likely to be very different. Same process, different mindset, likely different outcome.

Developing a scope / budget / concept for a twin as an Internal tool / project team

Most internal team projects are staged, with the minimum of work being done at each stage to validate if the next stage should be approved. Twins are no different.

Assumptions:

- You don't have a Problem Bank
- You do have a clear instruction on the idea but very little detail on how to achieve or the detailed what, except potentially a specific capability like "simulation"

In other words:

- You are focused on a solution and have been told to "figure out" what would work and if we should proceed

The process:

- Understand the real brief. Is this a request to solve a problem, or to deploy a Capability.

    - If it's a problem, move the process into Problem definition first. Get the right problem and validate it's a real Problem *and* it's the right problem.
    - If it's a Capability, bring the convo back to what problem(s) it's designed to solve, and how far along the Capability is. If the Capability is early / not procured, you still have time to anchor on real Problems that the Capability can solve. If it's already a done deal, see below on "Designated Capability".
- Find the right cross-functional people that need to be involved, and intro the Connected Map. Get buy-in on defining the Measures of Success and Desired Change before anything else, and anchor the team on the outcomes we want to achieve, before fixing scope in place.
- Bundle the draft Connected Action Maps and make these the basis of your concept design, retaining the other Connected Action Maps for Delivery.
- Validate your recommendations with your cross-functional team. Get one from each "world" to help you with your ~~pitch~~ business case.

Developing a scope / budget / concept for a twin as an External / product team

Genuinely new products are rare in teams developing products to take to market. If you're fortunate enough to be here, you may have a wide-open space to explore but you'll also be in this position because you have enough market feedback or customer requests or ideas from the founder to build "xyz." Likely there will be significant forward-looking ideas on how many customers will buy it and how much you can charge as well. In many cases, the benefits to your organization will have the highest scrutiny.

Assumptions:

- You have existing customers who put in lots of feature requests
- You have a founder / exec who has an "idea" to grow market share

In other words:

- You are focused on "finding" or creating the solution that will deliver the benefits to your business, and customer and sales feedback is a guide to what may work

The process:

- If possible, engage with potential customers and talk about problems. Real ones. They will very likely lean towards Capability requests, but you have a method for that too. Help them towards problems where you can, because you know that your method will work best with a real problem. Ask to talk to real-world problem holders. Suggest known problems from their industry.

- If you're answering a tender / expression of interest etc., you have a scope that you need to address. If it's sensible, address it. Easy. If it's not sensible or completely absent of any outcomes or just a list of standards, you need to dig in and start thinking. Here's some options:
  - Suggest a consulting engagement as the scoping / problem definition phase (all valuable and validated Problems go into the Customers' Problem Bank)
  - Suggest a free Connected Action Map workshop to get their real-world people engaged.
  - Develop a conforming bid using a Connected Action Map from a known industry problem, to show them how your way of working is superior to your competitors.
  - If need be, develop a non-conforming bid as well to show an innovative way of solving a similar problem, or an adjacent problem, to show that you are focused on high and repeatable ROI.

Procuring a new twin

For many organizations that wish to use twins and applied AI, the right delivery method will be to procure external capabilities, either as a service or a project.

Assumptions:

- You have defined the problems and sufficiently validated them, or at least the first problems to be solved, such that a budget for the twin can be established
- You have completed the Connected Action Mapping and have a series of maps showing feasible chains of solving the problems

In other words:

- You have a problem and you have validated various ways the problem *could* be mitigated or solved

The process:

- Decide how you are going to acquire the Data and make the changes in the real world. Develop separate scopes and budgets for this, even if you are thinking you can award to a single vendor. Don't get caught in the "software only" trap or the "hope it'll be ok" trap.
- Develop the Request for Proposal (RFP) utilizing:
  - the Valuable Problem definition
  - the bundled and pruned Connected Action Maps

- any constraints, specifications and other requirements
- a clear declaration of whether you want the vendor to:
  - Deliver the Connected Action Maps as a solution, OR
  - Use the Connected Action Maps as input to their own solution

- If you are seeking a set of Capabilities (a Wide twin), explicitly define the different data and output types, and especially the frequency and fidelity of data collection (it's not enough to say "OT and spatial data").
- Even if you are not specifying narrow problems, you should consider the likely growth of data and capabilities based on the problem you have identified. A key interim step here can be a small project to consider possible roadmaps of data and capabilities, especially if you have a Problem Bank, because this helps to ensure that the wide twin encompasses enough data types and capabilities, to solve the first sets of problems. I would advise that this is the danger point for teams who are vague on data, often just saying "Geospatial + BIM / 3D + OT" and then every twin platform vendor can honestly say they can handle this, but this high-level vagueness in no way implies the twin will solve any of the problems at all.
- If you are seeking to solve multiple specific problems, make sure the RFP makes this clear, and that Measures of Success are developed for each (this is often part of Delivery, but it's important to associate the approval of these as part of commercial milestones).
- Regardless of width / depth, I highly recommend you specify / require multiple iterations to improve outcomes, and ensure that your owners team budget and schedule similarly requires iterations. Remember, if you're truly measuring success as Desired Change in the real world, not compliance to scope or specifications, then you'll want these iterations even more than they do.

Appendix 3 includes some more information and a checklist for teams to consider when procuring twins.

Designing and building a new twin

Once you get the green light, you are in Delivery mode. At this point, you very likely have a scope / concept and hopefully some problem definition. If you have followed the DTDP, you have at least some direction on ecosystem change and hopefully a validated Problem.

An interesting wrinkle here is that in many organizations, the people making the decision on "what" to build have not at all considered "what actually" to build. They have approved investment, and approved return targets, but there's a huge grey fog of what's actually going to change. This is important because the assumptions made at this concept stage might be significantly altered or even invalidated when getting into the weeds.

But before building – design the change. As noted previously, fresh canvases are never blank. The business case has set multiple constraints in place and ideas in motion. Expectations have been set. Now you need to use these forces as levers to create positive and measurable change. Note that I mean this literally: forces have been sent in motion that will demand change. You are the change maker. This is the point of harnessing and directing these forces to begin creating positive expectations of change from those who will be most affected. Use executive buy-in to create the mandate for worker change and use the DTDP to ideate and align change with those who need to implement it.

Theres three main paths that this can go:

- Fresh canvas
- Designated capability
- Designated data

Fresh canvas

Time to design. DTDP all the way. Take the problem, validate it if you can or take the Validation and roll straight into Feasible Ecosystem Change.

Assumptions:

- You have a direction on ecosystem change or a Problem
- You have set expectations "up" that some things will change but you have not set expectations "sideways" to workers and technology teams about what will change
- If you have done Concept phase, you have Connected Action Maps, if not, you're starting at that point

In other words:

- You have direction but not substance

The process:

- DTDP, Working Backwards from a Problem
- Connected Action Maps
- Solution Design
- Change Design
- Approval to Build
- Design / Prototype
- Build
- User Testing and testing
- Change Management execution
- Go-Live
- Support

Outputs:

- Connected Action Maps
- Solution Design
- Change Design
- Design
- Change Management Plan
- Code / Integrations / Databases / Models
- Business Process rewriting and rollout
- Training

Desired outcomes:

- Live solution and change occurring in the wild with Measurements and user feedback flowing back

Designated capability

The customer (internal or external) has designated a specific Capability that must be a part of the solution. They may have a new in-house model, or a specific simulation or analytics tool that is mandated to be part of this business process, or it may be six months into a three-year SaaS contract. Whatever the reason, you need to find a way to make this capability "useful."

Assumptions:

- You have a direction on ecosystem change or a Problem
- You have a designated Capability that must be used

- If you have done Concept phase, you have Connected Action Maps, if not, you're starting at that point

In other words:

- You have direction but not substance, and you have an anchor point

The process:

- If the Capability is supportive, i.e., an analytics tool that has no impact on the actual Problem
    - Set it into your Connected Action Map as a fixed Capability, and ensure that all use cases utilize it. This should be fairly simple for authentication or reporting or business intelligence
- If the Capability is critical, i.e., a simulation tool whose outputs will be inputs into your model
    - Set it into your Connected Action Map as a fixed Capability, and run two motions – Forwards and Backwards
        - Forwards: Start with the Capability and work forwards to Decisions and Actions and Desired Changes. Attempt to solve the Problem using the Capability as the integral part of the solution. Remember that other Capabilities will be required, which is fine – work with the team to try and define a solution and change that gets as close to the Problem as possible.
        - Backwards: Work backwards from the Problem and see if the designated Capability is required to actually solve it. If it is, use the one designated, (obviously), but if it isn't, note that as well.
        - Bundle the Forwards and Backwards Maps to see if the Capability is actually *necessary* and *valuable:*
            - If you can solve the Problem without it, and without introducing additional complexity in the same domain space, suggest this
            - If you need to alter the outputs of the Capability to solve the Problem, show the proposed inputs and outputs to achieve the Decisions and Actions, so that the rationale for changing the mandated Capability is clear
- Prioritize the Connected Action Maps
- Solution Design
- Designated Capability use, inputs and outputs and any modifications required, for Approvals

- Change Design
- Approval to Build
- Design / Prototype
- Build
- User Testing and testing
- Change Management execution
- Go-Live
- Support

Outputs:

- Connected Action Maps
- Designated Capability requirements, inputs / outputs and modifications
- Solution Design
- Change Design
- Design
- Change Management Plan
- Code / Integrations / Databases / Models
- Designated Capability modification / change in process etc.
- Business Process rewriting and rollout
- Training

Desired outcomes:

- Live solution and change occurring in the wild with Measurements and user feedback flowing back

Designated data

Similar to the designated Capability, the customer (internal or external) has designated a specific data set that must be a part of the solution. This is less common than data models but I am seeing it more often, with the rise of data science teams and data investments needing to be justified (I once had a brief of "We have paid good money for this data precisely because we know you'll need it to solve this Problem, so make sure it is part of solving it). Whatever the reason, you need to find a way to make this Capability "useful."

Follow the designated Capability process, but for Data. It can be a bit janky, and I once saw a tiny dashboard off to the side that contained the designated Data but it wasn't part of any real workflow. I dislike this purely because it offends my sense of duty (letter versus spirit of a law), but you will be the one on the spot and so you'll need to follow your own heart.

Iterating on an existing twin

You have a good twin, it's solving a Problem, your model is accurate, people are using it but more importantly people are using the outputs to change what they would have done otherwise. People are excited and want more. Or, there's a huge problem sitting over / around your little Problem, and it's time to engage with the real monster. Either way, it's time to invest to iterate.

Beyond the usual, "add more Scope" or "update a model," we can use the concept of Narrow and Wide twins to bring two different motions here:

- Deepen
- Widen

Deepen

Deepening a twin or applied AI means solving an existing Problem or problem class more completely. Look to adjacent problems of the same class, or the larger problem class to which the existing twin Problem belongs.

Solving adjacent problems may require more or improved Capabilities and Data. The real-world teams and processes, however, should be substantially the same. Better yet, with a measurable win in hand, the real-world team members are your advocates for additional adjacent problems to be tackled with their help.

Deepening a solution can be thought of as deliberately varying the real-world focus left or right, and varying the virtual world capabilities and data to enable this.

Widen

Widening a twin or applied AI means adding additional Capabilities or Data to solve the same Problems at other locations / sites or different problems that require the same Capabilities / Data.

Solving the same Problem in different locations will require asset / location / site specific data streams along with he proven models and Capabilities of your solution. There is often a need to repeat the entire process of buy-in, and Connected Action Maps with real and virtual world players from the new teams, but with measurable results and advocacy from the original delivery, these things become easier, if not quicker. Change still takes time, and people need time to accept change.

Widening a solution can be thought of as deliberately varying the virtual world focus to adjacent Capabilities and Data, and varying the real-world Decisions and Actions to enable these improved Capabilities.

A note on synchronization

A particular trap for young connected players is partial decoupling from the real world. You cannot assume that the people responsible for changing the real world (replacing assets, buying new equipment, varying operating procedures etc.) are going to check in with all the connected solution teams to make sure they have or are or will re-synchronize their data feeds with the changed real world. They make decisions in their own time and way and you make yours. Progressive decoupling can cause many issues, but it can also present subtle false positives. When value starts to level off, or more correctly, the rate of change of value decreases, this is a sign to check both solution completeness as well as decoupling. A substantially solved Problem can look exactly like a partially decoupled solution in the wrong light.

Confirm the why of changes before deciding to grow or fix your solution, or to reinforce or alter your change or Measurements. Small changes in the real world can have massive impacts on data models, while large changes that are not measured go completely unobserved by de-coupled data models.

Part 8 – The future

Focuses on the practicalities of delivering digital twins and applied AI, emphasizing iterative improvement, adaptability to constraints, and achieving real-world change through connected solutions.

In the realm of digital twins and applied AI, there are many pushing the boundaries and many struggling to take a first step. I have personally seen large organizations where these two situations coexist. This book is wide, with specific (narrow details), and aimed at those who live in large organizations and desire to create connected change. By necessity I have glossed over 100s of details and potential situations that you may encounter. As a practitioner, I encounter new ideas, new models and new twists on old failure modes every week. This realm of explicitly connecting new capabilities with real-world work is big. Very big. There's a LOT of space to explore and spread your wings.

Disruptions and enhancements

Human work

The great potential disruption we face at the time of writing (early 2025) is the disruption of real-world work. There are many forms of "work," and the confluence of multiple technologies is leading to great tremors in the force. I posit that the gulf between technology and the real world, rather than model accuracy and capability, is going to throttle the speed of adoption more than any single technology. The investment into AI and robotics dwarfs the investment into transforming how we work with technology by perhaps 1000 to 1. Humans, with their highly trained and arguably over fitted models, are the almost fixed constant in the world of work.

GenAI

Gen AI is moving fast. Far too fast for anyone except an agentic newsletter to keep up with. I love working across models and changes and RAGs and agents, but I resist being pulled into any one for longer than about six months, at least for now. That's just long enough to build something, iterate it, play with it, and discard it for the next shiny thing. It's far too short a period for an organization to implement and discard though. I highly recommend to builders to keep building, but I recommend to organizations to build to easily replace whatever models they're using today. Replacing models quickly and creating rapid and effective outcomes in the real world, is where money is made for organizations who do real work.

Agents and intelligent automation

There is a lot of confusion at the moment as to what agents are, could be, should be, will be. Agentic workflows are very exciting and will perhaps be the actual killer application of AI in the late 2020s. I think there is a lot of cross over with control systems and architecture, and it saddens me to see so many neophyte agent builders ignoring the huge body of work on controlling and managing the real world. Similarly, a huge amount of real-world work is still done in excel, and with machines that have no digital capabilities at all, inside organization structures and governance that demand that humans take specific legal responsibilities for outcomes and risk and injuries. Agents with agency, and machines with agency, and humans collaborating with agents, and having their own agency reduced, are all going to occur in parallel. Without a doubt AI is still only getting started, and the impact on Decisions will be massive and irreversible.

Robotics

The leviathan is awakening. Robotics gives digital eyes and brains the means to create direct real-world change to isolated / unconnected systems. Combine this with autonomy, and we have real agency. Ironically, it is feasible to create isolated non-human agency... whether that's "general intelligence" or "super intelligence" may be of less import than how much agency it has. It also raises the very real specter of humans sharing the world with non-human entities, and working alongside entities who live in the RACI and the delegation of authority and are present in metaverse meetings... the whole debate on how "AI" they are will be moot. They'll be co-workers, and we'll need to keep evolving as individuals and organizations to make this work. Robots with agency are even earlier on the adoption curve than agents and their impact on Actions will be massive and irreversible.

Metaverse

The mighty metaverse. I will state, categorically, that I really don't think the virtual meeting room with life like avatars is the killer metaverse application. I spend an inhuman amount of time on teams, zoom and similar and I cannot imagine how bored I will be in a "virtual boardroom" talking to the same 10 people over and over again.

I think the real use of the metaverse is to place geographically remote people into specific visual contexts that improve group decision making. Boards reviewing safety incidents with immersive playbacks and agentic investigators, providing real context and satisfying individual inquiries to gain enhanced individual situation awareness and data histories. Military, police and emergency response command and control. Predicted scenario description and analysis. There's quite a few I can think of. Also, I'm sure MSFT will put a metaverse option in Teams so please don't build this and then get wrecked by them.

Skating to the puck

So, what's my advice to players in this funny confluence of worlds?

Know your domain (and limitations)

Strong coupling that leads to positive repeatable outcomes in the real world demands an understanding of that portion of the real world. The real world is big. It's also messy. At the lowest level, it's also odd and probabilistic (quantum), and much of our ways of working are empirical, not first principles driven. That is to say, they work, and we can show they work, but when pushed to show why and how they work, there's a lot of hand waving and gap filling by humans. There's also a huge amount of waste and distressing repeats of poor outcomes.

Your choice on what part of the real world to change has a massive impact on what kind of work and decisions are made and what kinds of abstractions and uncertainties exist and are papered over by humans. Hospital HVAC / emissions = easy. Optimization of patient health across many disparate government agencies in real time = hard. They're both "healthcare," but they're different worlds, and there's huge overlapping adjacent problems in every direction.

There are very few people who have real and demonstrable experience solving problems by designing change across the real and virtual worlds. There are millions of management consultants who have implemented digital transformations and new software implementations globally. There's millions of architects and construction workers who have built high-rises using specialized software and hardware tools. 99.999% of them did what they were told and had absolutely no skin in the outcome, and did the same thing the same way the next time for a different organization with different problems. We paper over the details and measure the abstracted financial outcomes and those who didn't create the new problems are left to deal with it any way they can. We have built the modern world this way, and it works, and there's a huge amount of waste and distressing repeats of poor outcomes.

If you choose to enter this world and play for keeps, then I urge you to narrow down to a portion of the real world where real and measurable change can be created in the next 12 months, and which has many adjacent problems that people will pay you to solve for them. Create momentum through real change and leverage new technology to create more and improved change. There's no shortage of problems to solve... and no shortage of new and exciting technology to try out... and I suspect if you position yourself to create outcomes, rather than deploy capability X, you will differentiate yourself in a very positive way.

There's also the old adage of loving the problem. This is often misinterpreted as "you need to be obsessed with something and I'm not obsessed with anything." That's not what it means at all. Obsession with a topic is not loving a problem. Loving a problem means you love the feeling of making progress on solving that problem. It means you love creating outcomes, for real people who have real problems. Remember I spoke of empathy and courage? Here's where they really come in handy. If you love the problem, you can pick yourself up every time you fail, and get back into it, excited about what you learned and determined not to repeat that mistake. If you love the problem, you can pick up and discard shiny things very quickly, based on whether they help solve the problem or not. Best of all, the people you work with will see and feel your genuine desire to create change. You can't fake that, or at least not for long, and trust me it's very draining to "fake it til you make it." Better to love the problem and be on a journey of solving it in better and more complete ways. Even better yet, you can love more than one problem, and there's no shortage of problems to solve. In fast moving and uncertain worlds, I find that true sustainability is loving to help people by solving real problems for those people.

Problems I love

Speaking of... here's the problems I love. I read and write and work on these, and chase work in these areas, and find people who also love these things and we have great conversations, and I learn, learn, learn:

- Enhanced situation awareness
- Probabilistic versus Logical decision making and governance
- Predictions, Prescriptions and Prescience
- Hybrid decision making (AI + humans)

I think the catchall is that last one. Hybrid decision making. There's a possible future where machines make the vast majority of decisions for us, and most machines and systems are autonomous or at least semi-autonomous. Between now and then is a huge journey to autonomy, where humans and machines need to figure out how and what and where and when and why and how much we collaborate and work together in parallel or sequentially and who is responsible for what when etc. Society itself needs to alter irrevocably to enable this, as does leadership, strategy, general, organizational and resource management and governance. Good space to play in if you love that kind of thing.

Summary

Summarizes the iterative approach to delivering interconnected solutions, highlighting key lessons, real-world integration, and maximizing ROI through measurable, adaptive change.

Conclusions are always difficult. As professional product builders who strive to create ecosystem change, I hope you can see that there are not many "conclusions" to our line of work. There are periodic budget conclusions. There are deprecations of old tools. But the vast majority of the problems we chase do not "end". They morph, they grow and decline and grow, but they are fed by work and energy inputs and friction and entropy. They end when the real world stops producing useful outputs. In other words, they don't end, they just change, and in the changing, unexpected things happen.

How then to summarize a book about things that don't end?

Fundamentals

The digital twin ecosystem comprises the real world, virtual worlds (existing and new), and their interconnections. We need to design change across them all to maximize the probability of achieving our desired change in the real world.

Digital twins are not just virtual representations, but patterns for creating real-world change. The interconnection of virtual capabilities with real-world change is vital and is what separates twins and applied AI from "software" and "models" and "processes" alone.

Strong coupling between virtual and real worlds is crucial for effective narrow digital twins, while loose coupling enables wide twins to deploy new capabilities at low cost. We design to achieve outcomes at acceptable time, cost, risk and change management – we don't gold plate to maximize fidelity.

"Banking" real and validated problems provides a far better prioritization signal than technology capability programs or vendor ideas. Clear and measurable problems don't imply "solvability," nor are they the only needs for an organization – but they do provide clear ROI and help teams focus on real problems, rather than shiny things.

Invest to define and validate a real Problem. Specificity forces consideration and helps to discard non-problems and break up bundles of problems. The Problem is **[What]**, it affects **[Who, Where and When]**. We need to **[Change]**, because **[Why]**.

Digital twins and applied AI should be explicitly designed to create change in the real world that can be measured and improved in the virtual. Benefits come from strong Virtual to Real connections, synchronization and measurement of change comes from strong Real to Virtual connections. ROI comes from having both.

The real world is not siloed, but our organizations and solutions often are.

Digital twins are best used to solve specific problems within larger digital transformations by implementing domain-specific AI solutions. Digital twins cross and interconnect organizational silos well, while applied AI solves domain specific problems well. Together, they solve down domains and across organizational boundaries.

The complexity of real-world systems often exceeds our ability to model them completely or sufficiently accurately. We still must make and measure changes in order to improve. We measure and iterate to discover and exploit emergence of changes in the real world.

We are proposing that we will design and deliver changes to the real and virtual worlds, through closely connected data models and associated capabilities.

We are proposing that we will deliberately budget and plan to iterate, because we know that deliberate change in ecosystems creates unintended consequences, no matter how well designed / intentioned / analyzed / executed our work.

We are proposing that we will seek to maximize the desired changes and minimize the unintended changes, over a period of time, in order to deeply solve specific problems or to maximize the value of specific designated Capabilities.

The Digital Twin Design Process (DTDP) offers a structured yet adaptable approach to creating and managing digital twins, focusing on maximizing the probability of repeatable, high-ROI outcomes. It emphasizes solving valuable Problems, enabling feasible changes in ecosystems, and ensuring the usability and viability of solutions. Central to the DTDP is its flexibility, allowing practitioners to adjust its steps based on real-world constraints and situations. The only rigid element of the process is the

Connected Action Map, which maps real and virtual-world actions to ensure logical coherence and peer-reviewed effectiveness.

The DTDP teaches us to: define the desired change across the whole chain of data-capabilities-decisions-actions (i.e., virtual and real), and measure activity and outcomes at each step, in order to iteratively improve elements and chains to improved desired changes.

At the heart of the DTDP is the drive to integrate real-world change with virtual capabilities. This involves iteratively designing, delivering, and improving solutions to adapt to new problems and unintended consequences that arise during implementation. The process systematically measures and improves real-world changes through virtual representations, aiming to leverage positive outcomes while mitigating risks and costs.

The DTDP underscores the importance of designing not just software solutions but also real-world changes. By connecting concept, delivery, and improvement phases, the process ensures solutions evolve in alignment with real-world needs. Its ultimate goal is to create interconnected, adaptive systems that consistently deliver measurable value in real-world applications.

Defining a twin like or applied AI solution as a *Product* sets the bar high for human centered solutions, usability and support. The irony of Applied AI is that 99% of use cases in the real world have the "AI" steps sandwiched between multiple human steps in any given workflow, setting real limits of actual change and value creation. Designing the end-to-end solution for the entire chain from AI to real world and back, regardless of how many higher order steps there are, is the path to maximizing desired change.

DTDP Summary

At its highest level, the DTDP seeks to maximize the probability of repeatably achieving positive ROI outcomes. It does this by:

- Focusing efforts on valuable Problems (which have high potential to create returns)
- Designing Feasible and coherent changes in the real and virtual worlds
- Developing solutions & change that are Usable and Viable

In Concept / Scoping, we iterate Feasible Ecosystem Change until we have a bundled set of chains that conceptually solves the Problem. High-level estimating of solution and change may be enough to support the business case – otherwise we execute Usable and Viable steps to develop a complete design and plan.

If Procuring, we use our Concept as the basis of a Scope of Work to give vendors the clearest possible direction and requirements to solve our Problems in feasible, usable and viable ways.

If Delivering, we use our Concept to verify Feasibility, and then we dive into detailed Usability and Viability to design, build and deploy our solution and create our Changes. Detailed design and solution design may force changes to our feasible chains. So be it. Refer to the Connected Action Maps to assess impacts or repeat the exercise to identify alternate feasible ways of creating the Desired Change.

When Iterating, take feedback from the field and revisit the Connected Action Maps to modify or develop new chains to deepen value or widen capability. Concept – Procure / Deliver and repeat.

If it's your first twin, or the first digital twin or applied AI in your organization, or if you have the choice:

- Build a narrow twin on a small validated Problem and deliver ROI, then
- Build an adjacent narrow twin on an adjacent problem that requires only incremental investment (e.g., uses 80% of data from first twin and / or the same data model and / or an additional data set to retrain your existing model) and deliver subsequent very high incremental ROI, then
- Build a wide twin around your narrow twins that provides a foundational Capability aimed at the same problem class, that requires successive wide and deep changes to overcome, and use that to find out what you need to create a genuine interconnected applied AI solution that substantially solves the problem class.

In a wide + narrow world, I like to proceed like this:

1. Iteration 1

    (a) Use the DTDP and work backwards from a horizontal problem class to create a narrow use case

   (b) Start from the narrow Capabilities and work forwards towards the problem class to create greater context
   (c) Bank potential adjacent problems

2. Iteration 2 / 4 / 6
   (a) Take operational feedback to extract an adjacent problem that likely needs existing Capabilities
   (b) Use the DTDP and work backwards from the adjacent problem to create a new narrow use case
   (c) Start from the combined narrow Capabilities and work forwards towards the problem class to create greater context
   (d) Deliver new change and solution

3. Iteration 3 / 5 / 7
   (a) Take operational feedback on how an existing narrow use case could potentially be more complete (deepened)
   (b) Review the Connected Action Maps to modify Change or improve the Solution
   (c) Deliver modified changes and solutions

Love the problems you invest into and share that love by helping real people solve real and valuable Problems.

Appendix 1 – Checklists

More advice and guides on specific areas

Visit the website to download guides, templates and checklists.

www.designingdigitaltwins.com

Digital Twin Design Process (DTDP)The DTDP is iterative, but iterative processes can be confusing.

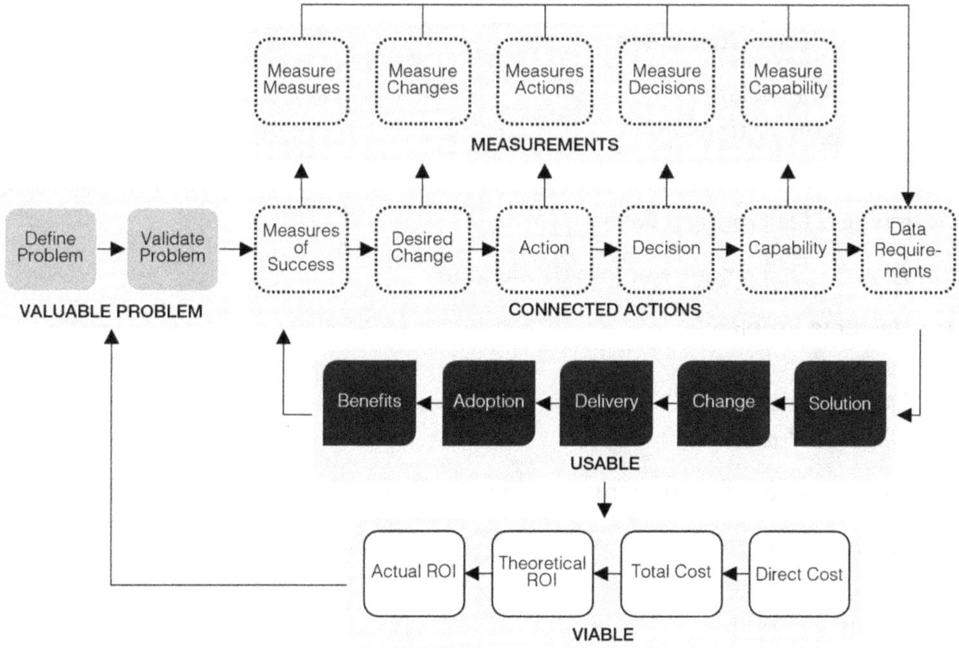

The linear paths are shown below.

Building a Problem Bank

- Valuable Problem

Scoping a Concept

- Valuable Problem
- Connected Actions

Preparing to Procure

- Valuable Problem
- Connected Actions
- Solution Design (optional)

Designing the Twin use cases

- Valuable Problem
- Connected Actions
- Measurements

Designing & Delivering a Twin

Iteration 1 – Deliver and Put into Production

- Valuable Problem
- Connected Actions
- Measurements
- Usable Solution

Iteration 2 – Use Measurements to make changes to improve real-world change

- Connected Actions
- Usable Solution
- Viable Solution

Iteration 3 – Validate or Extend Problem Solving and make iterative improvements to effectiveness and efficiency

- Valuable Problem
- Connected Actions
- Measurements
- Usable Solution
- Viable Solution

Iteration n – Measure and Improve as required

- Connected Actions
- Usable Solution
- Viable Solution

Extending / Deepening a Twin

- Follow process for Designing & Delivering a Twin

Roadmapping Problems

- Problem Bank
- Connected Actions
- Develop logical sequences of:
    - Problems to solve
    - Data to be acquired / added / improved
    - Additional Capabilities vs Problems
- Map paths of Problems vs Value created

Connected Action Mapping

Visit *www.designingdigitaltwins.com* to download connected action map resources.

The Connected Action Map process is:

- Work backwards from the Problem to develop multiple Connected Action Chains:
    - For a given Problem, develop Measures of Success.
    - For those Measures, determine what the Desired Changes in the real world are that would move the Measures in the right direction.
    - Ideate the Actions and Decisions required to create the Desired Changes.
    - Ideate what Capabilities are required to initiate / create / enable / allow the Decisions to be taken that create the Actions.
    - Analyze the outputs of the Capabilities to determine what Data is required as inputs.
- Prune chains that are infeasible, unsupported or otherwise low probability.
- Bundle chains with coherent Actions that have very high probabilities of creating the Desired Change.
- Work forwards from Data, grouping Data to Capabilities etc. to check the feasibility of the bundled chains and see if any other changes or ideas emerge.

- Develop Measurements for each link in each bundled chain to measure activity, inputs and outputs if possible.
- Deliver all of the outputs to the solution design or Procurement stage.

Ideally, you can work backwards from a Defined Problem.

In practice, if you start with "specified" Capabilities & Data:

- Add the Capabilities and Data to the Connected Action Map.
- Work backwards as per above, and see what chains involve your specified Capabilities & Data.
- Where feasible chains utilize specified Capabilities & Data, you have an easy win.
- If no feasible chains utilize your specified Capabilities, leave those chains in place (they are, after all, the ideated feasible chains to solve a real Problem), and research how others are using those Capabilities in similar industries or for people with similar problems (remembering that many problem classes are not unique to any one industry, e.g., predictive maintenance has a lot of common problems across all industrial orgs).
- Work forwards from your Capabilities to ideate what Decisions and Actions could be taken and what Desired Changes could be made.
- Work backwards from Measures of Success to connect the Desired Changes to Measures / Problems, and then keep working backwards to check the feasibility of the "specified chains."
- Iterate working backwards from real Problems and forwards from the specified Capabilities to establish Connected Action Map chains that are coherent and contiguous.
- If you truly cannot find any chains that connect real Problems to specific Capabilities, then you may well have to build a wide twin with no real problems. It happens, and at least you tried to avoid this. The added benefit will be that you have seeded your Problem Bank, and have multiple potential Connected Action Maps already done. If I was the product manager, I would immediately shift the most promising of these into position as the follow on or extended use cases for the wide twin, to try and ensure that they will be built as soon as possible after the initial wide twin.

Connected Action Map tools

The simplest tool to use for mapping is Miro or any other online "whiteboard" type tool, as it is extensible and malleable and remote participants can see and hear everything going on and can log in to the board and directly participate.

At its simplest, I usually set up four spaces on the canvas:

- Problem
- Connected Action Map
- Bundles
- Parking Lot / Notes

Templates for Problem Definition and Connected Action Mapping exercises can be found at *www.designingdigitaltwins.com*.

Problem

With Defined and Validated Problems, the problem space for Connected Action Mapping is not needed. I usually include it though because throughout the process it's very common for more details to emerge about the Problem, or for adjacent / associated problem information to be brought up. I have found separating this out helps people to separate out "bringing up issues" and "solutionizing".

Put the Problem Definitions and any links to Validation or other work front and center, so people can keep referring back to THE Problem.

Define the problem as you see it:

Re-state the problem starting with the other prompts (who/when/where/what):

The Problem is ***[What]***, it affects ***[Who, Where & When]***.
We need to ***Change***, because ***What***.

Connected Action Map

At its simplest, the Connected Action Map is a large space with the Connected Action Map steps along the top, and dividing lines "down the page", to create vertical areas for each step (Measures of Success, Desired Change etc.) so that participants can "post" suggestions into each area, and create connections between each step (to create the chains).

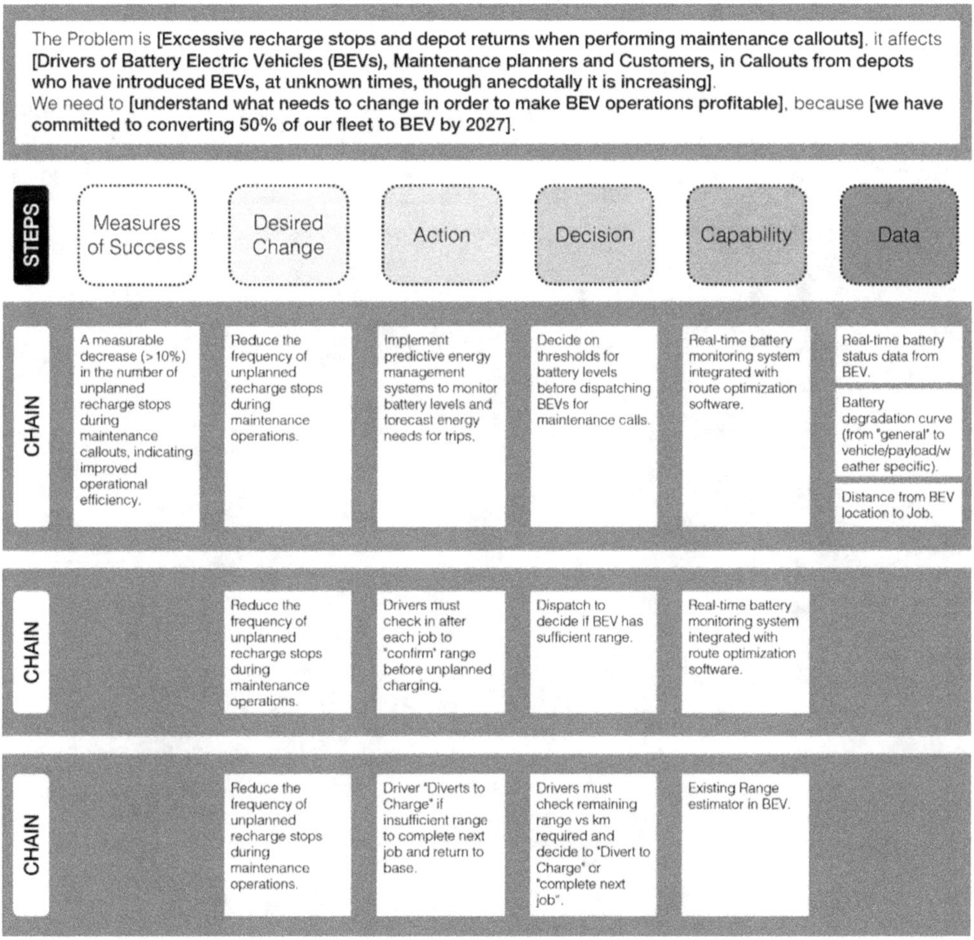

The Map is very simple, by design. There's no magic wand here… but of course Miro has some great AI functionality that allows you to summarize work done, as do many other similar solutions.

To Prune, I usually copy the raw chains that we want to keep down below, and leave the approved chains in place, but I have seen teams drag pruned chains down to leave approved in place. Either way works.

Bundles

I recommend Bundling the approved chains in a separate area, and the only difference here is the order. Start at the Data and Capabilities, and work "forwards" to Decisions & Actions, and hence Desired Change and Measures of Success.

Bundle 1 - Reduce the frequency of unplanned recharge stops during maintenance operations

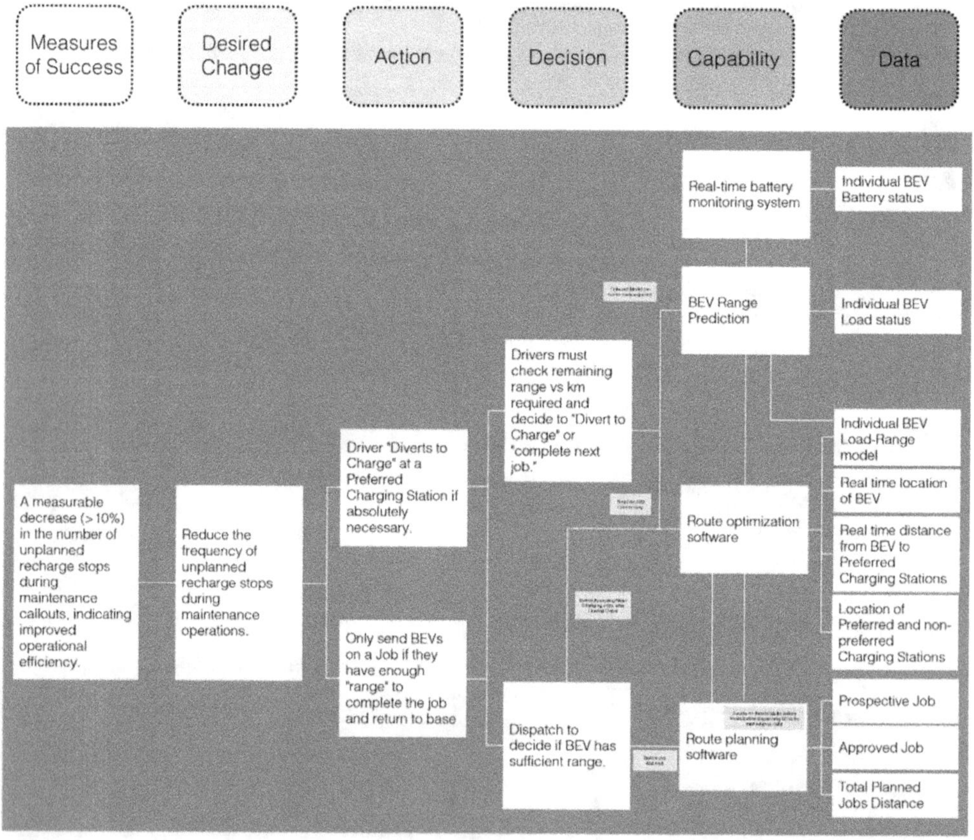

The Problem is **[Excessive recharge stops and depot returns when performing maintenance callouts]**, it affects **[Drivers of Battery Electric Vehicles (BEVs), Maintenance planners and Customers, in Callouts from depots who have introduced BEVs, at unknown times, though anecdotally it is increasing]**.
We need to **[understand what needs to change in order to make BEV operations profitable]**, because **[we have committed to converting 50% of our fleet to BEV by 2027]**.

Parking Lot

The proverbial "parking lot" is an important area, as many issues and ideas will come up during workshops. Give people a space to park things regardless of importance or source, and later on you will have some great ideas and insights into the teams. It also can help workshops flow along when an intractable idea or issue appears, and one or more participants cannot move past them. Get it into the parking lot, and commit to following up later with them to understand it better.

A word on Left-Right and Right-Left

I am Australian, so I read left to right. The "working backwards" from left to right makes sense to me, but if you come from a culture where the reverse is true, feel free to reverse the direction of steps, and put the Measures of Success on the right and work backwards to the left.

Appendix 2 – Problem Definition Checklist for Product Owners

*The Problem is **[What]**, it affects **[Who, Where and When]**. We need to **[Change]**, because **[Why]**.*

1. **Understand the Problem Context**
   - What is the problem?
     - Clearly articulate the problem in specific terms
     - Use a standard template: The problem is What, it affects Who, Where & When]. We need to Change, because Why
   - Who does it affect?
     - Identify specific individuals, teams, or user groups impacted by the problem (e.g., users, stakeholders, customers)
   - Where and when does it occur?
     - Define the locations, scenarios, or timeframes where the problem manifests
   - Why does it matter?
     - Explain the urgency or significance of addressing this issue (e.g., impact on business metrics, user satisfaction, financial outcomes)
2. **Assess Business Impact**
   - What business metrics are affected?
     - Identify measurable business outcomes impacted by the problem (e.g., revenue loss, operational inefficiencies, safety issues)
   - What evidence supports the business impact?
     - Provide data showing how the problem affects financial or operational metrics
   - How does solving this problem align with organizational goals?
     - Ensure alignment with strategic priorities or broader initiatives

3. **Investigate Root Causes**
    - Have you analyzed root causes?
        - Use frameworks like Root Cause Analysis or Design Thinking to identify underlying causes
    - Are there interrelated problems?
        - Consider whether this issue is part of a larger system of interconnected problems
4. **Define User Problems**
    - What are the user challenges?
        - Document user pain points and frustrations related to the problem.
    - Are user problems linked to business problems?
        - Clearly connect user challenges to their impact on business metrics
    - Have you gathered user input?
        - Conduct interviews, shadowing, or observations to validate user experiences
5. **Specify Process and Operational Impacts**
    - Which processes are failing or conflicting?
        - Identify operational inefficiencies or process breakdowns contributing to the problem
    - Are there edge cases or exceptions?
        - Document unusual scenarios that highlight process limitations
6. **Validate Problem Scope and Scale**
    - Is the problem measurable?
        - Identify metrics that quantify the scale and frequency of the issue.
    - Who experiences it most frequently?
        - Specify individuals or roles most affected by the problem (e.g., "Jim in maintenance")
    - What is the cost of inaction?
        - Estimate financial or operational losses if the problem remains unsolved
7. **Avoid Premature Solutionizing**
    - Have you avoided jumping to solutions
        - Are you describing your favored solution in "problem" language?

- Focus on understanding and validating the problem before brainstorming solutions
- Are ideas documented separately?
  - Maintain an "Ideas" file for potential solutions without letting them distract from defining the problem

8. **Engage Stakeholders Effectively**
   - Who should be involved in defining the problem?
     - Include:
       - Problem owners (budget holders)
       - People who live with or are impacted by the problem
       - Individuals who have previously tried solving it
       - Upstream and downstream consumers of affected processes
   - Have you aligned with user work environments?
     - Spend time observing users in their real-world contexts for deeper insights

9. **Evaluate Problem Feasibility for Solutions**
   - Can this problem be solved with existing resources / tools?
     - Determine if a digital twin, AI, or other technology is necessary—or if non-technological solutions suffice
   - Are there cultural / political barriers to solving this issue?
     - Assess whether non-technological factors (e.g., organizational silos) are contributing to the problem

10. **Make a Go / No-Go Decision on the Problem**
    - Is there enough clarity to proceed?
      - Ensure problems are defined in terms of measurable business and user metrics
    - Does solving this problem justify investment?
      - Confirm that expected benefits outweigh costs and risks
    - Is further investigation needed before moving forward?
      - Decide whether additional time / resources should be allocated for deeper analysis

Appendix 3 – Procurement

This section outlines a methodology for those procuring twins to evaluate and select solutions that deliver measurable real-world impact.

Procurement is a primary mechanism for many twin users to acquire twin capabilities. Poorly designed procurement processes often lead to misaligned solutions, wasted investments, and operational friction.

Key Procurement Considerations

Strategic Alignment and Problem Validation

Procurement must begin with a **value-driven problem statement** that defines the real-world outcomes the solution must achieve (e.g., 15% reduction in unplanned downtime, 20% improvement in asset utilization). This requires collaboration between operational teams, finance, and technology stakeholders to map pain points to quantifiable metrics.

Technical Architecture Evaluation

Asset owners should assess solutions against six core technical criteria:

1. **Interconnection Robustness**: Verify bidirectional data flows (real-to-virtual and virtual-to-real) with synchronization frequencies matching operational decision cycles (e.g., sub-second for control systems vs. hourly for predictive maintenance) - how and when will the right data be acquired and what is the allowable time between collection to making Decisions and taking Actions? The key question is: can we get the right data and make the changes in the real world (Decisions & Actions) in time to solve the problem?
2. **Ecosystem Integration**: Open APIs and pre-built connectors for critical systems (CMMS, SCADA, ERP) will help avoid full-platform replacements. Similarly, for legacy applications or isolated data models that are required, the vendor needs the capability of creating integrations.
3. **Model Transparency**: Require documentation of AI training data sources, validation methodologies, and ongoing monitoring processes for model drift.

4. **Change Measurement**: Ensure the solution includes instrumentation to track both solution adoption (user actions) and real-world impact (equipment performance shifts).
5. **Fidelity Scalability**: Confirm the solution allows gradual increases in data resolution without requiring full reimplementation.
6. **Governance Controls**: Mandate role-based access, audit trails, and version control for AI models / digital twin configurations.

Vendor Qualification Framework

Effective vendor selection requires evaluating four capability dimensions:

Dimension	Evaluation Criteria
Domain Depth	3+ years of industry-specific deployments; case studies with comparable asset profiles
Technical Maturity	Existence of DevOps pipelines for model updates; cybersecurity certifications (e.g. ISO 27001, SOC 2)
Change Management	Documented user adoption rates >70%; training programs integrating with existing workflows
Commercial Model	Clear ROI timelines (≤18 months); flexible licensing aligning with solution maturity/iteration stages

Implementation Risk Mitigation

Consider a staged validation process to de-risk delivery:

1. **Concept Proof**: 8–12-week sprint to define and validate Problem and to validate core AI / digital twin functionality against historical datasets.
2. **Limited Pilot**: 3-month live deployment on 1 Problem, against 2 assets/sites with parallel manual process (Decision & Action) tracking.
3. **Scaled Rollout**: Gradual expansion tied to achievement of predefined success thresholds.

Contractual Safeguards

Procurement contracts should include:

- **Performance Clauses**: Financial penalties or "included" (i.e. no additional charge) re-work/re-training for missing accuracy thresholds (e.g., <90% prediction accuracy)

- **Data Portability**: Mandatory data schema exports and model weight transfers upon contract termination
- **Innovation Escalators**: Commitments to annual or semi-annual capability upgrades reflecting model / AI advancements.

Example Checklist for Procuring Twins

Pre-Procurement Planning

☐ Document operational pain points mapped to strategic objectives

☐ Conduct Problem Definition and Validation

☐ Conduct Connected Action Mapping and develop bundled feasible chains

☐ Establish cross-functional evaluation team (operations, IT, legal, finance)

☐ Define minimum viable interoperability requirements with existing systems

☐ Develop a solution design OR specify that the successful vendor must develop a solution design

RFP Development

☐ Specify required synchronization frequencies (R-V and V-R) for critical data types

☐ Require evidence of model performance in comparable noise / drift environments

☐ Demand transparency on computational resource requirements (cloud vs. edge)

Vendor Evaluation

☐ Conduct scenario-based testing with historical outage / incident data

☐ Audit vendor's model retraining processes and change management playbooks

☐ Validate cybersecurity protocols through third-party penetration testing

Contracting

☐ Include service-level agreements (SLAs) for model accuracy, uptime, and support response times

☐ Negotiate rights to independent solution performance audits

☐ Define clear ownership boundaries for generated IP / derivative models

Implementation

- ☐ Establish baseline metrics for both solution performance (e.g., prediction latency) and operational outcomes
- ☐ Implement dual-track validation (solution outputs vs. real-world changes)
- ☐ Schedule quarterly business reviews to assess value realization

Post-Implementation

- ☐ Monitor solution "decision yield" - % of recommendations driving verifiable actions that create the Desired Change
- ☐ Track synchronization decay rates across critical data streams
- ☐ Conduct annual total cost of ownership (TCO) analysis vs. achieved ROI

Critical Failure Modes to Beware of:

1. **Feature-Driven Procurement**: Selecting solutions based on technical capabilities rather than problem-solving feasibility
2. **Static Synchronization**: Failing to re-evaluate data fidelity needs as operational environments evolve
3. **Governance Neglect**: Allowing uncontrolled model / dashboard proliferation without centralized oversight
4. **Adoption Myopia**: Over-investing in technical deployment while under-resourcing change management.

By anchoring procurement processes to real-world value creation and systematically addressing implementation risks, asset owners can transform digital twins and applied AI from isolated IT projects into strategic operational assets. The checklist above provides a battle-tested framework developed through analysis of successful deployments across mining, energy, and the manufacturing sectors.

Appendix 4 – FAQs

Frequently Asked and Infrequently Asked but Important Questions

Q. What is a digital twin, and how does it differ from other virtual representations?

A: A digital twin is a virtual representation of a specific portion of the real world, designed with two-way interconnections that synchronize at defined frequencies and fidelities. Its purpose is to create measurable and repeatable changes in the real world, which can then be improved upon in the virtual space. Unlike static 3D models or simulations, a digital twin is inherently dynamic, strongly connected to real-world data, and focused on solving real-world problems rather than just visualizing or simulating them.

Q: Why are digital twins critical for solving cross-silo problems in industrial organizations?

A: Digital twins excel at addressing cross-silo challenges because they integrate data, processes, and systems across traditionally isolated domains. In industrial organizations, silos such as maintenance, operations, or technology often operate independently, leading to inefficiencies when problems span multiple domains. Digital twins provide a framework to bridge these gaps by connecting real-world systems with virtual capabilities like AI, enabling actionable insights and coordinated solutions that improve outcomes across the entire ecosystem.

Q: How do digital twins and AI work together to create value in the real world?

A: Digital twins often incorporate AI capabilities to analyze data, predict outcomes, and optimize processes. While AI provides probabilistic insights and advanced analytics, the digital twin serves as the ecosystem that connects these insights to actionable changes in the real world. Together, they enable organizations to design solutions that are not only technologically advanced but also directly tied to measurable improvements in physical assets, workflows, and decision-making.

Q: What are the main challenges organizations face when implementing digital twins?

A: Organizations often struggle with:

- **Siloed Thinking:** Teams focus on their own domains without considering cross-functional impacts.
- **Weak Interconnections:** Many so-called "twins" lack strong two-way connections between real and virtual worlds, reducing their effectiveness.
- **Overinvestment in Visualization:** Excessive focus on high-fidelity 3D models can lead to "gold plating" without delivering ROI.
- **Change Management:** Resistance to new workflows or insufficient integration into existing processes can hinder adoption. To overcome these challenges, organizations must start with clearly defined problems and ensure their digital twin design aligns with measurable real-world outcomes.

Q: How do you determine whether a problem is suitable for a digital twin solution?

A: The suitability of a problem for a digital twin depends on its complexity and the need for interconnected solutions. A valuable problem should:

1. Require measurable change in the real world.
2. Involve multiple systems or domains where traditional siloed approaches fall short.
3. Justify the cost and complexity of building a twin by offering significant ROI or strategic benefits.

By validating problems through frameworks like the Digital Twin Design Process (DTDP), organizations can ensure they focus on impactful solutions rather than chasing shiny technologies or low-value opportunities.

Q: I don't know anything about digital twins and your book looks ridiculous. Just tell me what to do.

A:

1. Don't try and define what you think a digital twin is.
2. A great digital twin creates real change, measures that change, and improves that change. Aim everything at this.

3. Decide if you're trying to solve a real problem or trying to deploy new capabilities. Don't try and do half of each or you'll end up doing neither.
4. If you're solving a problem, work backwards from the problem to identify what needs to change in the real world, and then what technology you need to make that change.
5. If you're deploying capabilities, identify the key data types you use to operate every day and ensure your new capabilities can use these data types, and explicitly think about how this data gets from inside your twin to the real world to create change.
6. Plan to build something small, and test how it works in the real world, and plan to add more data or extend to other area / assets. Budget to do this in stages, and don't try and "one shot" it. Things will go wrong, but more importantly, you'll learn a lot from doing this and you want to use those learnings to improve what you do.
7. Don't worry if people say your thing isn't a digital twin, or doesn't have enough AI in it. The purpose of a system is what it does – make sure it does something that changes the real world, and measures that change, and improves that change.

The end

Thank you for reading "Designing digital twins". I hope you have learned some things and I hope you feel better equipped to wrangle these cyber-physical and cybernetic crossovers that many people think are "all sorted". Drop me a line if you need help with something or want to bounce an idea off me. I am already writing the next book, on applying "physical AI" to real-world Problems, because I am seeing a lot more of that in our day job at Geminum and nearly every physical AI requires non-AI and legacy systems and non-autonomous / non-AI systems to work with and around it... it's a fun world to be in, and the next few years will only get more interesting. Live well!

About the author

Rob is passionate about solving real-world problems with smart, practical technology. With over two decades of experience in engineering and digital innovation, Rob has become a trusted advisor for businesses navigating the fast-changing digital landscape.

As the CEO of Geminum, Rob helps industrial organizations connect people, processes, and data using digital twins and applied AI to unlock efficiency and drive results. He's known for making complex concepts clear, approachable, and actionable – whether he's speaking at global conferences or working alongside industry leaders.

Rob's journey began as a mechanical engineer tackling operational challenges on the ground and in the design office. Over time, he saw how emerging technologies simplified and enhanced collaboration and decision-making. His experiences led to the world of digital transformation and B2B SaaS, before taking the plunge to found and run a tech co focused on creating connected change for industrial organizations.

These experiences shaped the insights in 'Designing Digital Twins,' a book designed to help anyone – from business leaders to tech enthusiasts to maintenance managers – understand and design digital twins to effectively enable AI and transform how we work and solve problems.

www.ingramcontent.com/pod-product-compliance
Lightning Source LLC
LaVergne TN
LVHW010714061126
851857LV00014B/1176